The Struggle for Secession, 1966-1970

"Both parties deprecated war; but one of them would *make* war rather than let the nation survive; and the other would *accept* war rather than let it perish. And the war came. . . .

"Neither party expected the war, the magnitude, or the duration, which it has already attained. Neither anticipated that the *cause* of the conflict might cease with, or even before, the conflict itself should cease. Each looked for an easier triumph, and a result less fundamental and astounding. Both read the Bible, and pray to the same God; and each invokes its aid against the other."

Abraham Lincoln, *Second Inaugural Address*

The Struggle for Secession, 1966-1970

A Personal Account of the Nigerian Civil War

Ntieyong U. Akpan

Chief Secretary to the Government and Head of the Civil Service of Eastern Nigeria (which declared itself 'Biafra' in 1967) 1966-1970

FRANK CASS : LONDON

First published in 1972 by
FRANK CASS AND COMPANY LIMITED
67 Great Russell Street
London WC1B 3BT

ISBN 0 7146 2930 8

Printed in Great Britain by
The Garden City Press Limited
Letchworth, Hertfordshire, SG6 1JS

Contents

List of Maps

Acknowledgements

My first and greatest acknowledgement goes to my devoted wife, Margaret, without whose encouragement this book could not have been written. At a time of great mental and spiritual depression, arising from unemployment and uncertainty about the future—and without a sure place of abode—she urged me to save myself from physical collapse by employing my mind in the writing of this book. I am grateful to her, not only for her encouragement and initiative in this matter, but also for her suggestions and good memory.

I am grateful to the kind friend who lent me one of his typists to do the typing and I thank Miss Abimbola Akinpelu for her hard work and perseverence in uncongenial surroundings. I am also grateful to Mr. Efiong Udeng for the occasional assistance he gave Miss Akinpelu, and to my two young cousins, Ubon and Akaninyene, for helping in checking the typing.

All quotations from General Ojukwu's speeches and statements are largely from his collection of speeches, published by Messrs. Harper and Row of New York in 1969. The originals of the speeches are, however, extant in the files.

Lagos: 1970. N. U. AKPAN

Introduction

I dedicate this book to Truth, Honesty, and Unity—the unity of Nigeria, and maybe even of Africa. Truth, of course, can be bitter and hurtful. But it is not my intention to hurt or embitter. At the same time I am not so naïve as to think that nobody will be, notwithstanding my intentions. I am absolutely satisfied that my motives are completely altruistic.

This is a story of the greatest tragedy that can befall a people—a story of extreme human suffering and losses, to which the most innocent were the greatest victims—a story of human, moral and physical disaster. Parts of this story will sound like fiction or a novel. Where that is the case, readers should regard it as a matter of style and no detraction from its reality and truth. Where names are mentioned, they are the names of real persons, alive or dead.

I had two alternatives—to write or not to write this book. When I decided to write, I vowed to my God and conscience to be dispassionate, courageous, truthful, honest and fair. And even where my assessment and judgment of people and events may be wrong (for, after all, I am only human) this cannot and should not detract from the tenets of my vow.

The book contains my reminiscences of the Nigerian Civil War and of the tragedy of "Biafra", a name assumed on secession by the people of what used to be Eastern Nigeria. It is *not* an apologia. I am not writing to defend myself or others. If I make any defence at all, it is for the common man and woman of that area of our beloved and flourishing country which found itself engulfed in the disaster and tragedy of these events.

Nor am I out to condemn or implicate anyone. That is why I have refrained from mentioning names of individuals, except where absolutely necessary or under innocuous circumstances. I was Chief Secretary to the Military Government, Head of the Civil Service, Member and Secretary to the Cabinet of Eastern Nigeria, and held those positions in the secessionist Biafra until the end of the Civil War. I write, therefore, as one closely associated with the side whose actions led to the civil war and which eventually lost. I write because it is I who can best tell this aspect of the story.

I believe that the facts of the tragedy of the Nigerian Civil War can produce lessons and warnings for Africa and mankind. I write because I owe a duty to the dead and the living in this task. And I write now because I am aware that many people have embarked upon such a task, and many of these are people who base their accounts on hearsay, second-hand information or incomplete records perhaps found after the civil war. Under such circumstances their conclusions may be wrong, and such conclusions could perhaps be to the detriment of innocent individuals. It is my hope that this book will enable those now engaged on research about the conflict to get the right orientations.

I tell only that of which I knew, either because I was personally involved or had direct or reliable access to the facts. Others will have their own parts of the story to tell. The world needs their accounts told with truth, courage, honesty and without undue embellishments. Only in this way can we face the mistakes of the past and the needs of the future, the needs not only of the direct victims of the tragedy, but those of the country as a whole.

Could I have written this book if the end of the war had been different—if Biafra had survived? The honest answer is that I would have done so, perhaps in a more unrestrained way—except that I would probably have left its publication to my children!

Although my aim is not to criticise, blame or condemn, I know that it would be difficult to avoid inferences being drawn in that direction. Naturally, if I am to be true to my conscience, fair to my readers, and provide the right scope and factual basis for the necessary lessons to be drawn, certain people are bound to be offended or embarrassed by many things brought out in this book. But I have nothing personal against anybody: my duty and loyalty to the country, and hopes for the future, override and surpass old loyalties and personal feelings towards any individual.

He who aspires to be a public figure or servant must know that his life and his personal conduct are no longer his own exclusive preserves but those of the public as well, to which he has given himself.

The principal and nerve character in the Biafran drama was Emeka Odumegwu Ojukwu, and the whole story is inevitably centred around him. Readers will arrive at different judgments and conclusions concerning my treatment of this character. That cannot be helped. Some will say that I have been too kind, and others that I have been too cruel, towards him. I cannot prevent anyone from reaching his own conclusions. That is precisely why this book is written. For my part I have, to the maximum of my ability, kept my promise and personal vow to be dispassionate, honest, courageous and fair. My only plea is that readers should judge the book and the story as a whole, not by isolated statements, paragraphs, chapters or even sections. In order to free myself from prejudice, emotions and sentimentalities, I allowed nearly nine months to elapse between the end of the civil war and the writing of this book.

In spite of his last cowardly behaviour, many people will continue to admire Ojukwu for his intelligence, energy, clear and quick wit, resolution, consistency and calculating strategy. But controversy will rage on how he used these qualities, how disinterested he was in applying them, and how far personal ambition, love of power and ostentation, miscalculations, family and extraneous influences ordered his actions and thoughts. And how far he bore personal responsibility for the suffering, deprivations and death of those who had placed their faith and destiny in his leadership. Much has been said in this book about his methods and approach, his choice of associates and advisers, his weaknesses and other things which contributed to the tragedy of Biafra and his own downfall.

There are two important points which must be mentioned here, lest they be overlooked. Their mention here will put readers in the right frame of mind to read and judge what is contained in this book. They are about the civil war and secession. Bloody conflict and secession had become the two probables in Nigeria depending on timing and circumstances—bloody conflict, following the killings of 1966 and the massive return of Eastern Nigerians, particularly the Ibos, to Eastern Nigeria; secession, motivated by feelings engendered by events associated with the 1963 census, the 1964 Federal elections and the 1965 Western Nigeria elections.

Even if there had been no secession, there was bound to be a fight—if not a full-scale civil war—in Nigeria. The killings in the North, particularly those of September 1966 and afterwards had, understandably, so enraged and embittered the Ibos that practically all of them—men and women, young and old, soldier and civilian—were bent upon revenge against the Hausas (a generic term for the inhabitants of that portion of the country which used to be known as Northern Nigeria).

I preached a sermon once in the Nsukka University Chapel and, referring to the sad events of the year 1966, called for Christian charity, love and forgiveness. Immediately after the service of worship, hostile and disapproving groups of women surrounded me and remonstrated against that portion of my sermon concerned with love and forgiveness. They considered it inhuman that one should even suggest that the Hausas should be forgiven and loved after what they had done. Said an elderly woman, "As far as what the Hausas have done to our people is concerned, we shall neither love, nor forgive, nor forget. If that is what will send us to hell, then we are prepared." The speaker was applauded by others. If that could happen at Church and among enlightened people, then one can imagine the general feeling elsewhere.

The military and civilian killings of Nigerians by Nigerians in 1966 constituted (apart from the civil war) the worst tragedy for this country. There was no human being with a soul, blood and life who saw but was not revolted at what happened. And this was true even of the Northerners resident in the East. I have never been able to forget the shock I received when I went down to the railway station one evening early in October 1966 to meet a friend coming from Port Harcourt. Before the arrival of the Port Harcourt train, a train from the North carrying refugees had pulled into the station. What came out of that train is beyond description. Some got out with severed limbs, others with broken heads. But the most chilling sight was a woman who came out completely naked, clutching in her hand the head of her child killed in the North. This particular sight aroused the crowds standing in the station to a frenzy. They began to beat up all the Northerners within sight and rampaged through the entire town of Enugu, attacking Northerners, and destroying and looting their property. The hostility spread to Port Harcourt and Aba. The B.B.C. later announced that a number of Northerners had been killed. I cannot confirm or deny this, but would not be surprised judging from the mood of the people during that unfortunate late afternoon. It was later reported that a subsequent train to Enugu carried a coach full of headless bodies. The story was that the train had been stopped at Oturkpo and the male passengers called out and beheaded. The heads were taken, it was reported, and bodies sent down as "presents to Ojukwu". Again, I cannot personally confirm or deny this story, but it was told to me by very responsible persons as an eye-witness account.

Unfortunately not many in the rest of Nigeria fully knew the horrible situation. This could be seen from the obvious horror which struck the Obas and Chiefs of Western Nigeria who visited Enugu a few weeks later, and were taken to the general hospital to see the wounded and maimed. They were all so shocked that they could not enjoy the hospitality offered them, and before returning home they surrendered everything they had, collectively and individually, in the form of money to the Rehabilitation Commission. The same feeling was evident in the team of top civil servants who visited Enugu from Lagos and were taken to the same hospital. But what they saw was only a fraction of the story.

Writing at the time, Mr. Colin Legum of the *London Observer* said:

"For fear of promoting an even greater tragedy, the Nigerians have been sheltered from knowing the full magnitude of the disaster that has overtaken the Ibos in the Northern Region. The danger is that the truth will not be believed and so no proper lessons learnt, once the horror is over.... Men, women and children arrived with arms and legs broken, hands hacked off, mouths split open. Pregnant women were cut open and the unborn children killed."

I have recalled how hostile women mobbed me for calling for Christian charity, love and forgiveness in a sermon in Nsukka. There were places in Eastern Nigeria where nobody could have had the temerity to preach such a sermon during the period October-December 1966 and leave the pulpit unscathed, if alive.

Individual civilians were determined to avenge the deaths of their parents, husbands, wives and children; soldiers, the deaths of their colleagues; and the Ibo people the honour of their race. "How dare anyone even conceive that Ibo blood could be shed in such a wanton way, and imagine that nothing would be done about it—impossible!" their leaders kept on saying. (This, it must be stated, was reported to be the type of feeling in the North following the killing of the most prominent Northern political and military leaders in an Ibo-led army mutiny—as the event of January 1966 was officially described. The killing of Easterners in the North and elsewhere later that year was partly motivated by that feeling.) I have been told by reliable sources that, in anticipation of that revenge, some Ibo leaders had decided to raise at least one million pounds through levies from every town and village in Iboland, with which to acquire the necessary wherewithal to carry out their aims as and when circumstances presented themselves.

Thus, even if there had been no secession to induce the Federal Government to start the war, there would sooner or later have been civil or tribal war started by the Ibos. The difference would have been that such a war would not have been as serious as the one which occurred, would have been more easily contained, would have been less destructive, would have lasted only a short time, and would never have assumed international importance.

Governor Ojukwu in fact made it clear to Chief Awolowo and others of the National Conciliation Committee, which visited Enugu from Lagos months before the civil war, that the place of meeting between the people of the East and those of the North would be the battle-field. I do not know whether the visiting team from Lagos grasped the full significance of that ominous statement.

One needs to have been in Enugu and other main towns in the East on July 6th, 1967 to appreciate the paradoxical jubilation and enthusiasm with which the people welcomed the news of Federal

Military initiative. (The tactics had all along been to induce the Federal Government to fire the first shot.) The enthusiasm was symbolised in the Governor's broadcast of June 30th, 1967, six days before the start of the civil war:

> "Our soldiers are ready.... If Gowon should make the mistake of crossing into our territory, even by a few yards, we shall immediately go into open, outright, and total war against Nigeria.... This will be an opportunity for us to do honour to the memory of the thousands of our kith and kin savagely murdered last year by avenging their death.... Fellow countrymen, proud and courageous Biafrans, this is your moment."

Governor Ojukwu himself was not averse to a fight between the East and the North. Indeed, he considered it his duty to his people to avenge the death of those, including his military colleagues, who had been killed in the North. The point is that neither he nor others ever thought that the fight would assume the magnitude and proportions which it did. Nor did the Federal Government!

The second point is that while every Ibo person, with the sympathy of many non-Ibos, itched for a fight with the Hausas because of the events of 1966, the majority of them, if given a chance to express their opinion, would have rejected secession outright. Most people regarded secession, when it came, as unfortunate, while others felt that the situation might be readjusted when civilian rule returned.

But, again, in spite of the reasons given for the secession which occurred in 1967, an eventual secession of the East from the rest of the Federation was likely, even if there had been no provocation in 1966. In 1965, anticipating a possible review of the Nigerian Constitution, the Okpara Government of Eastern Nigeria sent out a delegation led by Mr. C. C. Mojekwu, then Attorney-General and Minister of Justice of Eastern Nigeria, to visit many countries of the world and study their constitutional systems. Their subsequent report contained the following:

> "As the tour gathered momentum, it became abundantly clear, both from discussions had and solutions proposed to us, and on our conviction based on past and present events,[1] and future trends, that secession is the ultimate cure for our difficulties. In arriving at this conclusion, we have considered the population of Eastern Nigeria, her economic possibilities and scientific and administrative expertise, and her goodwill abroad."

1. The immediate past and present events were the census crisis of 1963, the Federal elections of 1964 and the Western Nigeria elections of 1965.

Other members of the Mojekwu world-tour delegation were Mr. J. I. Emembolu, later Attorney-General in the Ojukwu Military Government, and Professor Kalu Ezera, later one of Ojukwu's personal assistants.

The most fervent protagonists of secession were a few individuals with private and personal ambitions, and others who had come home after the massacres of 1966, embittered by the glaring atrocities committed against them and their kith and kin.

Among the latter were those who genuinely believed that secession was the only way of ensuring for themselves and their children security of person and property. They considered themselves rejected and unwanted by the rest of Nigeria. Those who had lost their homes and business undertakings (and there were many of these) in other parts of Nigeria could not imagine how they could ever be expected to associate themselves again with a section of the country which had acted so cruelly towards them.

There was a third group who saw in secession a means of being able to build up sufficient military forces to protect their nationals in parts of Nigeria and beyond. They could not understand what their people had done, in trading and other activities, which the Lebanese and the Syrians from far-away countries were not doing in Nigeria. Yet the Lebanese and the Syrians were never molested for fear that their respective countries might react diplomatically or with force against Nigeria.

Secession, the third group believed, would also give them an international presence and identity, which would in turn give them a voice in world organisations like the United Nations. This group pointed to small countries the world over, including such neighbouring ones as Equatorial Guinea, Gabon, Gambia and others, with populations of less than a million inhabitants, smaller in population and perhaps in area as well, than some administrative provinces in Eastern Nigeria. These countries had a voice and an international presence in the councils of the world, and could raise a hue and cry, and obtain action and attention from the United Nations if a single citizen of their country were molested, let alone killed, by citizens of another country. Eastern Nigeria had a population of fourteen millions, ranked quite highly among the most populated areas in the world, and yet could not reach out to the world when thousands of its people were wantonly massacred outside their region of origin.

Intellectuals constituted this last group, and spared no efforts in trying to prove how different the East was from the North, and to some extent the West, in culture, education, and other attributes. They showed how uncertain and insecure the Nigerian association had been for them over the years, and argued how viable, progressive and potentially great were the people of the East, particularly the Ibo race, if left alone to develop at their own pace. This they tried to prove during the civil war—and did indeed impress friends and foes in their dogged determination, resourcefulness, endurance and exploits.

I agree generally with Mr. Nelson Ottah (see his article in the *Drum Magazine* of June 1970) when he said:

> "Almost everybody was crying for a showdown—the intellectuals, professionals, big money men, housewives, motor touts, spivs and pimps. The Eastern Region at that time was ripe for the misfortune that followed. And Emeka Odumegwu Ojuku exploited the situation to suit his private ambitions.... History, I am sure, will be kind to him. After all, he did not do it because he was cleverer than his victims: he did it because his victims—primed with craze for revenge, escapism, greed and foolishness—were so ready for destruction and only needed a command. Ojukwu's greatest crime today is that he gave that command."

My reservations on the assessment of Mr. Nelson Ottah lie in his indiscriminate confusion and condemnation of all in the East (even the Ibos) in his judgment. Not everyone was motivated by greed, not all had the same influence in shaping the destiny of the people, nobody was willing for destruction, and the non-Ibos were certainly not enthusiastic about a situation which would expose them to domination and exploitation by others. The minority (non-Ibo) groups believed that their greatest chance and scope lay in the context of Nigeria as one country.

All the same, even among the Ibos, the great majority of the ordinary people could not see secession as the best answer to their problems and difficulties as members or even neighbours of the Nigerian Federation. I whole-heartedly shared and sponsored that view.

Ojukwu almost certainly did not initially believe in secession, but in the unity of Nigeria. This was evident both in his attitudes and postures. I am inclined to believe that, even after the decision to secede had been taken—and this was as early as August 1966, as will be seen later in this book—he occasionally had serious misgivings about such a course. But he had made himself a helpless prisoner—a prisoner of his personal glory, ambitions and idiosyncracies, a prisoner of the will and caprices of those he trusted and upon whom he heavily relied, a prisoner of fear and self-deception, and finally, a prisoner of the mob. All this will be brought out later in the book.

I agree entirely with Mr. Nelson Ottah that the people were

efficiently primed for what eventually befell them. How this was done will be shown in subsequent chapters of this book. I also agree with Mr. Mojekwu and his world-tour team that Eastern Nigeria had a lot of goodwill and sympathy from some countries and peoples of the world even in secession. This was manifested during the civil war. But the book will disappoint readers in that it cannot bring out the details of that goodwill and sympathy, because such details were understandably denied me. All the same, discerning readers may be able to judge and discover. These details are in fact beginning to be exposed and explained, mostly by outsiders.

Biafra is the simplest name by which to identify the area of the secessionist regime. The name is therefore used many times in this book, though more cumbrous and verbose terms such as "secessionist enclave" are also occasionally used.

Except where otherwise indicated, the term "Governor" refers to the Governor of former Eastern Nigeria, or Biafra, namely Ojukwu.

SECTION I

MILITARY TAKE-OVER

1 The Military Take-Over

As was a common experience in our family in Enugu, our house had been flooded with visitors, the majority of them unexpected, who had arrived the previous night. They included three men and four ladies with some children, the latter passing through to join their husbands and fathers. We already had quite a crowd in permanent residence, what with our children and relations. My wife was faced with the problem of sleeping arrangements. She had become an expert in this, and I did not have to bother in the least. After the evening meal, I took the male visitors to the club. On our return, my wife announced that the ladies would be sleeping with her in our own bedroom; the visiting children were already asleep with our own children in the children's bedroom; two of the men would have to sleep in the out-houses, from which the occupants had been temporarily evicted for the night; and I would have to sleep with a cousin of mine, who had come from Ibadan, in the small annexe downstairs.

At a quarter-to-six the following morning, Saturday, January 15th, 1966, we switched on the transistor radio beside the bed, tuning into the Eastern Nigeria Broadcasting station. What we heard was quite unusual. The announcer, in an extremely panicky tone, was calling out his own name and telling listeners that a group of soldiers had moved into the studio and surrounded him. There was silence. No music, no sound.

My partner jumped up and sat on the bed. "Da,"[1] he called, shaking me as though I had not heard what had happened, "something has happened. Could it be a coup?" It was the last thing I would have thought of. We got up, still confused and anxious. "I must go and find out," my cousin said, trying to dress and without even bothering to wash his face or clean his teeth. There were signs of returning sound on the radio. It was music. I cannot now recall what sort of music it was. At exactly six o'clock a voice came over the air. It was the terse voice of the Officer Commanding the Enugu Army Garrison. He announced that he had assumed all Governmental powers and control over Eastern Nigeria. It was a very short speech lasting about two minutes. So it

1. A mutual Ibibio nickname used by friends and equals.

was a coup. Our conclusion at that particular moment was that the Federal Government under Sir Abubakar had decided to take over the N.C.N.C. Government of Eastern Nigeria. A complete breakdown of law and order in the country had been threatened by the bloody and destructive disturbances which had been raging in Western Nigeria since the previous general elections, involving the N.C.N.C. and its allies against the N.P.C. and its allies.

My visitor still went out to see what was happening in town. He later returned to report that soldiers were everywhere, many of them surrounding the E.N.B.C. (Eastern Nigeria Broadcasting Corporation) buildings. Nobody was allowed to go to or through the Independence Layout, the residential quarters of Eastern Nigerian Ministers.

I was in my office at eight o'clock as usual. There was consternation everywhere. Groups of people were to be seen talking and speculating. In the office I learnt of a rumour that the Prime Minister and the Premiers of Northern and Western Nigeria had been killed. Other military and civilian names were also mentioned. A few of these rumours later turned out not to be true.

Later that morning, all the Permanent Secretaries were summoned to the Premier's Office where the then Chief Secretary to the Premier and Head of the Civil Service (Chief J. O. Udoji) told us that information had been received from Lagos that the Military had taken over the Government of the Federation. He had been to the Premier's Lodge and informed the Premier, Dr. Okpara, accordingly. He advised us to go back to our respective ministries and tell the senior staff what had happened, and then await further instructions.

The date was January 15th, 1966. Archbishop Makarios of Cyprus, who had attended a meeting of Commonwealth Prime Ministers in Lagos, had been feted as the guest of Government at a dinner party given by the Premier of Eastern Nigeria the previous night. He had left that morning, and had been seen off at the airport by the Governor and Premier of Eastern Nigeria. Those who were at the airport reported that soldiers arrested Dr. Okpara, the Premier, as soon as the Archbishop's plane had left.

An hour or so after the Chief Secretary had spoken to us, another message came that all the Permanent Secretaries should be at the army barracks by 11 a.m. to be presented to Lt.-Col. David Ejoor. We proceeded there as directed, for the most part timorously, not knowing what might happen to us there. For most of us it was the first time that we had entered the barracks, save possibly on the few occasions we had been there to watch a play or listen to a concert in the garrison theatre. Our experience at the gate was not a very

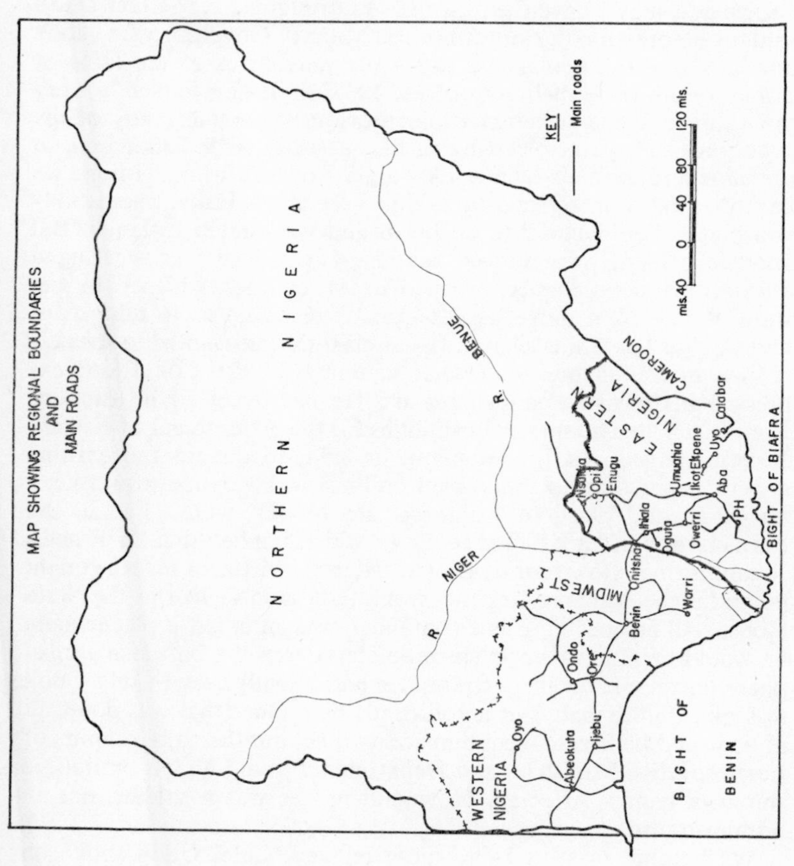
MAP SHOWING REGIONAL BOUNDARIES
AND
MAIN ROADS
NORTHERN NIGERIA
R. BENUE
R. NIGER
KEY
Main roads
mls.40 0 40 80 120 mls.
CAMEROON
EASTERN NIGERIA
MIDWEST
WESTERN NIGERIA
BIGHT OF BENIN
BIGHT OF BIAFRA
Oyo
Abeokuta
Ijebu
Ondo
Ore
Benin
Warri
Onitsha
Oguta
Ihiala
Owerri
Nsukka
Opi
Enugu
Umuahia
Ikot Ekpene
Uyo
Calabar
Aba
PH

reassuring one. One of the soldiers at the gate nearly shot a civilian for having the temerity to resent insults heaped on him by another soldier, a private. Like most others, the poor civilian did not yet fully appreciate what had happened until some passer-by pushed him away and told him to be careful. Helplessly and uncomprehendingly, the miserable fellow walked away grumbling.

We eventually arrived at the Officers' Mess, where we found Lt.-Col. Ejoor waiting for us. Beside him stood Chief Udoji. "Your Excellency, may I have the pleasure of introducing . . ." Chief Udoji said, as he presented us in turn to the Military Governor who shook our hands with a genial and shy smile, waving us to the table of drinks opposite to help ourselves. Lt.-Col. Ejoor looked a very young man. I had never met him previously, though many of my colleagues had. After receiving all his guests, Lt.-Col. Ejoor went to the table and took his own drink—a glass of soft drink. "I hope we haven't caused an offence by taking beer and whisky," somebody whispered. He intended to be jovial and we wanted to laugh. But another person, who noticed that Lt.-Col. Ejoor was wearing a businesslike countenance, warned us in another whisper to beware. We checked ourselves. Lt-Col. Ejoor asked us to take seats, and we did. There was silence. It was clear that he wanted to speak.

In a measured and somewhat halting voice Lt.-Col. Ejoor expressed his pleasure at meeting us. He had received instructions from Lagos to assume responsibilities for the government of Eastern Nigeria. It was not his intention, he said, to disturb the existing system, other than to remove all politicians. Everyone would keep his office and place of residence. He himself would live in the barracks and did not intend to move, which implied that Sir Francis Ibiam, former Governor of Eastern Nigeria, whatever his role might be under the Military Regime, would continue to live in the State House. All he needed, Ejoor continued, was an office, a place where he would be able to work, since he considered the barracks atmosphere unsuitable for the purpose. He had already asked Chief Udoji to look into the matter of an office for him. Once that was done, all of us would be free to meet him at any time, but the daily running of our respective Ministries and Departments would be left entirely in our own hands. After all, he wound up, he was a soldier, not an administrator.

We became reassured and quite relaxed. Chief Udoji spoke on behalf of us all, pledging full loyalty and cooperation. As civil servants our role was to serve faithfully, loyally and devotedly any government in power. We then went back to our drinks, chatting freely with each other and with the Military Governor until we left.

The day passed, with everyone wondering what would happen

next. On the afternoon of the following day January 16th, 1966, it was formally announced that the Council of Ministers in Lagos had handed over power to the Nigerian Army and that the Nigerian Armed Forces had accepted an invitation "to form an interim Military Government for the purpose of maintaining law and order and of maintaining essential services". That Government was to be headed by Major-General J. T. U. Aguiyi-Ironsi.

Not much could be done by way of office work during the following two or three anxious days. Those of us who owned transistor radio sets carried them with us to the office and kept them going low as we did whatever we were able to do. We heard that a meeting of senior army officers was being held in Lagos, and that Lt.-Col. David Ejoor had left for the meeting. Meanwhile, from Radio Kaduna we had heard, almost about the time we heard the Lagos statement that the Nigerian Armed Forces had accepted the invitation to form an interim military administration, that Major Nzeogwu had set up, for the Northern Region of Nigeria, the "Supreme Council of the Revolution". Two rival military governments for the country! Fear, tension and anxiety increased among the people. There was real fear of civil war, which continued unabated until one or two days later when it was announced that Major Nzeogwu and his "Supreme Council of the Revolution" had agreed to dissolve and submit to the authority of the Military Government in Lagos. About this time too, we heard of the formal appointments of Military Governors for the four Regions of the Federation. Lt.-Col. Chukwuemeka Odumegwu Ojukwu was appointed Military Governor for Eastern Nigeria while Lt.-Col. David Ejoor was appointed for the Mid-West.

Col. Ojukwu arrived in Enugu on January 19th, 1966 to assume his appointment. Many of us turned up at the airport and watched the ceremonies. A day later, all Permanent Secretaries were instructed to proceed with the senior officials of their respective ministries to the old Government House, to meet the Governor. Everyone assembled in time. Col. Ojukwu walked in, serious and unsmiling, and took his seat. His A.D.C. stood behind him. The atmosphere was clearly different from our previous experience with Lt.-Col. Ejoor five days before. Chief Udoji, as head of the civil service, introduced us in turn. Each of us stood up and bowed. Col. Ojukwu merely looked on without a word or smile. The introductions ended, and Governor began to address us.

He spoke to us about the aims of the military regime—the usual things about the eradication of corruption, inefficiency and so on. He then said that he was a hard worker and liked work. All of us must be prepared to do the same, or else.

One thing he said struck me particularly on that first occasion. He warned against gossips and jealousy. If it became necessary that jobs and positions should go to persons from one family or area, rather than complain and gossip, others should try to find out how it came about that so many people should be qualified from the family or area for such positions, and then work hard to produce such people from their areas or family. He alluded somehow to President Kennedy and his brother Robert who was Attorney-General in the Kennedy Administration.

There was also a small incident which left lingering impressions in my mind from that first meeting. One of the professional officers said something or asked a question which the Military Governor did not particularly like. The Governor's reaction was one of stern rebuke and abuse to that poor official. All of us recoiled and nobody dared ask any more questions or make comments. The unfortunate question or comment was in connection with the civil service which the Military Governor had hinted would be pooled, with the possibility of some of us being sent to Lagos or elsewhere, something to which the ill-fated Decree No. 34 later gave legal effect.

"Why the seriousness and lack of humour?", I asked myself as I observed and listened to the Military Governor. Why was it necessary to give an innocent official such public embarrassment merely because he had said something the Military Governor did not like? Was that his true character, or was it a mere façade intended to put everyone in his place, or was it a means of hiding a complex or weakness? I recalled an incident of my primary school days, when a new headmaster, on the very first day he entered our school, severely flogged a child for a very trivial offence and struck terror in our hearts, but who later turned out to be the kindest headmaster we had ever had, and who hardly used a cane, or allowed any other teacher to use one, on any pupil. I hoped that this first impression of our new Military Governor would prove similarly misleading.

On the evening of January 25th, 1966, the Military Governor made his first broadcast to the nation over the television and radio networks of Eastern Nigeria. After condemning, in the strongest possible language and gestures, the persons and misdeeds of the now discredited former politicians, Col. Ojukwu made the following announcements:

> "In the Eastern Provinces, all executive powers are now vested in the Military Governor. In the day-to-day business of Government, I have appointed an Executive Committee which will assist me. The Executive Committee will be composed of: (1) the Military Governor, (2) the Commanding Officer of the Army in the Eastern

Provinces, (3) the Commissioner of Police, (4) the Chief Law Officer, (5) the Chief Secretary, (6) the Permanent Secretary, Ministry of Finance.

"All other permanent secretaries will be co-opted (when necessary) to participate in the discussions of the business of their respective ministries.

"It is our intention to stamp out inefficiency, corruption, and dishonesty in all facets of public life, to create the consciousness of national unity, and to lead the citizens of Nigeria as one disciplined people in purposeful march to maximum realisation of the country's potential.

"The citizens of Nigeria must therefore realise that we are determined to turn our back forever on the unproductive drift of yester years. To this end the following will come into immediate effect:

> All the powers and functions formerly vested in or exercised by the former Governor, Premier, and Ministers have been vested in and will be exercised by the Military Governor.
>
> The Regional Public Service Commission shall no longer be responsible for the appointment and promotions of senior staff in the public service of the Eastern Provinces. In future the Public Service Commission will act in an advisory capacity to the Military Governor in relation to the appointment, promotion, and discipline of senior members of the public service of the Eastern Provinces.
>
> All Provincial assemblies in Eastern Nigeria are abolished.
>
> The former regional Governor, Premier, Ministers, Provincial Commissioners and Parliamentary Secretaries shall, if they have not already done so, vacate their former official residences and surrender any government property, including cars, in their possession forthwith.
>
> The post of Agent-General for Eastern Nigeria in the United Kingdom is abolished.
>
> All photographs of the former President, Prime Minister, Regional Governors, Premiers, and Ministers shall be immediately removed from all public buildings in the Eastern Provinces.
>
> The photographs shall be replaced with the photographs of His Excellency, the Head of the Military Government and Supreme Commander of the Nigerian armed forces, Major General J. T. U. Aguiyi-Ironsi.
>
> No person in the Eastern Provinces, except the Military Governor, shall fly any flag on cars and private residences.
>
> The salaries of all members of boards of statutory corporations and companies, solely owned by the Government of Eastern Nigeria, are hereby suspended until further notice. They will, however, be entitled to their present sitting allowances.
>
> All debtors to Government or Government-sponsored financial institutions are warned in their own interests to liquidate such

debts without delay in order to avoid the use of drastic measures in their recovery.

The public is hereby warned against bribery, nepotism, and other forms of corruption in public life. The warning is directed principally to the holders of public offices in the police force, civil service, judiciary (including customary court judges) local government bodies, statutory corporations, and trade unions.

All doctors, pharmacists, nurses, and other workers in hospitals are reminded of their responsibility for the health of the members of the public.

The Military Government will not tolerate acts of irresponsibility, dereliction of duty, and corruption in government hospitals, maternities, health centres and dispensaries. The Military Government will deal firmly with any case that comes to its notice.

The public is warned against careless talk, acts and gestures contemptuous of all sections of the public, calculated to incite or cause disaffection among any section of the community. Such acts will be deemed to constitute an offence against public order and will be dealt with summarily with firm measures.

The activities of the regional and provincial scholarship boards are suspended until further notice. In the future, scholarships will be awarded purely on the basis of merit to enable us to solve our urgent high-level manpower needs.

The law establishing the University of Nsukka will be reviewed to ensure that matters academic are left entirely in the hands of the academicians, subject to the overall direction of the country's manpower needs as recommended by the National Universities' Commission.

The appointment of chairman and members of statutory corporations will be reviewed and any future appointments or re-appointment will be based entirely on qualifications and merit."

I watched the Governor from beginning to end on the television. Again what struck me was his aggressive, grave and pompous display, which did not particularly become him. He appeared to have rehearsed that speech a number of times before delivering it, and his aim was to make an impression. But what impression? I could not say. Beneath his articulate forcefulness and gesticulations, I could discern some signs of weakness which the embellishments of speech and action were trying to hide. I had not known him intimately, although I had some acquaintance with his family and people when I served as an administrative officer in Onitsha division, with special responsibility for the southern district of that administrative division which included Nnewi. I met him casually in Enugu, but a little more closely in London when he was undergoing his army officers' course there and I was serving as the

Principal Secretary in the Eastern Nigeria Commissioner's Office, where he occasionally called. I knew his father, for whom I had great respect. Before the Governor's arrival in Enugu, someone had told me that his father had asked him to tell me and others known to him to give Emeka every help and cooperation he needed in his difficult assignment. I was, therefore, naturally anxious to know something about his character and disposition and, as an administrative officer trained to deal with people, I knew that one way of learning this was through a person's words and demeanour.

A few days later, I asked for and received an audience with him, not privately but in my official capacity as the permanent secretary, Ministry of Education. We had a general discussion and I found him quite a different person from what I had observed on the day he met us as a group. He was quite relaxed, though still official. I complimented him on his speech and wished him success in his assignment. I said I was particularly impressed by the Military Government's intention to wipe out corruption. I handed to him copies of speeches I had made on church and social platforms on the matter. I also handed to him some files on the Ministry which were of urgent interest. After further chat, I left, convinced that he could be a good actor, and this to me was a useful initial discovery.

2 Emeka in the Saddle

As the Military Governor of what used to be Eastern Nigeria, Lt.-Col. Emeka Ojukwu was determined not merely to govern, but to reign as well. He proceeded at once, by word and action, to establish this fact beyond dispute. With the suspension of parts of the Nigerian Constitution and the removal of ministers from offices, the former Regional Governors were retained and redesignated "Advisers" to the new Military Governors. In other words, unlike the political office holders, they were not in disgrace.

One of the very first acts of Col. Ojukwu was to order Sir Francis Akanu Ibiam, former Governor of Eastern Nigeria out of the State House. The order had in fact been given and the State House had been vacated before the Military Governor's maiden broadcast naming those who were to "vacate their former official residences and surrender any government property, including cars, in their possession *forthwith*". It was the manner, not the idea itself, of evicting Sir Francis Akanu Ibiam from the State House that caused some concern among many people. Sir Francis was still to enjoy his salary and most other perquisites of his former office. Nobody could dispute the Military Governor's rights to the State House, but certainly Sir Francis should have been treated with greater decorum and consideration. He could have been invited to move into the old Government House, which was later to lie vacant and unused, instead of being given ordinary civil service quarters. All his previous cars having been removed, he was left for a few days without any means of transport. The Military Governor, however, had nothing personal against Sir Francis, but merely wanted to show evidence of his all-embracing authority. If he could do that to the former Governor of the Region, a man of universal respect in the country, then how much more could he do to ordinary people who might oppose him.

There was also the Military Governor's open hostility towards Dr. Nnamdi Azikiwe, President of the Republic of Nigeria until the coup of January 15th. He openly accused Dr. Azikiwe of all sorts of things, and then shabbily removed him as Chancellor of the University of Nigeria at Nsukka, cut off all incomes accruing to him from his properties in Nsukka, and ordered the African

Continental Bank to recover forthwith all overdrafts or loans outstanding against Dr. Azikiwe or any companies and business establishments with which he might have been associated.

"No person in the Eastern Provinces, except the Military Governor, shall fly *any* flag on cars or private residences." This order overlooked the presence of foreign consulates and of the British Deputy High Commission whose heads were by international convention entitled or required to fly their national flags on their cars and places of residence. There was also the right of the commissioner of police and some categories of army officers to fly flags on their cars. These people continued to exercise that right. All the same, the original instruction pointed to one direction—the pre-eminence and absolute powers of the Military Governor.

His authority was next directed against the civil service. As has already been shown, one of the decisions announced in his maiden broadcast to the nation on January 25th was the abolition of the executive powers of the Public Service Commission, which was now to "act in advisory capacity to the Military Governor in relation to the appointment, promotion, and discipline of senior members of the public service". That appeared irregular and contrary to the Constitution. Decree No. 1, suspending many parts of the Nigerian Constitution, never suspended the parts affecting the position and powers of the Public Service Commissions. However, the Military Governor assumed the executive powers of the Public Service Commission, and later was on several occasions to exercise those powers without even seeking the advice of the Commission.

From the start he made it clear that the control and supervision of the ministries was to be concentrated in his own hands. He virtually became the head of the civil service as well. He was not initially enthusiastic at the idea of having a Chief Secretary or Secretary to the Military Government and Head of the Civil Service. He practically abolished the post for Eastern Nigeria in his first budget proposals, but the Supreme Military Council held at Lagos later overruled him and reinstated the post when the budgets for all the regions of the country were considered by that body. Having been frustrated on that score, he decided to emasculate the position and office of the Secretary to the Military Government by making the State House the real centre of power and control. Permanent Secretaries were to go to him with all their problems, administrative and ministerial, and not to the Secretary to the Military Government, whose duty it should be to coordinate the executive and administrative functions of the ministries.

He cut down the number of ministries from fifteen to twelve, which was not a bad idea, although later (when he declared secession) these were again considerably increased. He then proceeded to re-appoint and re-allocate permanent secretaries. In this exercise he removed practically all the substantive permanent secretaries except myself and one or two others, and replaced them with new and junior officers, all of them two steps in rank below that of permanent secretary, but acting with full salaries in the post of permanent secretary. The substantive permanent secretaries were posted to other duties outside the mainstream of government service, such as those of chairmen of government-owned industries. The few of us who were left in ministries were removed from our former ones. I was transferred from the Ministry of Education to that of Commerce and Industry. Ojukwu did not trust any of the existing regional officers to be his secretary and had to go to Lagos to bring one from the Federal Service.

I do not know whether there was anything personal between him and the head of the regional civil service at the time. But it was clear that Ojukwu did not want to have him. It is possible that this was an expression of his aversion to working with people older than himself. He got the Military Government in Lagos to appoint the then head of the Civil Service as chairman of one of the newly established "Working Parties" based in Lagos. His departure raised the problem of a successor. I happened to be the next man to him, who had on previous occasions always acted when he was away. I must say I personally shared everybody else's belief that I would be called upon to act. The Military Governor had in fact given me a hint along that line sometime before.

From all later indications and events, it appeared that the previous holder did not want me to succeed him. But this could not be avoided if merit and the normal procedure were to be followed. The Military Governor did not, apparently, want to offend the person he was doing all in his power to be rid of. At the same time he did not know how he could justify not promoting me. He called for my confidential files and for days pored over everything about me, including my junior service records. Could it be that he was trying to see if he could discover something to hold against me and which he could show as a reason for denying me what everyone considered to be, and what was in justice, my right? He was clearly in a dilemma.

Eventually, he decided to play the Pontius Pilate by shirking his duty to justice and, lacking the courage to accept responsibility for his actions, he decided, as a way out, to pass the buck. He accordingly decided to resort to a most irregular and extraordinary procedure, namely a system of promotion in the civil service by means of a rigged election.

I was on tour when I was urgently summoned back to Enugu. Reaching there, I was asked to proceed to the State House where I was wanted by the Military Governor. At the State House were all the acting permanent secretaries as well as provincial secretaries specially brought down from their offices in the field, duly assembled. I could not understand, but suspected something underhand. Of a crowd of over thirty persons, only about two were substantive permanent secretaries, while the rest were all officers of deputy permanent grades drawn from Ministries and field administration. Chief Udoji arrived last and later marched us upstairs to the Military Governor. Before doing this, he had had a preliminary discussion with Ojukwu.

The Military Governor received us and then told us that Chief Udoji was proceeding to Lagos to be chairman of the "Working Party on Primary and Secondary Education in Nigeria" which had been set up by the Military Government. It was therefore necessary that someone be appointed to act in his place. He had decided to leave us to choose our own leader. I was stunned and wanted to speak and tell the Military Governor that I would not like to be a party to such an irregular procedure, the effect of which would be to destroy the civil service. Once such a dangerous precedent was set for the highest appointment in the regional civil service, why should it be stopped for others? Positions in the civil service would be open to canvassing, campaigning, bribery and corruption. But I was not allowed any time to speak. The Military Governor handed to each of us a piece of paper and asked us to put down two names, other than our own, of people we would like to be our leader. We did as required and handed over the papers to the Military Governor who stared into the face of each one as he took the ballot paper from him. With Chief Udoji, he counted the votes, and I lost to Mr. C. C. Mordi by two votes.

I must say that I considered it a great personal achievement, knowing that the whole exercise was directed against me. I am one who absolutely eschews tribalism and religious bigotry, but I could not help noticing, nor can I help mentioning here, that of all those who voted only one was not Ibo and only two not members of the Roman Catholic Church. I had just emerged, as permanent secretary, Ministry of Education, from a very serious dispute with the Roman Catholic authorities over the question of establishing school boards in the region in accordance with the recommendations of the Adefarasin Committee on conditions of service for teachers in voluntary agency schools. The Catholic Church's hostile opposition to the measures nearly led to serious civil disturbances, making even Chief Udoji, the head of the civil service, defy all conventions and publicly oppose the Government. The bill establishing school boards was, in spite of all odds, passed just before Christmas, 1965. Such was the gravity of the situation that the Minister and I had decided to resign if the bill were rejected. Before the bill could receive the assent of the Governor in order to become law, the Military took over, and the Military Governor never assented to the bill. It was probably for that reason that I had to be removed from the Ministry of Education lest I should keep on pressing for the bill to be made law. I later learnt from some of those who had taken part in the ballot that they had been instructed beforehand how to vote. There had been a preliminary ballot which produced a tie between me and Mr. Mordi, but instead of the Military Governor giving his casting vote, he called for a subsequent ballot. The fact that Mr. Mordi, of all persons, was selected lends great weight to the story about previous instructions on how to vote. Although the oldest amongst the permanent secretaries, Mr. Mordi was the most junior in appointment as permanent secretary. He had served directly under me both in London and on different occasions in Eastern Nigeria. He is a Roman Catholic and a very close and intimate friend of Chief Udoji. An honest, harmless and guileless man, I can say that he could not willingly have involved himself in any plot to do injustice to a colleague and I was personally sorry for him in the embarrassment into which he was thrown.

This unfortunate incident revealed the Military Governor as a person of weak character, in spite of every attempt to conceal it. It was this weakness and lack of courage which his relatives and close associates subsequently exploited to their personal advantage and gain, and at the expense of the common good. This subject will be dealt with at greater length elsewhere.

Against every advice and warning I decided to fight this outrageous irregularity. In this I knew that the whole of the country's civil services would be behind me. Already the incident had been received everywhere with great shock, and there was general open condemnation. I wrote a strong letter to the Military Governor, stressing not just the irregularity of the procedure, but its dishonesty, spite and corruption—the very vices which he had been preaching against and which the Military Government had vowed itself to eradicate. I analysed the votes as a proof that the election was rigged.

I did it, well aware of the possible consequences of my action. I was prepared to be detained, dismissed, or even shot. I sent the letter to him, and then showed copies of it to various people, including my wife. Practically everyone was disturbed, and vehemently wished that I had not sent the letter. My explanation and excuse was that I had to do it, not because I was personally affected, but in the interests of justice and integrity in the civil service to which I had devoted my career. I did not expect the Military Governor to change his decision, after having accepted the verdict of the vote. Weakness often goes with stubbornness, which was part of Emeka's character. I expected some drastic action against me which might give further publicity to the whole mess. But no reaction came from the Governor, although I was sure he had duly received and read the letter.

Nothing, however, in my action was intended to mean a claim to the office as of right. The governor had the complete and absolute right to choose anyone he liked to be his Chief Secretary. Had he done this, that would have been the end of the matter. If others had agreed to fight the case, I would have kept quiet. But nobody was prepared, not even the civil service association, to take the risk.

Somehow, the story of what had happened got to Lagos, where everybody was disgusted. On the suggestion or recommendation of someone in Lagos, the Supreme Commander agreed that I should go to Lagos for an assignment in the Cabinet Office. I accepted the transfer with mixed feelings, paid a visit to Lagos and was promised an official residence. Back at Enugu I informed friends and started to pack. Some send-off functions were arranged and just as arrangements for our departure to Lagos were to be finalised, the Governor called me to say that I was not to go. He had returned from Lagos the previous night, and while there had informed the Supreme Commander that he needed me in the East. He had now appointed me Chairman of the Eastern Nigeria Marketing Board (which also implied membership of the Nigerian Marketing Company), and member of his Executive Council. This was to be in addition to my post as Permanent Secretary, Ministry of Commerce and Industry, which also involved my control of a number of government boards and companies and membership of others. I thanked him but added that I would have preferred to be allowed to go to Lagos.

This happened about April/May 1966. In August, I was informed that Mr. Mordi, who had been acting as Secretary to the Military Government, was going to be given another assignment and I was appointed substantively to his post. (Chief Udoji was now finally retiring.) When the appointment actually came, it became necessary to restore the pre-coup title of "Chief Secretary" to avoid confusion in the minuting initials of "S.M.G." which could as well apply to the Secretary to the Military Governor as to the Secretary to the Military Government. (These two Offices actually existed in Ojukwu's set-up.) We shall see how little the Governor regarded or respected the civil service as an organisation.

It is impossible to give an accurate assessment of Col. Ojukwu's personal popularity when he arrived in Eastern Nigeria as Governor. Whoever was appointed was bound to ride the surging tide of the popular welcome extended to the military regime. In any case, the people had no choice, and even if they had private misgivings about the appointment of any individual as Military Governor, they could not express such feelings openly. The Governor was therefore welcomed with all enthusiasm. As an Easterner, better understanding was expected from him. But it was not long before people started to whisper aloud, wondering about his actions and behaviour which ran counter to the professed aims of the military regime—and not long before he became probably the most unpopular Military Governor in the country.

The first of these actions were what appeared clear acts of nepotism which both the Governor and the regime as a whole had condemned in no uncertain terms. After announcing the removal from office of all political appointees, the Military Governor announced the re-appointment of his own father as the Chairman of both the Eastern Nigeria Marketing Board and of the African Continental Bank. That these appointments had been political (clear personal merits possessed by the holder notwithstanding) was not in doubt. And even if this were not so, common sense should have warned him that the re-appointment of the Military Governor's father would be misunderstood. But the Military Governor did not stop there. Among the new permanent secretaries appointed was a relation of his to be brought down from Lagos. (The Federal Public Service Commission eventually stopped this.) A very young lawyer (a charming and intelligent young man) was brought in from private practice to hold appointment in his office as legal secretary or adviser—an act which greatly offended the senior civil service lawyers in the Ministry of Justice. And while former Ministers were hounded out of their official residences, the Attorney General and Minister of Justice in the discredited civilian government, his relation, was allowed to stay on for some time in his official residence.

It was no secret that his own relations or people from his clan, even though they might have been well known former politicians and held ministerial appointments, were the real power behind the throne. Proper official advice submitted to the Governor from ministries could be overruled as a result of counter advice by these people who had no proper official positions. All this led to much frustration and resentment not only within the civil service but also outside. It was one clear aspect of the Military Governor's weakness, and a contributory factor in his subsequent tragedy, that he allowed himself to be influenced so absolutely by relatives and others who had no real official responsibilities or any real knowledge or experience, let alone objectivity. And yet in his maiden speech to the nation, the Military Governor had spoken of the public service "being increasingly demoralised because nepotism had become rife".

In that very speech the Military Governor also condemned the former politicians for constructing palaces "for the indulgence of ministers and other holders of public offices—men supposed to serve the interest of the common man. Expensive fleets of flamboyant and luxurious cars were purchased" (for the use of those evil politicians now swept out of power). But the Military Governor's precept in this regard was different from his practice. He had moved into the old State House in the face of open suggestions that it could be converted into a hospital. He went about in a Rolls-Royce belonging either to the state, or to his late father. When travelling out of his residence, and much more so if on a visit outside the township, the retinue and motorcade accompanying him were no less flamboyant than the most ostentatious ever seen in political days. In his residence he drank mainly champagne and served this lavishly to visitors. A leading journalist and public figure from Lagos wrote strongly against this ostentation and lavish living in one of the national newspapers. Added to all this were his personal arrogance, presumptuousness, rudeness and off-handed attitude towards even the highest-placed civilian in public life.

He preached fervently against all forms of corruption and abuses of office, and handed out very harsh punishments to offenders; but his private failings, and his apparent impotence in restraining grasping close friends and ambitious relations robbed his public utterances and actions of much effect and impression.

And yet, I believe that Col. Ojukwu sincerely wished to carry out the aims and aspirations of the military regime. The spirit was willing, but the body weak in the face of the temptations of power and luxury. He passionately believed at that time in the concept of one Nigeria, and meant to do everything to preserve it. This was much in evidence. For one thing, he initially regarded himself as nothing more than the representative of the head of the *only*

Military Government for the country which was based in Lagos. As far as he was concerned, the former regions had been abolished and the country was virtually under a unitary form of government and administration. That is why he always spoke of the ill-fated Decree No. 34 as "formalising as an interim measure the unified nature of army command for the convenience of the Military Government in Lagos". When persons of Eastern Nigerian origin fled the North as a result of the May 1966 disturbances and killings, Col. Ojukwu personally sent them back with assurances of safety. He believed in the creation of states as a means of unifying Nigeria. The appointment of the Emir of Kano as the Chancellor of the University of Nigeria was another proof of his practical belief in the unity of Nigeria. The circumstances of his upbringing contributed greatly to this attitude. He was born in the North and had his education in Lagos and Britain, and never really lived in the East except when he served for a short time in the civil service before joining the army.

He was a very hard worker, clearly intelligent and alert. He was generally distrustful of people, and for this reason tended to take on much more work than any single individual could cope with. His distrust of people, including his official advisers, induced his increasing reliance on the small body of personally selected officials and relatives close to him. The result was that too much importance and power centred on these people. For instance, whereas the head of the civil service was not allowed to see the recommendations or advice tendered to the Governor by the Public Service Commission, a mere assistant secretary in his office had the responsibility of going over those recommendations, which might involve reading the confidential reports of his senior officers, and then advising him further on whether to accept or not to accept the recommendations from the Public Service Commission—that is, of course, where the Governor did not already have alternative ideas from extra-official quarters.

Until January 1969 the State House was the nerve centre of every government action. It was there that questions of policy were determined for the Chief Secretary's office and ministries to execute. The Chief Secretary knew nothing concerning overseas communications, even though selected and trusted junior officers under him had regular access to every such communication. In January 1969, some functions and officers hitherto in the State House were, along with those in the Chief Secretary's office, placed under the general supervision of the Chief Secretary, under the umbrella of one Cabinet Office. The Chief Secretary was supposed to be the head of this new outfit, but the Governor continued to deal directly with individual officers. For instance, the person in charge of security, though technically within the Cabinet Office, was operating from a separate building and dealing directly with the Governor to the exclusion of the Chief Secretary.

For the most part of his service as the Military Governor, Col. Ojukwu was, without knowing it, a prisoner of intimidation and fear—intimidation by his close relations (including childhood guardians) and fear arising from those intimidations and his natural desire to live. Those relatives, professing to be more interested in the Governor's personal safety than anyone else, were always crying wolf, with success, where there was none. They would not allow him to travel except where they approved. Mention may be made of three typical cases of such intimidation. One concerned the first visit the Governor was to make to Calabar. After everything had been arranged, and the Governor was to leave the following morning, relatives assembled that night to dissuade him from going. The following morning, one of his intelligence officers who had been to Calabar returned to say that the Governor would be killed if he dared go there. It took a lot of pleading from me and others involved in the arrangements before the Governor would go. As it turned out, he so liked the place and people that he stayed an extra day!

The same people almost stopped him from going to Aburi after all arrangements had been completed. It was not until after security men had been sent to Accra days before and had returned to report that the Governor would be safe, that he eventually went.

But the most ridiculous and embarrassing act of intimidation related to the executive jet ordered for the Governor's use. On its way to the East the pilot, owing to some misunderstanding, landed in Lagos. For this the Governor was advised to reject the plane. A number of reasons were given for the childish and ridiculous action, one of them being that the plane would have been "bugged" while in Lagos. The assurances of both the dealers and the pilot that nobody in Lagos had even got near the plane, which was kept locked by the pilot all the time it was at the airport, did not make any impression. Another executive jet, which soon proved unsatisfactory, was bought. In the end, the very plane which had been rejected because it had landed in Lagos was accepted, after it had been flown back to Britain.

More telling evidence of Ojukwu's weakness was his aversion to advise, particularly if proffered by senior people. The reason was twofold: he wanted to be the sole governor, and he wanted to show those who might regard themselves as older and therefore more experienced that he could do without them. It was a tactic of keeping himself uninfluenced except by those he chose. He deceived himself into believing in his actions and views, and whether they were intuitive, deliberate or reflex, he considered that they must be right and the best. "Let me do (or handle) it my own way," he would say. "Can you name one instance where I have gone wrong or my tactics did not prove the best?" But the truth was that he never allowed other views or tactics to be put to the test. Where he happened ultimately to accept another person's views, he would start by arguing against such views and maybe rejecting them, only later to give instructions based on those views as if they had originated from him.

The fact was that his tactics and methods were not necessarily better than any other, and even where they produced good results, this did not mean that others might not have produced better results. A classic case was that of some expatriate oilmen, the majority of them Italian, captured by the secessionist forces during one of their incursions into the Mid-West. The captured men had been brought into Biafra where they were kept and well cared for in a strictly guarded and secret place. The capture and fate of these men became a matter of world-wide concern. The Governor handled this incident alone, keeping his plans to himself except perhaps for the few he knew would agree with him. The result of his actions was in this case far less favourable than if plans suggested by others had been followed. At the Executive Council the Governor merely referred the expectant members to "rumours which were going on about some oilmen". Even though it was common knowledge that such people had been captured and had been seen in Biafra, the Governor refused to tell his cabinet what exactly the position was. All he did was to warn members to keep cool while he was handling that "very delicate matter" himself. In the end his shock tactics nearly lost him his friends and supporters in Africa and Europe, and considerably injured his image. One could discern all along that the Governor wanted to release the oilmen, and, although he did probably in the end succumb to pressure by his more die-hard confidants, it is possible that he was not personally keen even on ransom. Then why all the fuss about trial, condemnation and threatened execution? Why the recalcitrance and rude obstinacy towards his strongest supporters in Africa and even in the face of a personal appeal from the Pope and personal visits to Biafra by top ministers from the Ivory Coast, Gabon and Italy? Surely if he had accepted the advice that an immediate announcement of the number and names of those captured should be made, and the International Red Cross informed, his stature and even the cause of Biafra could have been enhanced.

The Governor was a prisoner of self-deception. According to A. W. Tozer, "Of all forms of deception, self-deception is the most deadly, and of all deceived persons the self-deceived are the least likely to discover the fraud." So it was with the promising Military Governor. Half way in office, he came to regard himself as a messiah of the people. He overrated his popularity, intelligence, and personal qualities and as a result lacked humility. He took special delight in the hero's songs composed for him. Many flattered him for favours and patronage while others simply feared him. Those who had his ear never told him the truth either about himself or about what was going on. Those of us who tried were either not believed or simply hushed up as alarmists and worse. Behind it all was fear and a personality complex.

A question which has been anxiously and constantly asked by outsiders, particularly since the end of the civil war is: "How can any reasonable person be expected to believe that Ojukwu could have done all he is accused of without the support of leading personalities?" It depends on what is meant by "all". Policy decisions and their execution are two different matters. In government affairs the real crux is in policy-making, while those paid to carry out policy must do their work or suffer. Clever and highly intelligent though Ojukwu was, he would have had to be more than human to do all the thinking and planning alone, although in most cases the initiative was his. It was his ardent belief and faith that a leader must really lead. But in looking for those who might have helped him to think and plan, one must look quite outside what one might, for lack of a better term, call "the establishment", for which the Governor did not have any particular respect, believing rather in *ad hoc* methods.

Those who were carrying out the Governor's policies naturally included those in the establishment, but they played minor roles except when ordered to carry out specific assignments. For instance, no member of the establishment had anything to do with or even knew much about the buying of arms, or the acquiring and expenditure of foreign exchange. These were rigidly exclusive fields for the trusted few outside the establishment. Policy-making, was, as I have said, the Governor's personal preserve, and for help and advice on this score he could draw from anywhere according to his fancy, the project, or the occasion.

But all this does not answer the important question of how to believe that such eminent and intelligent members of the establishment could carry out Ojukwu's policies in the way they did unless they absolutely agreed with such policies. Incredibly (especially to those outside) they did. The Governor was a good student of power tactics. As pointed out elsewhere in this chapter, he started by shocking people out of their balanced sense of the norm, and those to whom the message went most strikingly were members of the civil service and other public establishments—the police, the judiciary, and even the army. He started by devaluing the persons and positions in the public services. To some extent he virtually depersonalised individuals of influence and authority, whether public servants or former politicians. The situation was once graphically represented by Chief Patrick Okeke, Biafra's Inspector General of Police, when he ruefully said to me, "What sort of life is this? Nobody is any longer anybody in this Biafra. We are virtually without mind, without will, without personality as individuals." It was the tyranny of the gun.

To reinforce his will and methods (and this was boldly evidenced after the second coup in July 1966), there were the "agents of terror"—private informants, agents, paramilitary secret organisations and, later, the special tribunal. Telephones were tapped. Mine was one of them, but it was done so crudely that I discovered the trick and had to make a personal protest to the Military Governor! Consultative assemblies and councils of chiefs and elders were nothing but rubber-stamps passing pre-ordained resolutions. The cabinet was merely deliberative to the end. The decisions were quite simply the Governor's.

Now, what about the army? Here again it appears that the Military Governor was determined from the very start to reduce this to an instrument of his personal will. We have seen how he constituted his Executive Committee when he first arrived in Eastern Nigeria. Only one military member was included. As a result of events following the coup of July 29th, 1966, army officers of Eastern Nigerian origin streamed back to the East. Among them were men like Lt.-Cols. Imo and Hilary Njoku, who were senior to Ojukwu in the military hierarchy. For a while these and a host of other military officers had nothing to do. Some of them, Imo and Njoku for instance, wanted to be associated with what was going on. They suggested that some of them be brought into the Executive Committee (to give it a truly military character). But the Governor kept on dodging the issue by continuing always to "consider the matter". He wanted to be the sole "boss of the show" and was uncomfortable at the very idea of having military officers, senior to himself, on the Executive Committee.

Eventually, he made Njoku military commander and put Imo in charge of civil defence. He also established what he called "the strategic committee" and made the two of them members. But that committee was a sham. It contained some civilians, including myself in my capacity as chief secretary. The committee met occasionally, but never really discussed anything of substance. The Ad Hoc Constitutional Conference had failed, and people really wanted to know what was going to happen next, and where we were going. Were we really interested in settling the disagreement with the Federal Government peacefully through negotiations? If so, what exactly were our demands? In the event of there being a fight if peaceful negotiations failed, were we prepared? The Governor would not give any clear answers or indications to these questions, nor did he allow any serious discussions on them to take place. Only about the possibility of a fight did he say that efforts were being made to acquire arms. Efforts by whom and arms from where? He would not disclose.

As time passed dissatisfaction and frustration grew within the army. Sensing this, I suggested that some of the officers be brought into the Executive Committee and given some supervisory responsibilities over ministries or groups of ministries. Others could be posted to provinces and administrative divisions to assist in the civilian administration. I did this out of a genuine sense of fear of what might happen if the frustration resulting from idleness were allowed to gather momentum within the army. The Governor did not accept the suggestions, but did not openly tell me so. The next thing he did was to instruct the army to direct its full attention to recruitment and training. This was done, and such out-of-the-way places as farm settlements were selected as places of training with sticks and dummies.

Finally, the army officers could wait no longer in silence. They decided to meet the Governor in a group. I do not know what transpired at the meeting. But people present at the meeting informed me that the Military Governor was quite prepared for them. As normal with him on such occasions, he seized the initiative at once by talking, and morally blackmailing the officers. But the meeting did not bring satisfaction, and the Governor sensed the danger, as did many people close enough to notice what was happening. It is most likely that the army had decided to force the issue in its own way. Always alert, the Governor was too clever for them, and his tactics were both dramatic and unconventional.

In a few hours during the evening, he had the parents and relatives of Lt.-Col. Njoku brought to Enugu. He also sent for leading personalities, men and women carefully selected, as well as bishops and chiefs. Before them he blandly accused Njoku of plotting to overthrow him by force. Not that he cared about himself, he said with emotion, but only for the disaster and tragedy that such a move would bring to the people of Eastern Nigeria, particularly the Ibos, for whom he was fighting! Women began to weep and invoke everything against any person conceiving such an evil idea. The bishops began to pray solemnly. Njoku was bereft of words. Activity continued during the whole night and the following day, mainly by bishops and some selected leaders. Njoku had to give promises and undertakings, both orally and in writing, never to do anything to disrupt the government. But the Governor could not take chances. With Njoku in the country and about, he could not feel comfortable or safe. He therefore decided that Njoku must leave. An excuse for this was not difficult to find. Njoku had been with the former Supreme Commander in Ibadan when the latter was abducted by the army. He was wounded but managed to escape. His bones needed treatment and this was a good enough reason for sending him to Britain. Immediately Njoku had gone, the Governor reorganised the army by splitting Njoku's former responsibilities and making himself the over-all commander. In order to create rivalry among the senior officers he promoted Imo, Njoku and Effiong to the rank of Brigadier with the same seniority. By accident or design, Njoku returned to Eastern Nigeria about the very day on which the civil war started. He was given charge of the fighting but under the over-all control of the Military Governor. Even thus, he was not to last very long.

The Governor had all along, since the July 1966 coup, been living in fear. That fear now became real and open. He distrusted the army officers, hence the establishment of the "directorate of military intelligence", a cover name for what turned out to be an all-pervading secret service. For a long time he never slept at night, and in order to keep awake, senior government officials and others had in turn to keep vigil with him in the State House. One incident during that time may be mentioned. Imo was in charge of civil defence. One day it was decided that there would be a practice that night involving the firing of guns and a total blackout. If the Governor knew of the arrangements he possibly did not catch the part about gunfire and a total blackout. I am inclined to the view that he was told, but did not read anything sinister into it, until his friends and relations cried danger. There was panic, and the Governor not only called off the exercise just as it was about to start but sent out personal patrols into the town. We did not sleep at all that night, but drowned our tiredness in drink.

A born actor, Col. Ojukwu, like a chameleon, could turn his mood, posture and action to suit any environment. Among leftists and radicals, he could act their part so perfectly and convincingly as to make them accept him almost unreservedly. Among rightists and conservatives he could do the same. Though by no means a religious man, he could put on a façade of piety and religiousness in order to win the sympathy and respect of visiting bishops, as he won those of local ones by ending all public speeches with prayers to God. As a result, it was always difficult, even for those closest to him, to understand, predict or place him exactly in any given situation.

The intention of this chapter has been to give readers an insight into the personality of the chief character and driving force in the story told in this book. The points raised here will recur as we proceed.

Emeka is in the saddle, and holding firmly the reins of affairs affecting the fourteen million people of Eastern Nigeria, who must helplessly go wherever he leads them—through hills and dales, over rough and smooth, towards life and death.

3 The Kidnap

Following the military take-over in January 1966 the Nigerian Constitution had been suspended in parts, mainly those parts relating to politicians and political institutions. The term "Regions" was suspended in favour of "Groups of Provinces". The term "Federal" was dropped. Military Governors were appointed for the regions now known as Groups of Provinces. In harmony with the unified nature of military command and administration, the "Military Government" was based in Lagos with Major-General Aguiyi-Ironsi as its head and Supreme Commander of the armed forces. The Military Governors of the four Groups of Provinces were to regard themselves as representatives of the Military Government in Lagos. Former regional ministries and government departments were in effect arms of the Military Government in Lagos, and this was particularly the case with economic and development ministries and government departments. Estimates for services in the four "Groups of Provinces" were subject to scrutiny and approval by the Military Government personified in the Supreme Military Council, of which the Military Governors, and the Administrator for the Lagos territory, as well as the top brass of the Armed Forces and the police, were members.

On May 24th, 1966 the Head of the Military Government, with the prior approval of the Supreme Military Council promulgated and published Decree No. 34. On the face of it this decree merely formalised the administrative system which had come into vogue with the military take-over in January. But it also empowered the Military Government to move public servants to serve anywhere in the country. That this must have been the intention of the military administration from the start was indicated by the Military Governor of the Eastern Group of Provinces when he spoke to top Civil Servants (as mentioned in Chapter One) on his assumption of duty. But it had not been done or openly intended until the publication of that decree. At the same time, too, the Head of the Military Government announced that Military Governors were to be rotated. Wisely or unwisely, when the Military Governors were first appointed, they had been posted to their respective native "Groups of Provinces".

Earlier, in February, the Military Government had set up study groups to work "towards national unity and peace". The groups established included "The Constitutional Review Group", "The Working Party on Primary and Secondary Education in Nigeria", "The Working Party on Technical, Commercial and Vocational Education in Nigeria".

It is clear that some sections of the Nigerian population, particularly in the North, saw danger and a threat in these new measures, which they regarded as a means of perpetuating Ibo domination of the country. The feelings in the North at that time were crystallised in an article published by the *New Nigerian* of August 22nd, 1966 in the name of Abubakar Tuggar, part of which read: "The appointment of various study groups to examine ways and means of unifying the country into one solid whole, the declared intention of the former Military Government later to abolish the Regions, and the issuing, haphazardly, of decrees that took the form of extreme centralisation were signs of things to come. But the proclamation of decree No. 34 which transformed Nigeria into a unitary state overnight seemed to be the last straw which broke the camel's back . . . What mattered to the former Military Government was the selfish ambition of some tribesmen to dominate the whole country by all means, fair or foul . . . As a master plan continued to unfold itself we saw being undertaken mass recruitment into the army—with the long arm of tribalism playing its full part, of course—to precede the appointment of Military Prefects and provincial Military Courts so that the former Military Government would be able to take its administration from the national down to the village level. Thus a reign of terror, having been created, was to be perpetuated."

Tuggar's article, written after the overthrow of the former Military Government, explains the reasons behind the tragic incident, as well as the background to the disturbances and killings which had earlier taken place, from May 29th onwards.

These disturbances were confined to Northern Nigeria, and were directed principally against the Ibos, very many of whom were indiscriminately killed, even in churches and hospitals. May 29th was a Sunday, and reports from independent and reliable eye-witnesses spoke of crowds of hostile Northerners breaking into churches, in the midst of worship, attacking and killing the worshippers. And Christians in the North are, by and large, Southerners.

The publication of decree No. 34 is generally regarded, and has been accepted, as the immediate cause of the hostility. Abubakar Tuggar's article confirms this and also gives the impression that the hostility was planned and organised, which is what both Easterners then resident in the North and those at home were telling the world. The Northerners pleaded provocation as a justification for their action. Apart from the decree No. 34, they accused the Ibo Easterners of provocative and insulting utterances and behaviour, including heaping abuse on the memory and photographs of the late Premier of that Region, killed in a military coup led by Ibo army officers. All this may be true, or partially true. I have no means of categorically confirming or denying the allegations. The fact is that the killings and molestations actually took place. It is also a fact that Easterners other than the Ibos were killed. Relations of mine by marriage lost their lives in the disturbances.

As a result, many people from Eastern Nigeria resident in the North fled home to the East, many of them abandoning their jobs and all their possessions. One thing which struck me about the Military Governor of the East was his attitude towards the disturbances. He considered them unfortunate happenings, but personally induced those who had fled the North to return with assurances and promises of safety. Most of those who returned to the North on the basis of those assurances were subsequently killed during the September/October disturbances. Col. Ojukwu never forgot the death of those people and was never able to absolve himself from personal guilt and responsibility. I recall occasions when he had to recount the incident. He must have been inwardly determined to avenge the deaths of those people if those responsible were not punished.

A month after the May 29th disturbances and loss of life, the Military Governor entertained the Emir of Kano, His Highness Alhaji Ado Bayero at a state banquet to mark the latter's installation as the new Chancellor of the University of Nigeria, Nsukka, an appointment made by Governor Ojukwu himself the previous March. In the speech delivered at the end of the banquet, Col. Ojukwu referred significantly to the May incidents, and these were some of his moving words on that occasion:

> "I know that those events have greatly distressed you, as they do all well-meaning Nigerians and friends of Nigeria . . . we must accept the sad events as a challenge to all who have dedicated their energies to the tasks of unity for the country. . . .
>
> "Lives and property have been lost; many have been made homeless; others have been bereft of their loved ones; confidence

has been shaken; fear has replaced faith in one toward the other. These are sad reflections which must remain a source of guilt and shame for all who, by deliberate acts and insinuations, were responsible, directly or indirectly, for them . . . we cannot restore the lives which have been lost nor the blood which has been shed. But we should not ignore the fact that they have been valuable lives and blood. It must, therefore, be our prayer that the innocent blood thus shed will be accepted as the supreme purchase price for the solid and everlasting unity of this country, and that the events which had led to the situation will, for ever, be the worst that this country should experience."

The incidents of May 29th caused a lot of concern to the Military Government, as they did to the people of Eastern Nigeria who demanded that justice be done, or they be allowed to fight it out with the North. In this latter case the Military Governor had to intervene with personal assurances that "appropriate steps were being taken". While the Supreme Military Council was meeting in Lagos to consider the situation and how to tackle it, a meeting of Northern Emirs and Chiefs was also reported. The Supreme Military Council decided to set up a commission of inquiry whose impartiality was unquestionable. A British High Court Judge was accordingly named as Chairman. The Northern Emirs were reported to reject not only the "obnoxious" decree No. 34 but also any idea of investigation into the May disturbances which might lead to the punishment of those concerned.

The Military Government apparently did not want such an open confrontation between itself and the natural rulers and chiefs of the largest Region of the country. So Major-General Aguiyi-Ironsi as the head of that government, decided to tour the country and explain, visiting the North first. He started his tour of the country on July 25th, after issuing invitations to chiefs and natural rulers all over the country to meet and advise him in Ibadan on July 28th.

I must mention here that the attitude and efforts of Col. Ojukwu during this period convinced everyone that he sincerely believed in the unity of the country, and was dedicated to that end. The few Northerners with whom I have spoken do not deny this fact although they hold the view that his efforts towards this end were motivated by his belief and expectation that "his tribesmen would dominate the country forever"—to use their exact words.

Major-General Aguiyi-Ironsi arrived in Ibadan as scheduled and addressed the Emirs, Chiefs, Obas and natural rulers from all over the country on July 28th. While in Ibadan he stayed as the honoured guest of the Military Governor of the Western Group of Provinces, Lt.-Col. F. A. Fajuyi. On the morning of July 29th, elements of the Nigerian Army kidnapped both the guest and the host.

The news of the kidnap reached the general public of Eastern Nigeria on July 30th. I first had a hint of it when I went to the State House that morning in connection with the affairs of my ministry. There I was told that something very serious had happened and the Governor had convened a meeting of the Executive Committee for eleven o'clock. It was only twenty minutes to that hour by my watch, and so, as a member of the Executive Committee, I decided to wait without bothering to see the Military Governor, who was reported to be in a very black mood.

We found the Military Governor a very disturbed man. The meeting was short. All that he told us was that the Supreme Commander had been kidnapped by Northern Nigerian elements of the army. He was in touch with Ibadan and elsewhere and would keep everyone informed. "One thing is clear, however," the Governor said ominously, "these people are quite bent on annihilating the Ibos."

That afternoon we learnt that the Governor had suddenly left the State House for an undisclosed destination. There was panic, and every one started moving out of the government residential area. Not having anywhere to go within Enugu or the suburbs, I decided to stay put in my house with my family. But anxious and frightened friends would not allow us to do so. By 11 p.m. that night I decided, on the basis of *vox populi vox dei,* to leave. But for where? Our Canadian friend had a ready answer in his garage in the Queen's School compound. That settled, we had to decide where friends and relatives staying with us should go. Finally I found myself, wife and children spending an uncomfortable and dreadful night huddled together in the friend's garage where two camp beds had been improvised. Other inmates of our house and compound scattered in different directions—most did not have people to whose houses they might go and so had to crouch under trees and shrubs around the compound, while others had to sleep on church verandahs and in market stalls. The following day we all decided to go back to our residence and face the consequences, whatever they might be.

The Eastern Chiefs and natural rulers, who had gone to Ibadan, returned early in the evening of July 30th with varying eye-witness accounts of what had happened. Late that night I learnt that the Governor had returned to Enugu and was staying in the Police

Headquarters. When I saw him the following morning I noticed that he had moved house and office there. The whole place was crammed with the Governor's staff and relatives. He was almost continuously on the telephone to Lagos.

In the afternoon of July 31st, he called a meeting of the Executive Committee to bring members up to date. He informed us that Brigadier Ogundipe whom he had contacted and urged, as the next senior military personnel after Major-General Aguiyi-Ironsi (whose whereabouts were still unknown), to assume control of the army and of the Military Government, had told him that the situation was out of hand and that he was not in a position to do anything. He had contacted Col. Gowon who, according to information, was then in the Ikeja barracks, and he too had said he was not a "free agent". The position was therefore absolutely confused. The Governor then asked us to go but to remain within call as it might be necessary for him to get in touch with us hourly.

The next meeting was held that evening. The Governor now told us that the position was becoming clearer. Major-General Aguiyi-Ironsi and his host Lt.-Col. Fajuyi had been kidnapped by a group of Northern officers and men of the Nigerian army; Ibo army officers had been killed in all the garrisons in the North, the West and Lagos; he mentioned some names. He further informed us that Col. Gowon had told him that the Northern Region of Nigeria wanted to secede from the rest of the country and that the only condition for ending bloodshed was that the Republic of Nigeria should be split into its component parts, and that all Southerners resident in the North should be repatriated to the South and vice versa. Col. Ojukwu had discussed the matter on the telephone with Brigadier Ogundipe and had agreed that if that was all that the North wanted in order to end the bloodshed they should be allowed to go. This decision had accordingly been conveyed to Col. Gowon. As he was still talking to us the telephone rang, and we heard the Governor say in a stern voice, "Yes, if that is what they want I agree. Let them go!" He dropped the telephone and told us that he had been talking to Brigadier Ogundipe. We met again later that night, but the position had remained virtually the same, except that our Governor could no longer contact Brigadier Ogundipe on the telephone. We stayed with the Governor until past midnight before we went home, leaving him with his body-guards and relations, and not sure what might happen next or even on our way home. The atmosphere was still heavily charged with fear and tension.

When we met next morning, August 1st, we heard that Col. Gowon (as he then was) would broadcast to the nation that afternoon. We assembled at the appointed time and together heard the broadcast at the Regional Police Headquarters. As I shall be quoting part of that broadcast in a subsequent chapter, as well as describing the reaction at Enugu, I shall not go into those matters here. Suffice it to say that Col. Gowon announced that he had assumed the positions of Supreme Commander and Head of the Military Government of Nigeria.

SECTION II

THE GERMS OF CIVIL WAR

4 Futile Negotiations

(a) The Meeting of the Representatives of the Military Governors

The next few days saw continuous telephone contact between Enugu and Lagos. Col. Ojukwu was demanding the removal of the Northern Nigerian elements of the Nigerian army stationed at Enugu, and the return of the Eastern Nigerian elements of the Nigerian army to Enugu from wherever they might be. But the removal of Northern troops from Enugu was the most immediate necessity, to enable the Governor to return to the State House. Many things were discussed on the telephone between the two colonels during those days. There were times when the conversations were heated and tones high and urgent. It was apparent that Col. Ojukwu was not willing to accept Col. Gowon as Head of the Military Government and Supreme Commander of the Armed Forces.[1] He repeatedly asked and shouted, "Where is the Supreme Commander?" I believe our Governor also spoke on occasions to his counterparts in Benin and Ibadan.

A few days later we were told that it had been agreed that representatives of the Military Governors should meet in Lagos on the 9th August to discuss and advise on what to do immediately in order to stop further bloodshed and reduce tension. Professor Eni Njoku had already been sent to Lagos, and the Governor now named Mr. C. C. Mojekwu and myself as his representatives, and ordered us to proceed to Lagos where we would be joined by Professor Eni Njoku, who was already there, for the talks. I did not know why I was chosen—it might have been in anticipation of my imminent appointment, which the Governor had apparently decided to make, as the Secretary to the Military Government now that the former substantive holder was retiring, or that I was the handiest member of the minority ethnic group in the Region, to send along with the other two who were Ibos. My feeling at the time was, however, that I had been chosen because I had been the most outspoken at the recent discussions (see Chapter on Secession). I was nonetheless happy

1. The term "Commander-in-Chief" came later after the Aburi meeting.

to undertake the assignment. Many were genuinely and greatly worried about our safety. I recall Mr. Mojekwu writing what appeared to be last instructions to his wife as we were about to board the plane.

Before our departure the Governor gave us detailed points to be included on the agenda of the meeting. So detailed were the instructions that they ran to twenty-two items. It is interesting to mention these points since they subsequently constituted the basis of our stand both at the Ad Hoc Constitutional Conference and at Aburi, and clearly show how even in those confused days, the Governor had firmly made up his mind on what he wanted and whither he was going to lead the people of the East. The points were:

> (1) Repeal decree No. 34 and return to Regional autonomy. (2) The Central Executive Council should be enlarged to include wider shade of opinion. (3) Armed units in each area should consist of people drawn mainly from the inhabitants of the area.* (4) All Northern soldiers in the East to be removed with immediate effect.* (5) Rights of equality of all Nigerians. (6) Review of the present constitutional system as begun by the review panel. (7) Meeting at a place unanimously accepted by all the members (of the Supreme Military Council), but meeting not yet necessary until preliminary agreements are implemented.* (8) What has happened to the Supreme Commander and Lt.-Col. Fajuyi and Brigadier Ogundipe?* (9) Names of casualties (of the July and subsequent disturbances) to be listed. (10) Immediate compensation for the families of those killed in the recent disturbances. (11) We must continue the Northern enquiry and the venue should be Lagos not Kaduna. (12) Find a way of giving Regions the right to make arrangements for internal security.* (13) Autonomy of Regions in police and security measures. (14) National Government to give money for resettlement of refugees and compensation.* (15) Military inquiry into the reasons for the disturbances. (16) Release of detainees of January 15th disturbances.* (17) Road blocks and train searches to be stopped. (18) There should be a standing committee of elders, leaders, chiefs to be called upon for advice as and when necessary both in the Regions and in the Centre.* (19) Exchange of Eastern personnel working for the Federal Government.* (20) Make Lagos a free area with free port facilities.* (21) Compensation for all escapees. (22) No change (in boundaries of) Regions.*

Naturally, all these points could not be discussed at the kind of meeting to which we were going, if only because of lack of time and the fact that it was an emergency. However, we did succeed, as we shall see, in getting favourable decisions on those points which were discussed at the meeting, namely, Nos. (1), (3), (4) and, in modified forms, (6) and (7). As we shall see in a subsequent chapter, practically all the twenty-two points were later to be raised and carried almost a hundred per cent by the Governor at the Aburi meeting of January 1967.

We arrived at the Lagos airport, Ikeja, on the evening of August 8th, and found the place filled with armed soldiers. I stepped out of the plane and passed through the columns of soldiers without any incident; but my colleague, Mr. Mojekwu, was accosted by the soldiers who suspected him of being a soldier, and demanded that he produce his identity card. Mr. Mojekwu was naturally frightened but was quick-witted enough to treat the matter with some humour. Patting his stomach he smilingly asked the grim-faced soldiers, "Can a soldier have a tummy like this?" It worked. The soldiers smiled and let him pass, and that smile reassured us that they were after all human.

A police driver, an Easterner, had been sent for us. Although he had our names and identities mixed up at first, he eventually took us to where we were supposed to stay, along the Marina. The police driver happened to be one of those who had accompanied Major-General Aguiyi-Ironsi to Ibadan and so was able to tell us what he saw. He also confirmed the stories we had heard before leaving Enugu, that some prominent persons from the East had been called out of their houses at night and killed. Such were our fears and apprehension for our lives that we decided not to stay where arrangements had been made for us. Our excuse was that we had already booked accommodation at the Ikoyi hotel, which was not true. We subsequently drove straight to the Ikoyi hotel, booked and paid for accommodation there without intending to use it. We then decided to separate and sleep at different places and meet in the morning at the hotel in order to be taken to the meeting place. Since Professor Eni Njoku was not present at Enugu when the Governor briefed us on the points to raise, we had to find him and brief him that night for the following morning's meeting.

That evening of August 8th, the new Head of State and Supreme Commander of the Armed Forces broadcast a statement of policy to the nation. The tone of the speech was more reassuring to the country than the one of August 1st. The main points of the broadcast were:

(i) He was doing everything possible for a return to civilian rule as soon as it could be arranged.

(ii) The Military Governors of the Eastern, Western, Mid-Western and Northern Provinces had all agreed with him that there was urgent need for discussions, "at the appropriate level, to pave the way for the people to express their views as to the form of association they desire for themselves".

(iii) "This great country of ours has much to benefit by remaining a single entity in one form or another."

(iv) Immediate repeal of decree No. 34 as well as the "modification or nullification of any provision of any decree which assumes extreme centralisation". The Military Governors had all agreed that a new decree be issued to repeal decree No. 34 and return to the *status quo ante*.

(v) "An immediate meeting of the already proposed Advisory Committee to follow up deliberations already in progress." One of the first tasks of the advisory committee would be to pave the way for a constitutional review assembly reflecting all shades of opinion throughout the Republic.

(vi) The constitutional review assembly would, when established, make recommendations which would be subject to a referendum.

(vii) As a military man, he had no political ambition. His task was not to impose any form of government on the people, but to pave the way for the people to determine the form of government they wished for ensuring the stability and unity of the country.

Our meeting, which was due to start at eleven o'clock on August 9th, was delayed for more than an hour because the plane bringing representatives from the North did not arrive until 11.50 a.m. We were already in the conference hall when the Secretary to the National Military Government informed us of the delay. There were many armed soldiers around the building and inside the hall—which made us rather uncomfortable. At twelve noon, the Supreme Commander accompanied by the Inspector General of Police, the Head of the Navy, the Acting Chief of Staff, and the Military Administrator of Lagos arrived and addressed the delegates in the heavily guarded conference room.

Welcoming the delegates as "representatives of the Provincial Governors", the Supreme Commander expressed the hope that the meeting would "yield good results in the national interest". He referred to the events of July 29th, and said that it would be futile to pretend that serious damage had not been done to inter-people relations in the Republic. Whatever might be the arguments, it was only honest, he pointed out, to recognise and appreciate the feelings of bitterness on all sides. He appealed to the delegates to view "the whole situation realistically and in its true perspectives". Sentiments must not be allowed to cloud the main issues involved. He then commended the text of his policy broadcast of the previous night to the consideration of the delegations which were composed as follows:

North

Sir Kashim Ibrahim
Alhaji Usman Sarki, Etsu Nupe
Alhaji Baba Ardo—Attorney-General
Alhaji Mohamed Tukur Emir of Yakuri
A. A. Okpabi Oci'Idoma Ochi Idoma
Alhaji Yusufu Gobir
Mr. S. B. Awoniyi

West

Professor Akin Mabogunje
Dr. F. A. Ajayi—Solicitor-General

Mid-West

Chief T. E. A. Salubi
Dr. Christopher Okojie
Mr. D. P. Lawani

East

Mr. C. C. Mojekwu
Professor Eni Njoku
Mr. N. U. Akpan

It had been the understanding that the Governors were to send two representatives each. It was therefore rather a surprise to us when it was announced on the radio the day before the meeting that the North was sending two representatives, three assistant representatives and a number of advisers. All of them entered the conference room and took their seats. As a means of easing the tension with some humour, our delegation asked me to introduce myself, when my turn came, as the adviser. The Northern delegation explained that they had only two delegates, and that the others were advisers and had come into the conference room only because they had arrived from the airport direct and it had not yet been arranged where they should sit. As it turned out, the advisers all found themselves obliged right through the conference to "advise" the whole meeting by standing up to speak in their own right—and the meeting did in fact benefit greatly from their advice.

It had been left to the delegates to elect their own Chairman, and Sir Kashim was elected.[1] After two days of deliberations and arguments the meeting approved the following recommendations:

(1) Immediate steps should be taken by the Supreme Commander to post military personnel to barracks within their respective regions of origin.

(2) Having regard to its peculiar position the question of

1. The decision was that the chairmanship should rotate daily among the heads of the delegations. But as it became clear that the meeting would be a short one, Sir Kashim presided right through.

maintenance of peace and security in Lagos should be left to the Supreme Commander in consultation with the Military Governors.

(3) A meeting of this committee or an enlarged one should take place in a week's time to recommend in broad outlines the form of political association which the country should adopt in future.

(4) Immediate steps should be taken to nullify or modify any provisions of any decree which assumed extreme centralisation.

(5) The Supreme Commander should make conditions suitable for an urgent meeting of the Supreme Military Council as a further means of lowering tension. (This last recommendation was made even though everyone realised that no Military Governor would be willing to attend a meeting of the Supreme Military Council in Lagos at that time. The Eastern delegation had been insisting, in accordance with their mandate, on a meeting "at a place unanimously accepted by all the members of that Council".)

It is worth mentioning here that the Western delegation had said from the start that they were not in a position to participate seriously in the discussions since they had not been briefed by their Governor, who was then quite new. It was therefore agreed that the meeting should not enter into discussions about the form of a future association until the West was ready. It was for this reason that all present felt that the reconvening of the meeting, the composition of which might be altered or enlarged, should not be postponed for more than a week—hence the recommendation (3) quoted above.

The whole meeting had been conducted in a very cordial and calm atmosphere except once when, as the leader of the Eastern delegation, Mr. C. C. Mojekwu was pressing home some points rather strongly, and a member of the Northern delegation, Alhaji Usman Sarki, cut in and asked why the East had not taken the stand they were now taking after the event of January 15th. (In fairness to him, he subsequently apologised for butting in and making the heated remark.) During a preliminary "friendly" chat, a member of the Eastern delegation had told a Northern delegate, again Alhaji Usman Sarki, that the North would be given what they wanted, and Alhaji Usman had quickly replied that they should not be given what they wanted. When in the course of debate an indirect reference was made by the leader of the Eastern delegation to what the Emirs and Chiefs of the North were reported to have decided, the Northern delegation retorted that what we might have heard was the decision of the Chiefs, and not that of the Northern people. These points, trivial as they seem, are significant in that they showed the changing attitude of the North, and that was why I mentioned them in my notes.

(b) The Ad Hoc Constitutional Conference

It had been recommended by the meeting of Military Governors' representatives, that "this committee or an enlarged body should take place in a week's time to recommend in broad outlines the form of political association which the country should adopt in future". The recommended "enlarged committee" turned out to be the high powered Ad Hoc Constitutional Conference meeting a month instead of a week later. The delay appeared to have been agreed among the military leaders to allow for adequate preparation. Memoranda were to be exchanged among the delegations. We in the East worked very hard to crystallise our ideas.

There was a committee of leading persons under the chairmanship of the Chief Justice, Sir Louis Mbanefo. It was a voluntary meeting to consider a matter deemed to be of the utmost national importance. The Military Governor officially appointed what was called a "constitutional committee" under the chairmanship of the attorney-general, Dr. Graham-Douglas, but restricted it to considering the "*future constitution of Eastern Nigeria*". I was a member of both committees.

The Graham-Douglas committee met once or twice and then fizzled out because the chairman soon lost interest. The unofficial Mbanefo committee continued meeting regularly, without evoking any particular interest or respect from the Military Governor who, we later discovered, had already made up his mind on the issues involved, and was working with a "secret" committee, two of whose members had been invited by Sir Louis Mbanefo to join his committee and occasionally turned up to participate in the discussions. It now appears that they were both spying on us and picking our brains.

The Military Governor had on August 31st convened a meeting of the Consultative Assembly and in his opening address had asked them to consider for the impending meeting in Lagos "the position of the armed forces in any association, bearing in mind what I have said earlier, namely that the basis for unified military command in Nigeria no longer exists". He went on, "You have to consider what economic ties will bind the component parts of Nigeria, to ensure our unrestricted economic development and that our funds are not unnecessarily diverted to others. You have to consider where the responsibility for foreign affairs will lie and to what extent the region will cooperate in the formulation of foreign policy, bearing in mind the necessity of exercising full control over our economic and defence agreements, and to establish friendly relations with countries of our choice. You will have to consider the political arrangements for the supervision of the common services. You will also consider what type of constitution will be best suited to Eastern Nigeria."

The university intellectuals were busy, producing documents and theses—historical, economic, political—on the future association of Eastern Nigeria with Nigeria. They had returned to the East in large numbers and immediately started exerting effective and respected influence on the Governor They were all using their "knowledge, findings and research" to show that the Nigerian Federation had failed and should either be broken up or kept together by means of a very loose association. "Any state that cannot guarantee a citizen security of his person and his property has no right to demand his allegiance. Recent events have shown that security of the person and of property does not exist for a large section of the community." That was how one of them opened his memorandum entitled "Issues and Objectives".

In the end it was the views and stance of these people which prevailed, because they agreed with the Governor's own intentions, not with those of Sir Louis Mbanefo and his committee. It was during the final preparation of the documents, which involved my having to express in writing points and positions agreed for the delegates to take with them as briefs, that it dawned upon me that those concerned had lost interest and faith in the existence of Nigeria as a strong political unit. In the end I was completely ignored because of my doubts and scepticism about what was being proposed. The total aim of the memoranda of the East was the abolition of the central government for the country and its replacement with a loose and scarcely effective common services organisation. The former component parts of the Federation would, for instance, be able to keep their own independent armies and the police "for internal security". (Cp. the briefs given to the Eastern delegation to the meeting of August 9th, mentioned in the first section of this Chapter.)

It was not, however, the East alone which advocated a loose association. The Northern memoranda was also in favour of this and even included the right of any part to secede. The West and the Mid-West also wanted something looser than before. The significant point was that the Easterners had in the past consistently been the greatest protagonists of a united Nigeria, and it was because of their enthusiasm in this regard that some sections ironically suspected them of wanting to dominate the country. It was probably because of this complete volte-face that, paradoxically, they were suspected by those who had in the past been the strongest advocates of the loose-association now proposed by the East; and these had, therefore, to make a similar volte-face. Thus, they took up the extreme opposite position, including the idea of creating new states all over the country—a matter they would not even hear of in the past. It was these contradictory positions which eventually caused the impasse and failure of the first meeting of the conference.

Of the recommendations made by the representatives of the Military Governors at the meeting of August 9th, the most crucial one for the East was the posting of military personnel to their respective regions of origin. This had been only partially implemented, in that the Northern troops were removed from the East and Eastern troops were being returned from other parts of the country to the East. Northern troops stationed in the West were not removed. When the time approached for the Eastern delegates to leave for the meeting in Lagos, the majority of those selected to represent the East were reluctant to go "for fear of the Northern troops still stationed in the Western Region". They wanted these soldiers removed, in order that they might feel free and safe while in Lagos, otherwise they would not travel. In this they had a lot of public support. But the Military Governor was determined that they should go, and virtually forced them to do so. Early on the morning of September 12th, he broadcast to the people of Eastern Nigeria, assuring them that the delegation from Eastern Nigeria would be quite safe in Lagos. He had received that assurance by telephone, telegram and in writing. "As a soldier, Lt.-Col. Gowon must be trusted to keep his word of faith and honour."

The delegation from Eastern Nigeria comprised thirteen persons drawn from different parts of the Region, accompanied by two officials. It was to have been fourteen persons but one of them, a leading lawyer, stubbornly refused at the last moment through fear to go, and chose to remain behind "to assist" the Governor. He was one of those who played decisive roles in the affairs of the Region even though he held no official position, and had never even been a prominent politician. The team was led by Professor Eni Njoku with Mr. C. C. Mojekwu as his deputy. The delegation, through its leader, was instructed to adhere strictly to their brief and not to depart from it without reference to the Governor. Such was the Governor's determination to control the conduct and activities of the Eastern Nigerian delegation in Lagos that even their opening speech was drafted at Enugu for them. For reasons which I could only conjecture, the Governor also decided, for the duration of the conference, to keep in Enugu as his "guests" and continuous "advisers", a number of prominent and vociferous personalities from different parts of the East. Among those so invited from the Efik/Ibibio area was Chief E. O. Eyo, but Eyo quickly left the Region for Lagos the night he received, or had hint of, the invitation. The Governor saw the invitees only once during all this period, and that was when he welcomed them to explain the purpose of their presence in Enugu. Beyond that the invitees did and were told and asked nothing! They were given their meals and a daily allowance. They could not leave Enugu without the permission of the Governor. My conjecture afterwards was that the Governor wanted those leading persons there as a means of blackmail should they later reject what might be decided, or even disagree with the stand of the Eastern delegation in Lagos, particularly over the issue of the creation of new states. It was significant that the majority of those brought to Enugu were from the minority non-Ibo areas of the Region. An even more likely reason was that their presence would enable the Governor to keep up the façade of always acting in accordance with the advice and wishes of the people, a façade of which the much vaunted "Joint Meeting of the Council of Elders and of the Constitutional Assembly" was a classic feature.

Opening the conference on September 12th, the Head of State categorically ruled out any idea of breaking up the country. Part of his opening address read:

> "It is very clear to me that it will be economically and politically suicidal to harbour any idea of a complete break-up of the Federation. Therefore we seem to be left with the alternatives of:
>
> (*a*) a Federation with a strong central Government
> (*b*) a Federation with a weak central Government
> (*c*) a Confederation.
>
> On the other hand, it may be that through your deliberations, which commence here today, we may be able to devise a form of association with an entirely new name yet to be found in any political dictionary in the world, but peculiar to Nigeria."

Five days later, on September 17th, the conference was adjourned for three days to enable the Northern delegation to have further consultations both in Kaduna and Lagos. The delegation for Eastern Nigeria also took this opportunity to send one of their members home to brief the Military Governor. The Western Delegation did not altogether like the adjournment and their feelings were expressed by their leader, Chief Awolowo, who accused the North of trying to exploit the fact of their being "in control" of the country.

An example of how the Eastern delegates were to be delegates in the strictest sense of the term by acting always on instructions, occurred when the delegation, following the trend of developments at the conference, wanted to manoeuvre even within their brief. Mr. Matthew Mbu, one of the delegates, was sent to Enugu, to brief the Governor face to face on what was happening.[1] After receiving the personal report from Mr. Mbu, the Governor was not very happy that the delegation should try to show flexibility, and therefore sent Mr. Mbu back with the following written instructions to Professor Eni Njoku.

(1) The East should open the next meeting on Tuesday with a clear statement deploring the fact that a whole week had been wasted without a single decision being recorded. According to the recommendations of the meeting of the Governor's representatives on the 9th of August, the meeting now being held should have been held over a month ago. That meeting of the 9th of August seemed to have had a better appreciation of the grave urgency of the situation than the current meeting. We of the East had accepted the delay in convening the meeting because we learnt that the various governments were carrying out intensive consultations with a view to bringing to the present conference final briefs and proposals without having to call for adjournment for consultations. You will stress the point that this has been a source of real disappointment to the people of the East, whose delegation has thereby been compelled to waste four idle days in Lagos, in order that other delegations could return home for further consultations. You should insist upon adherence to the known programme, the first item of which is to decide on the type of association for the people of Nigeria which will eliminate all areas of conflicts, and provide peace and security for its inhabitants. Ours must be a Loose association of Autonomous Regions.

(2) There shall be a Central Authority, but this authority shall exercise powers and carry out functions delegated to it by the Regions and clearly specified in the Constitution. Such authority shall have equal representations from the component parts of the country.

(3) There should be provision for *secession,* as for automatic review of the constitution after a specified period.

(4) There shall be no Federal Public Service Commission. The respective Regions will expand their civil services having in mind the need to contribute their quotas for the central services.

(5) The question of central banking and coinage is something which must be very carefully looked into. I am worried by the news that the Federal Government, because of shortage of funds for its services, has authorised the printing of a large quantity of unbacked notes for circulation. Such a unilateral inflationary decision could damage the economy of the component parts. I shall send to the conference, when the time comes, economic experts who will advise

1. The Governor had in fact been fully briefed and advised on the phone by Mr. Mujekwu before Mr. Mbu arrived.

on detailed arrangement with a view to safeguarding our future in this respect.

(6) Railways. The maintenance of existing ones should remain the responsibility of the Central Authority. We must not commit ourselves about new railways which may be opened in the future.

(7) Existing ports should belong to the Regions, but other Regions will have free use and access.

(8) National Shipping Line should remain with the Central Authority, but not shipping generally.

(9) Navigation on the Niger, Benue and Chad to be national and controlled by Central Authority.

(10) Territorial waters should remain the responsibility of the Central Authority.

(11) Aviation—safety and maintenance of standards should remain the responsibility of the Central Authority.

(12) We must insist that the North keeps the Niger Dams.

(13) Foreign trade and external publicity should be Regional responsibilities.

(14) The Armed Forces (including the Navy) must be regionalised, with commands remaining with the Regions.

(15) Lagos. Our attitude remains that Lagos belongs to the West, but we must not declare this attitude too soon. Lagos must be used as a bargaining bait with the West, and we must use every tactic to prod the West into a position of having to approach us for a bargain here. One way of doing this might be to choose a strategic moment to remind the conference that, as for now, Lagos belongs to all as a Federal territory. This moment could be after the Lagos delegation have spoken, and we take the opportunity to raise the question of the status of Lagos, the position of whose delegation at the conference could be described as awkward, having regard to its present status as Federal territory. There is no question of considering Lagos as a state either now or for the future. You will use your discretion to decide how and when to use this stratagem.

(16) Mid-West. We should at an appropriate moment express our understanding and appreciation of the difficulties of this new Region, and propose financial assistance to them by means of capital grants.

Those extracts, apart from confirming the Governor's determination to secede (see Chapter on Secession) also reveal the character of a man who knew where he was going and how to get there. It shows how firmly he controlled everything personally. The surprising and most damning aspect of the matter is that, in spite of this unshakeable determination, he repeatedly told the world, his followers and even his senior officials, that the East had no intention of seceding "unless forced out".

As was bound to happen and might have been expected, the conference did not make much headway. Some agreements towards a loose association were reported at one stage, but the North later suddenly changed its mind, declared its support for a strong central government for the country, called for the simultaneous creation of states all over the country and, in spite of the fact that their original memoranda had provided for a secession clause, would not even tolerate a discussion about secession. On September 29th, accounts of fresh violence against the killings of Easterners were reported from the North. These had assumed far greater proportions than those of the previous May. The conference was adjourned until October 23rd. The Eastern delegation went home determined never to return.

On October 23rd, the other delegations assembled in Lagos as planned, but the Eastern delegation did not appear. They wanted the Northern troops still stationed in Western Nigeria to be removed and sent North, as had been recommended by the representatives of the Military Governors on August 9th, before they would return to Lagos for the meeting. Alternatively, they insisted, the conference should be held outside Nigeria. All subsequent persuasions, promises, and overtures failed to make the East change its mind. The conference again adjourned until November 17th. On November 16th, when it was absolutely clear that efforts to make the East participate would never succeed unless their conditions were accepted, and with the Federal Government unwilling to accede to the conditions, the Head of State adjourned the conference indefinitely, there being no useful purpose served by keeping it in existence. Earlier, Chief Awolowo had resigned as leader of the Western Nigerian delegation to the conference.

(c) *The Meeting of the Supreme Military Council at Aburi, Ghana, January 4th and 5th, 1967*

With the failure of the Ad Hoc Constitutional Conference, and its eventual indefinite suspension, the prospects of peace and unity for Nigeria seriously deteriorated. Many people both in Nigeria and abroad were alarmed by the increasing possibility that the East might secede from the rest of the Federation. It was this alarm and fear which brought the British High Commissioner in Nigeria, Sir Francis Cumming-Bruce, and the American Ambassador to Nigeria, Mr. Elbert Matthews, all the way from Lagos to Enugu, to persuade the Military Governor to work for a peaceful solution and the unity of Nigeria. They also issued a mild warning, in diplomatic fashion, against secession. The Military Governor gave them every assurance that the East had no intention whatever of seceding, unless forced to do so. But these experienced diplomats appeared to see deeper than the Governor realised, for, after the meeting, the British High Commissioner, on behalf of himself and the American Ambassador, wrote to the Governor an account of what they had understood from him, and what they had said to him, and reminded him at the same time of his undertaking to publish the exchanges. (See Chapter on Secession.)

As a gesture of goodwill and to show the East that the rest of the Federation cared about and regretted the atrocities directed against Easterners in a section of the country, a delegation of Western Nigeria Obas and Chiefs visited Enugu, as did a delegation of top Federal civil servants, trying to find out what exactly the East wanted in order to cooperate for unity and peace in the country.

As a follow-up to the visit by the top British and American diplomats already mentioned, the American Consul and the British Deputy High Commissioner in Enugu (Messrs. Robert Barnard and Jim Parker respectively) paid many visits to the State House carrying messages from their principals to the Governor. Nor were diplomats from other countries idle. They came to Enugu in turn with messages and pleas for the unity and peace of Nigeria.

In November 1966, seeing the dangerous trends in the East, I contacted my counterparts among the Secretaries to the Military Government in the North, West, Mid-West and Lagos, urging that we owed a duty to the country not to sit idle while it was thus burning. The first person I spoke to was Alhaji Ali Akilu of the North and I was encouraged by his ready acceptance that we should meet. He even offered to come to Enugu if necessary. Eventually all of us, the Secretaries of the Military Government, met in Benin. Such was the importance I attached to that meeting that I had to leave the dead body of my own sister in Enugu, in order to attend. At the meeting I was able to tell them, as forcefully as I could, of my fears and apprehensions. (Later, the Head of State in his usual generous way thanked me when we met in Aburi for my small efforts to bring about peace and understanding.) We all agreed that the situation was extremely serious and urgent. We therefore decided to do all in our power to bring about a meeting of the Military Governors.

Immediately following our meeting was that of the Advisers to the respective Military governors. They too agreed on the urgent need for the Military Leaders to meet, and accordingly pledged their immense influence to bring about such a meeting in order to save the country, and they issued a public appeal to this effect.

Lastly came the personal efforts of Mr. Malcolm Macdonald, that well-known veteran of British diplomacy. He visited the East more than once, commuting between Lagos and Enugu. He spoke to the Governor both in Enugu and at Onitsha. His efforts ultimately put the seal to all discussions and secret moves to bring about a meeting of Nigerian Military Leaders outside the country.

Thus it was the combination of many efforts, involving hard work and seasoned diplomacy, which eventually brought about the famous meeting of the Nigerian military leaders at Aburi, a meeting which has already assumed a prominent place in the history of Nigeria.

It does not appear that the Governor's personal advisers had much of a say while the discussions for the meeting were going on between the Governor and the different intermediaries. They no doubt knew about them, but probably did not believe that anything concrete would be achieved. I say this because, immediately the final arrangements were concluded, they raised the usual alarm about the Governor's personal safety in Ghana. His Nigerian enemies could quite easily arrange to kill or kidnap him there, they pointed out, mentioning the presence of many Hausas in Ghana—and Hausas, of course, were resolute "enemies" of Easterners and their leaders. Fortunately the personal advisers were a little late on this occasion. The Governor had already given his word to Mr. Malcolm Macdonald and, through him, to General Ankrah that he would attend the meeting. General Ankrah had not only guaranteed the Governor's personal safety and that of his aides, but had undertaken to send a Ghanaian Air Force plane to collect him from Enugu and take him back afterwards. All the same, to make doubly sure, security men from Enugu were sent to Ghana to check on the security arrangements before the Governor would go.

We arrived on schedule at Ghana airport and found security arrangements almost too rigid. The Eastern Nigerian delegation were received at a different time, and maybe even a different place from the other delegations. We arrived nearly an hour ahead of the other delegations, which arrived in the Nigerian Airways Fokker Friendship. After thorough searches of our persons and luggage, we were taken in helicopters and cars to Aburi, once more arriving before the other delegations.

The delegations from Lagos arrived wreathed in smiles and full of expectancy. A number of them, among them the Head of State and the Military Governor of the West, were particularly exuberant and warm, calling our Governor by his first name and even offering to embrace him. But our Governor was serious, unsmiling and cold, refusing in fact to accept any embrace. Eventually we all took our seats. Recording instruments had been installed. General Ankrah opened the meeting with advice and prayers that the discussions and deliberations be approached with a deep sense of fraternity, understanding and give-and-take. He was not going to chair the meeting, and would not even participate in the discussions in order not to detract from Nigeria's sovreignty, but would be on hand with some members of his National Liberation Council, in case their help and assistance were needed for anything. He had made available competent secretarial service for the meeting.

The meeting started without any officially accepted chairman, but it was obvious that Col. Gowon (as he then was) took precedence. Our Governor, however, would not allow this to be taken too far, for at the end of General Ankrah's introductory remarks both Col. Ojukwu and Col. Gowon replied in turn. I think it was Col. Gowon who spoke first.

Before the discussions began, Col. Ojukwu said there was something preliminary but vital which he would like done before anything else. All agreed that he should say what it was. In measured tones and with dramatic sincerity, he proposed that, as a means of inspiring confidence, they should all do two things: (*a*) re-affirm their faith in discussions and negotiations as the only peaceful means of resolving the Nigerian crisis; and (*b*) "renounce the use of force as a means of settling the present crisis in Nigeria and hold ourselves in honour bound by the declaration". It appeared quite innocuous and the meeting saw no objection to the proposals, which were at once accepted without argument. I shall return to this in the next chapter.

The discussions proceeded, and our Governor was clearly the star performer. Everyone wanted to please and concede to him, although on a few occasions Col. Hassan, the Military Governor of the North and Major Mobalaji Johnson, the Administrator of the Lagos territory threw in some harsh and contrary views. But on the whole the meeting went on in a most friendly and cordial atmosphere which made us, the non-military observers, develop a genuine respect and admiration for the military men and their sense of comradeship. The meeting continued so smoothly and ended so successfully, with champagne (lavishly provided by the host government) and toasts, that I, for one, became convinced that the military, among themselves, had their own methods. And it was for this reason that I fervently prayed and wished, even in the midst of war, that they should meet again. We (the Eastern Nigerian party) left first, and our Governor received an ovation as he walked to his plane.

The actual decisions of that meeting are well known, for they have been far too often quoted in different ways and circumstances. I shall not, therefore, go into their details here. All I need say here is that the Military Governor of Eastern Nigeria carried his points.

At this one meeting, he obtained almost all that he had wanted to achieve both at the meeting of the representatives of the Military Governors arranged on August 9th, 1966, and at the abortive Ad Hoc Constitutional Conference of the same year. Furthermore, he arranged that the body of the kidnapped and murdered former Supreme Commander should be exhumed and given a state burial.

"Why were those people so jubilant?" the Military Governor quietly asked me after our plane had taken off. "Do you think they have grasped the full implications of the decisions they have taken?" I did not think they had, and I told the Governor so, and he smiled with satisfaction and asked his A.D.C. to bring out a bottle of champagne. I must have spoiled the fun and made him wonder when, in the midst of the drinking, I said, "Your Excellency, I am honestly worried by it all." I had chosen my words carefully to ensure that he did not know exactly what I meant. Fortunately he did not pursue the matter; but I was honestly worried by the fact that those decisions could mean the end of what we used to know as Nigeria. However, as a civil servant, I took them as the decisions of those whose duty it was to make them, while it was my duty to carry out such decisions whether I liked them or not—or else resign if I felt so strongly against them and could afford it, but which I could not do under a military regime with its guns and absolute powers. It was in this spirit that I did all within my power to see that the Aburi decisions were implemented as the best way of preventing bloodshed and immediate disintegration of Nigeria, but diffidently hoping that with luck, a civilian regime might alter them.

It had been one of the understandings of the Aburi meeting that the first statement on the meeting and its decisions should come from Lagos—that is, from the Head of State, even though the Governor of the East still said he would not recognise Col. Gowon as such until he had been formally so appointed, and had undertaken to propose that at the next meeting of the Supreme Military Council in Nigeria. A carefully drafted communiqué had been issued in Ghana, and the Governor expected to receive praise and commendations from his mentors at home. Unfortunately, these he was not to have. For on arrival at Enugu airport all he heard from his arch-adviser was, "Thank God you have come back alive. That is all that matters." I was close-by and immediately asked if he had not heard all the Governor had achieved at Aburi. A direct telephone or wireless link had been installed between Enugu and Ghana and the Governor had been informing them of what was happening at the conference. "But you have not brought us *full* independence or sovereignty," was the reply I received.

The Governor was surprised and peeved. He drove home to the State House accompanied by those who had come to receive him at the airport. There he briefed them fully on the decisions taken, after which he was probably advised to inform the public, contrary to the understanding reached in Aburi, namely that the first statement on the outcome of Aburi should come from Lagos. Thus, soon after our arrival back home, the Governor called a press conference because "it has come to my notice that the public is anxious to have more details of decisions taken" and his hurry to make the statement was caused by "the misgivings which I understand are prevalent in the region as a result of this meeting". He went on, "I recall that just before my departure, when the public did not even know that our meeting was so close, students and other groups of individuals issued resolutions advising me against attending any meeting with my counterparts."

The Governor then analysed the implications of the Aburi decisions, stressing that the Regions would henceforth pull further apart than before. The Army had been "regionalised" and so on and so forth. This alerted and annoyed Lagos and all the other participants at the conference. They awoke to the fact that they might have been hoodwinked, and were annoyed that the understanding that the first statement should emanate from Lagos should have been disregarded by Col. Ojukwu without even the courtesy of prior information to the rest. There was much wrangling between Col. Gowon and Col. Ojukwu over the phone on the matter. The harm had been done, the cat was out of the bag. The confidence engendered at Aburi was undermined and was being replaced by awakening suspicions. A group of top Federal civil servants met to scrutinise the decisions and arrived at firm recommendations for their rejection. The storm began to gather, turbulent and fast.

(*d*) *Efforts to Implement the Aburi Decisions*

With his usual calculating and anticipatory mind, Col. Ojukwu knew that once the true implications of the Aburi decisions were appreciated in Lagos, his colleagues at the conference might consider themselves duped and so either stall on implementing the proposals, as happened in the case of the decision made on August 9th, 1966, about the posting of troops, or even repudiate the decisions, as indeed was virtually to happen in this case. He accordingly wanted to ensure that the others did not have time to have second thoughts on the decisions, and his strategy was to set deadlines for the implementation of those aspects of the agreements which meant most to him and his ultimate aims. Thus, he persuaded the meeting to agree that law officers of the Federation should meet on January 14th (that was about a week after the delegations' return to Nigeria), and list all the decrees and provisions of decrees which should be repealed to restore autonomy to the Regions. This done, the actual decree implementing the decision about this should be promulgated not later than January 21st, 1967. Since he also needed money, he induced the meeting to agree that Finance Permanent Secretaries should meet within two weeks and submit recommendations for the allocation of funds for the task of rehabilitating displaced persons.

Although the law officers met as scheduled, the decree was not promulgated by January 21st, 1967. Before then Col. Ojukwu had been importuning the Head of the Military Government to honour the deadline. But as we have seen, others were now having second thoughts. Later a draft decree came from the Federal Government but was clearly out of tune with the Aburi recommendations. The East naturally could not accept it. Tension heightened, arguments and even quarrels broke out, and worsened when on January 15th, the Federal Government launched a vicious pamphlet in answer to several which had been published by the East. The Federal pamphlet was entitled, "Nigeria '66". (Col. Ojukwu claimed that, in the true spirit of Aburi, Col. Gowon had told him in advance about the publication and he had persuaded Col. Gowon to agree to suspend it.)

On February 17th-18th Secretaries to the Military Governments, accompanied by legal and financial advisers, met in Benin to advise on how the Aburi decisions should be implemented. There had up till now been pressures on the Federal Government, by those who read the writing on the wall, to do something about carrying out the Aburi decisions in order to keep the country together. At that meeting I impressed upon my colleagues the need to implement the decisions in order to enhance the image and good name of the country. No matter what personal reservations one might have about the actual decisions, the fact remained that they were agreements freely entered into by those in whose hands lay the destiny of the country. I criticised my colleagues in the Federal Government for trying to change policy decisions duly taken by the highest authority in the land—the Supreme Military Council. As civil servants our duty was to carry out the decisions of Government, although we had also the right, indeed the duty, to analyse and spotlight the effects of such decisions.

The outcome of that meeting was Decree No. 8 which, in my

view, faithfully implemented the Aburi decisions. As was the practice, the draft was sent to all the Military Governors of the country. A meeting of the Supreme Military Council was fixed for Benin on March 10th. Benin had been chosen to enable the Military Governor of the East to attend, since he would not go to Lagos "because of the presence of Northern troops in the West". The East Military Governor had no intention of attending, because he had been advised by his constitutional experts not to accept the decree "because it had not fully implemented the Aburi decisions". What was more, the Military Governor had received "reliable information" that he would be kidnapped or arrested once he reached Benin. The Federal Government had in fact done everything to ensure the security of all attending. The world press was present. "How could one believe," I asked, "that, with all the glare, attention and interest of the whole world focused on what was going on, the Federal Government would be so reckless and mean as to arrange the kidnapping of the East Military Governor whilst attending a legitimate meeting arranged by the Federal Government to resolve the Nigerian crisis?" I incurred much displeasure with such an impertinent question, and also earned further suspicion and distrust.

The draft decree had gone to the Governor first, and he had handed it to the "legal experts" to examine. I saw a copy later, but in time for me to study and make counter-comments on the legal experts' comments, a copy of which had been sent to me. I do not have a copy of the legal experts' comments with me, but my own counter remarks may give an idea of what they said, which eventually led to the rejection of that decree by the Eastern Nigeria Military Government.

"Y.E.,

Lagos has now submitted a draft decree for the implementation of the Aburi agreements. It is now for Your Excellency to decide, taking all the implications into account, whether to concur with the publication of the decree or not.

In order for this to be done objectively, I suggest the draft decree be studied against the background of the Aburi decisions. Those decisions broadly involve the following:

(i) The restoration of the powers of the Regional Governments which had been suppressed or depressed by decree No. 1 following the Army take-over in 1966.

(ii) The vesting in the Supreme Military Council all the powers which used to belong to the Federal Government, prior to January 16th, with the proviso that any decision of the Supreme Military Council which affected the whole country must receive the concurrence of the Military Governors—in other words, in so far as those matters were concerned the Military Governors had the powers of veto.

(iii) The vesting in the Supreme Military Council of all powers of appointment into certain categories of posts in the Federal Public Service, namely:

(*a*) Diplomatic and Consular posts;
(*b*) Senior posts in the Armed Forces;
(*c*) Senior posts in the police;
(*d*) Superscale posts in the Federal Civil Service;
(*e*) Superscale posts in the Federal Corporations;

(iv) The reorganisation of the army.
(v) The resettlement of displaced persons.

The power to make the appointments at (*a*), (*c*), and (*d*) implied that the Federal Public Service Commission and the Police Service Commission were reduced to advisory capacities, in so far as these appointments were concerned. At the moment they have executive powers in respect of these appointments.

3. For the purpose of the present decree, the following decisions of Aburi meeting are not relevant:

(*a*) *Appointment to superscale posts in the Federal Corporations*
This will require the amendments of the different laws which established these corporations.

(*b*) *The re-organisation of the Army*
This must depend on whatever recommendations the military experts who were to meet will make, leading to the amendment of the Army Act as may be decided by the Supreme Military Council.

(*c*) *The resettlement of displaced persons*
This will involve the whole question of fiscal arrangements or formula for the allocation of revenue which were to be determined by the financial experts of the various Governments.

4. Having said this, it is for us to see whether those decisions, which can be implemented by the present draft decree have, in fact been implemented. My close study of the draft decree with the eyes of a layman, as carefully compared with the Aburi decisions, show that they have, in fact been implemented. The position and powers which had been detracted from the Regions by decree No. 1 have been restored. Executive and Legislative powers of the Federal Government have been vested in the Supreme Military Council, with the proviso as stipulated at Aburi. Appointments to Diplomatic and Consular posts, senior posts in the Police and superscale posts in the Federal Civil Service have also been vested in the Supreme Military Council.

5. I have this morning received a copy of the comments by the lawyers. In considering the comments of the lawyers, I submit that Your Excellency be guided by the following considerations:

(*a*) The fact that this draft decree presents a major victory for Your Excellency's stand and principles. I assess the success to be at least 95 per cent.

(*b*) The Federal Government has made this capitulation mainly because the whole world, through their accredited representatives, have brought pressure to bear on them in support of Your Excellency's moral stand. The feelings and reactions of these countries through their diplomats should not be ignored if something happened to show that their efforts have been in vain.

(*c*) Unless the departures in the draft decree have been very fundamental, it is advisable that we ignore them so as to avoid giving the impression that we do not want a settlement.

(*d*) Your Excellency's policy and public statements show that you are striving for a peaceful and just settlement of our difficulties through negotiation. The outright rejection of this draft decree will dash every hope of a peaceful settlement and avoidance of a violent conflict.

6. I will now make brief comments on the points raised by the lawyers. Reading them through, I see that they involved technicalities. I agree that decrees promulgated by the Supreme Military Council should be signed by the Chairman of that Council, but the Chairman has not yet been elected and to insist on this issue for this particular decree presupposes that the Supreme Military Council must meet and elect the Chairman, so that he might sign the decree. This will be contrary to the stand of this Government that there can be no question of Your Excellency's attending a meeting of the Supreme Military Council before this decree is promulgated. In any case, the Aburi decisions spoke of the Chairman of the Supreme Military Council, Head of the Federal Military Government and Commander-in-Chief as being one and the same person. The question of which of these three designations he should use in signing the decree is a matter of detail.

7. For the present decree, perhaps we could ask that it be promulgated by the Secretary to the Federal Military Government by the order of the Supreme Military Council. If the Federal Government should be difficult over this issue, then let it be signed by whoever wishes to sign it provided that the Supreme Military Council will take the earliest opportunity to ratify such a signature.

8. I now take the different parts of the lawyers' comments which imply some reservations.

Section 1:

The point that all the provisions suspended by decree No. 1 should remain suspended may be worth mentioning, but one wonders whether this is so fundamental or even so rigidly valid that we should stick to our guns. To carry it to its logical conclusion would mean that the Regions cannot get back the powers which Aburi said should be restored to them. Quite a number of provisions suspended by decree No. 1, particularly as they affected the Regions, have had to be restored—for example, the power to re-open the Agent-General's Office in London, establish High Courts, etc. Where the restoration affects the Federal Government, we should not lose sight of the fact that the Federal Government now means the Supreme Military Council.

Section 3(1):

The Legislative and Executive Powers of the Supreme Military Council and the proviso of Concurrence.

The first point made by the lawyers about the use of the words 'remain' and 'vest' require my observation. I honestly think that the word 'vest' is better than the word 'remain'. Although the latter was used in the official Minutes, it is a fact that the powers which are now to *vest* in the Supreme Military Council never belonged to that Council, in order to make the word 'remain' significant. I do not agree with the second point about limiting the powers of the Supreme Military Council, since this appears adequately done in the draft decree. In any case, are these points so fundamental as to make us reject the draft?

Section 4(1):

My comments showing that by the Aburi decisions the posts of Chairman of the Supreme Military Council, Commander-in-Chief and Head of the Federal Military Government are now vested in one person, apply to this section.

Section 6(2):

The composition of the Supreme Military Council was omitted because we, the officials meeting in Benin, thought it would be better so, and although it may make the draft untidy, it should be allowed to remain if they want it.

Section 6(3):

I do not see anything in the draft decree to imply that civilians have been introduced into the Council. I have not got a copy of the draft decree as I make this minute, but I remember that their attendance at the meeting of the Supreme Military Council is permissable, implying that the civilians (i.e. officials) may only attend that meeting if they are wanted by the military bosses and then only in their capacity as official advisers to the Military Government. In this connection, it is noted that the officials are the Attorneys-General and the Secretaries to the Military Governments. The 'caveat' included in the Aburi decisions was against politicians.

Section 6(4):

I do not honestly follow the lawyers' comments here. The examples given reflect the advice of the officials in Benin, but my discussion of this section with the Economic Adviser shows that the wording of the draft decree enumerating the subjects covers the case. I do not think that it would be very realistic to insist on the inclusion of the words 'administer all the existing laws', since, in fact, the Supreme Military Council does not and cannot administer existing laws, which is a matter for the courts and the executive officials of the Government. Like Parliament, they make laws for others to administer.

Section 7(1):

The Head of the Federal Government hardly has power within the draft decree to delegate. The only powers the decree gives him are the powers of the Prerogative of Mercy, which he can only exercise on the advice of the appropriate advisory body and the power to confer National Honours, which must be based on the recommendations of the Military Governors. The other power is that of the appointment of Federal Judges, on the advice of the Advisory Judicial Committee, which we can resist, I am sure, successfully.

On the question of delegation generally, this was in fact the advice of the Benin meeting in order to ease administrative machinery and the provisions in the decree are discretionary. I do not think we should flog this matter at all.

Section 8(1):

There is no specific mention of the Secretary to the Supreme Military Council as such, although one would expect that the Secretary to the Federal Military Government would be the one.

Section 9:

I agree with the law officers. The power to appoint Federal Judges was vested in the Prime Minister before the Army take-over. The decree says that wherever the word 'Prime Minister', 'Parliament', 'President' appear, the words 'Supreme Military Council' should be substituted. I think we can draw the attention of Lagos to this fact and ask them to amend this section of the draft decree.

Section 11(2):

Would not our insistence here lead to chaos? I understand this to mean that the coming into effect of this decree should not invalidate all the laws which had come into existence before 16th of January.

Section 11(6):

The suggested amendment by the law officers would appear to go beyond Aburi which limited the concurrence of all the Military Governors only to matters which affect the whole country. I honestly feel we should leave the wording of the draft as it is.

Section 12(1):

My comments on Section 16(6) equally apply.

Section 16:

If we must insist, it would perhaps be tidier to set out the decrees specified by the law officers.

SCHEDULE 1

S.1(1): My comments on Section 1 of the main decree apply.

S.32: I agree with the law officers.

S.69: As a layman I saw in the revival of this section the means to tie the hands of the Federal Government by ensuring that the concurrence of all the Military Governors is secured before anything affecting the whole country is done, as recommended by the officials in Benin. Section 69(6) appears to have done this.

S.101(1): Can we really reject the draft on this score? I think if we make the point, people in Lagos will not insist. After all, they have lost much more worthwhile powers.

S.107(1)(*a*): Again, does this not depend on which of the three designations vested in one person should be used?

S.110(1)(*a*): Certainly the Supreme Military Council must have someone to process the applications compile papers and offer advice on the qualifications and other matters before they can take a decision. In any case, this was the advice the officials gave in Benin.

Your Excellency, my views already expressed regarding other sections cover the remaining sections of the draft. My final submission is this. It has been a battle between this Region and the Federal Government to get this decree in its present form. The Federal Government has been defeated with heavy casualties. We have won a major victory and if we sustain minor casualties we should not throw away that victory. Nobody ever goes into a battle without expecting casualties. I should think that we have hardly sustained casualties in this case.

Sgd. N. U. AKPAN
S.M.G.
4/3/67"

I apologise to readers for having to bore them with the above lengthy extract. I do it to typify the sort of futile and frustrating battle I had to put up, in the honest belief that those with whom I worked sincerely wanted to resolve the Nigerian crisis peacefully. The person who put into words the "objections" of the lawyers was the lawyer who accompanied me to Benin and fully participated in the discussions leading to the recommendations faithfully embodied in the draft decree. The truth was, as I later discovered to my disillusionment, that they were not interested in anything but secession and eventual war. This matter is further developed in the next two or three chapters, particularly in the Chapter on Secession.

The Supreme Military Council met as scheduled in Benin, and passed the decree, without the attendance of the Military Governor of the East. The Military Governor of the East refused to accept the decree on the ground that it has not received his concurrence as required by the Aburi decisions, a concurrence he wilfully withheld. The next chapter explains the background and prop to the recalcitrance of the East and the strategy adopted to appear right, and to make others appear wrong.

5 Over the Precipice

With the removal of the Northern Nigerian elements of the Nigerian Army from Enugu in August 1966, the Military Governor of the East always claimed that the East was left practically without arms and ammunition. According to him, only one hundred and twenty rifles were left in the Enugu garrison, because the departing Northern troops had taken away everything else in the way of arms and ammunition. Troops of Eastern Nigerian origin who returned to the East, in accordance with the August 9th recommendations, had arrived without arms or uniforms. Most of them, of course, had to flee the North and other parts of Nigeria disguised in all sorts of ways; this I can confirm because Col. Philip Effiong who came to stay with us arrived in this way.

The Military Governor's efforts from August 1966 were directed towards the acquisition of arm for the troops in Eastern Nigeria. Practically all these efforts failed with heavy losses in funds. In desperation, individuals and organisations were encouraged to acquire weapons by any means, fair or foul. Gun makers in the East were encouraged to increase their efforts. But all along the Governor kept up a façade of almost having a surfeit of arms and weapons. This was the impression he gave everyone, including the army officers who tried unsuccessfully to obtain details. The rest of the country also believed the propaganda, and even went so far as to believe that the East also had a fleet of war planes, including jets! Non-Eastern Nigerians had been forced out of the Region early in October 1966, thus ensuring that no outsider knew the truth.

So, in spite of all the boasts and propaganda to the contrary, the East had no arms—or at least not enough—when the Governor went to the Aburi meeting. His initiative in the matter of arms and the renunciation of the use of force in settling the Nigerian crisis was both a diplomatic and a military strategy—diplomatic in order to project himself as peace-loving, and military, in order to play for time.

Col. Ojukwu did not stop at getting his colleagues to "reaffirm their faith in discussions and negotiation as the only peaceful way of resolving the Nigerian crisis" and of renouncing "the use of force as a means of settling the Nigerian crisis", but went further to get them to "agree to exchange information on the quantity of arms and ammunition available in each unit of the army in each Region and in the unallocated stores, and to share out such arms equitably to the various commands and "that there should be no more importations of arms and ammunition until normalcy is restored".

The first aim of these proposals was to enable the East to have badly needed arms for its unarmed troops, while the second was to manoeuvre the Federal Government into a position of disadvantage. By getting the Federal Government to stop further importation of arms until normalcy was restored, the East, whose efforts to smuggle in arms were being intensified, would be able to reach parity with the rest of the country in the possession of arms, and possibly even surpass them. If the agreement was implemented it would be possible to check the Federal Government which would be acquiring arms through regular and legal sources, while it would be well-nigh impossible to check the East which would be doing so through irregular and illegal sources. Any suspicions could always be countered by the claim that the East had neither the funds nor the channels to acquire arms.

Towards the end of January 1967, the East had its first signal success in the acquisition of arms. Two ship-loads of these were due in Port Harcourt. The joy at this news was beyond description. Such was the extreme importance attached to this news that the Governor decided to go himself to Port Harcourt to supervise the off-loading of the cargo and the arrangements for its removal inland. Before this a number of helicopters had been acquired.

The cargoes were off-loaded, and the Governor was well pleased and satisfied with them. Several lorries were hired and commandeered to take the goods, not to Enugu, but to somewhere in Nnewi. On that day the routes and highways taken by the arms and ammunition vehicles were virtually closed to normal traffic.

After that, the Governor toured different parts of the Region, including Calabar, to inform the unarmed troops that they were now soon to be real soldiers with weapons. A number of the weapons were issued not just to the troops but to the civil defenders as well. The aim was to make the availability of these arms as much in evidence as possible. Visitors to Enugu were sometimes worried by the free and careless way in which these weapons were deployed. A foreign journalist was even allowed to examine their make and origin, and later published that they had been imported from a country in Eastern Europe.

From this time the Governor's attitude towards Lagos changed.

He became more provocative, intransigent and defiant because he was now more confident. The public followed his lead, and the whole Region was now going slowly over the precipice.

Col. Ojukwu's strategy to prop up his irrevocable decision to remove Eastern Nigeria from the Federation and to fight the North when the opportunity occurred, was many-sided. (As far as the East was concerned their quarrel was with the North, identified as the "Hausas", although later, when it became clear that attempts to woo the West and Mid-West to join the East might not succeed, the rest of the country was grouped with the North as enemies.) This strategy was as follows:

(*a*) To always appear reasonable and anxious for peaceful settlement of the crisis and the preservation of the unity of Nigeria, while making the other side appear unreasonable and difficult. The passionate letters written to the Head of the Federal Military Government and copied to other military leaders was part of that strategy. I had a hand in drafting those letters without knowing the real intentions of them, but believing in the sincerity of what they contained. The Governor's intention from the start was to expose to the world the contents of those letters at a chosen moment, just to prove how sincere he was while the others were full of duplicity.

(*b*) To put himself in the right and others in the wrong. For this, he would take sufficiently provocative steps and find good reasons and justifications for them, while in fact aiming to push his opponents into a particular course of action to suit his purpose. This we did in many ways and innumerable circumstances. For instance, although the East had decided never to participate in further meetings of the Ad Hoc Constitutional Conference, conditions known to be unacceptable to the Federal Government were put forward, and when eventually the Head of State suspended the conference, he was accused of assuming dictatorial powers, and trying to impose a constitution on the whole country, contrary to the original intentions of the Military Government, and even to the previous declarations by the Head of State. In order to play mischief and lend colour to that charge, the Head of State of Nigeria was accused of being obsessed with a desire to free his Middle-Belt people from the "Hausa-Fulani" oppression by creating separate states. The provocative edicts mentioned elsewhere in this book were deliberately intended to provoke the Federal Government into expected actions, but the edicts were called not provocative but necessary to the East's survival.

(*c*) To use blackmail and propaganda. This was prevalent right through the crisis—and with good dividends. Any information about the Federal Government's plans and moves must be given the widest publicity, particularly if they were embarrassing. The aim here was also to frighten and discomfort the Federal Government, to create an atmosphere of mutual distrust among its functionaries, by making them always look over their shoulders with the feeling that nothing they did, no matter how secret, could be hidden from the all-seeing eyes of the Eastern Nigeria Government. This strategy eventually boomeranged, in that it made the Federal Government tighten its security arrangements and keep on changing their radio channels and wave-lengths.

(*d*) To use threats and intimidation. Examples of this were when the East threatened to shoot down any plane which might fly over "its territory", or sink naval vessels approaching "its waters", when in fact it had not the means at the time of doing such things.

(*e*) To appear always to be doing the will of the people, even against his own will and with the greatest reluctance. The principal agent of this strategy was the consultative assembly and the council of chiefs and elders. Originally the consultative assembly was a body of people personally selected by the Governor himself. Later it was enlarged with people chosen on a divisional basis. The council of chiefs and elders was wholly appointed by the Governor. At first the two bodies met separately, but later jointly. They had no independence or initiative. All the resolutions passed, and "advice" given, were exactly what the Governor and his advisers wanted. Indeed the resolutions were invariably drafted by a body of these advisers.

Other agents of this particular strategy were the public, trade unions, student organisations, and various mass organisations, particularly women. They were properly organised, and the person charged with that responsibility was a Mr. Alale (who was later executed along with Ifeajuna, Banjo and Agbam for trying to overthrow Col. Ojukwu). Alale was a known extreme leftist who had once been specially trained in "revolutionary" tactics, and had been in a number of foreign countries. A short while before he was given his assignment to organise the masses of the people of Eastern Nigeria to demonstrate and make demands, he had married a woman who claimed to be a relation of the Military Governor. Alale went around preaching hatred and contempt for the Federal Government, and even went to schools to persuade teachers to indoctrinate the children with prejudice against Northerners. In a lecture in one school, for instance, he suggested that children be taught to define a Northerner as "a person who lives in that part of Nigeria where Easterners are always massacred". Everything was done to incense the people against the rest of Nigeria, and it was during this time that the term "Nigerianism", defined as a connotation for corruption, inefficiency and all public ills, began to be used. The name of the Nigerian Head of State was made the very symbol of everything evil to the people of the East, and for this, public abuse and insults against his person and office became the order of the day.

It was not long before it became clear that the situation was getting out of hand. People sounded serious warnings to the Governor when it was known that the leaders of those demonstrations had ulterior motives: their own selfish and ideological objectives. The warnings also came from church and other leaders. The ultimate objective of the "revolutionary" leaders, they said, was to cause general discontent and confusion, which would spread from the East to the whole country, with a view to overthrowing the Military Government, including Ojukwu himself. Police intelligence also showed that they were in contact and communication with collaborators outside Eastern Nigeria. As usual, the Military Governor took no heed and dismissed us as alarmists. He even accused me of having a personal dislike for Alale, at whose wedding reception I had had the honour of chairing the proceedings.

I recall one evening when Sir Louis Mbanefo and I went to the State House to speak to the Military Governor about the dangerous trends, but we were barred from entry at the gate, no doubt on the orders of the Governor himself. We had before leaving phoned to tell him we were coming. The excuse was that he had gone to bed. The following morning a person who had gone later and was admitted to see the Governor told us so.

Eventually Col. Ojukwu discovered to his discomfiture that he had created a torrent now too strong for him either to withstand or put an end to. He had, therefore, to follow the current or be dashed to the rocks and broken to pieces. He had become a captive of the mob he had inspired.

The people's feelings and mood at the time were ripe for manipulation. They were full of uncontrollable bitterness against the people of Northern Nigeria for the killings of their kith and kin. For this reason, Alale and his group never lacked followers and zealots. Women abandoned their occupations and spent days in demonstrations, calling upon Ojukwu to give them arms—a matchet or gun would suffice—to go and "kill Gowon" and fight the North. Students abandoned their studies to undertake visits to different parts of the Region to preach hatred and violence.

6 Secession

> "I have now come to the most difficult but most important part of this statement. I am doing it conscious of the great disappointment and heart-break it will cause all true and sincere lovers of Nigeria and of Nigerian unity, both at home and abroad, especially our brothers in the Commonwealth.
>
> As a result of the recent event and other previous similar ones, I have come to strongly believe that we cannot honestly and sincerely continue in this wise, as the basis for trust and confidence in our unitary system of government has not been able to stand the test of time. Suffice to say that putting all considerations to test—political, economic as well as social—the basis for unity is not there, or is so badly rocked not only once but several times."

That was General (then Lt. Col.) Yakubu Gowon on assumption of office as Supreme Commander and Head of the Military Government following the kidnap of the former incumbent, Major General J. T. U. Aguiyi Ironsi by elements of the Nigerian army at Ibadan on July 29th, 1966. This portion of his first broadcast is relevant here because it was the anchor to which the protagonists of secession in Eastern Nigeria frequently moored their arguments and justifications. Every memorandum, statement or official publication having a bearing on the country's internal relationships quoted the section which stated that "the basis of unity is not there".

Earlier, our Governor and his "legal and constitutional advisers" (not bona fide official advisers of the Ministry of Justice) had been arguing that, with the kidnap of the Head of State and Government of Nigeria on July 29th, without an immediate appointment of a successor or successors, the existence of the Nigerian State, as constituted by the British, had lapsed. And as a result of this its component parts had automatically "resumed their sovereignties" as they had existed before the British colonial government. The answer of the then Attorney-General, Dr. Graham-Douglas, was that, carried to its logical conclusion, this would mean that the respective entities and chieftaincies with whom the British had entered into original trade treaties would resume such sovereignties, but not "Eastern Nigeria", which had never existed as such at the time, and so had no formal treaty with the British. In other words, it would be the riverain areas of Calabar and the Rivers which would rightly and automatically assume such sovereignties, and each its separate entity, for it was mainly among these people and chieftaincies that the British had negotiated treaties. Other areas of what came to be known as "Eastern Nigeria" were subsequently acquired, either by conquest or annexation. It was no wonder that Dr. Graham-Douglas was subsequently deliberately kept out of all preparations made for the Ad Hoc Constitutional Conference, and that he had to resign in disgust.

It was significant, if absurd, that to the end Governor Ojukwu always spoke of "Biafra having resumed its sovereignty"!

General Gowon's broadcast took place on August 1st, 1966. We have seen in Chapter Three that the Military Governor of Eastern Nigeria had at that time taken asylum in the regional police headquarters, and was in almost continuous telephone conversation with Lagos. According to him everything said over the phone in those critical days and hours was tape-recorded. I had no means of confirming this, but we heard the broadcast of the new Head of State which contained the extract quoted above. Reporting on the conversations which had taken place on the phone between him and Col. (as he then was) Gowon and others in Lagos, our military Governor told us that, according to all he could gather, the only way to stop further bloodshed was for the North to be allowed to secede.

On that August 1st, 1966, Col. Ojukwu also broadcast to the people of Eastern Nigeria on what had happened. He stated, *inter alia,* "However, the brutal and planned annihilation of officers of Eastern Nigerian origin in the last few days has again cast serious doubts as to whether the people of Nigeria after these cruel and bloody atrocities, can ever sincerely live together as members of the same nation.... As a result of the pressures and representations now being made to me by chiefs, leaders and organisations in the Eastern Group of Provinces, I am arranging for representatives of chiefs and organisations in these provinces to meet and advise me"

Before the "representatives of chiefs and organisations" could meet, the Military Governor had obtained "advice" from a group of persons. On the morning of the day on which the meeting was convened the Governor assembled members of the Executive Committee as well as all the permanent secretaries in his office at the police headquarters. The only member of the

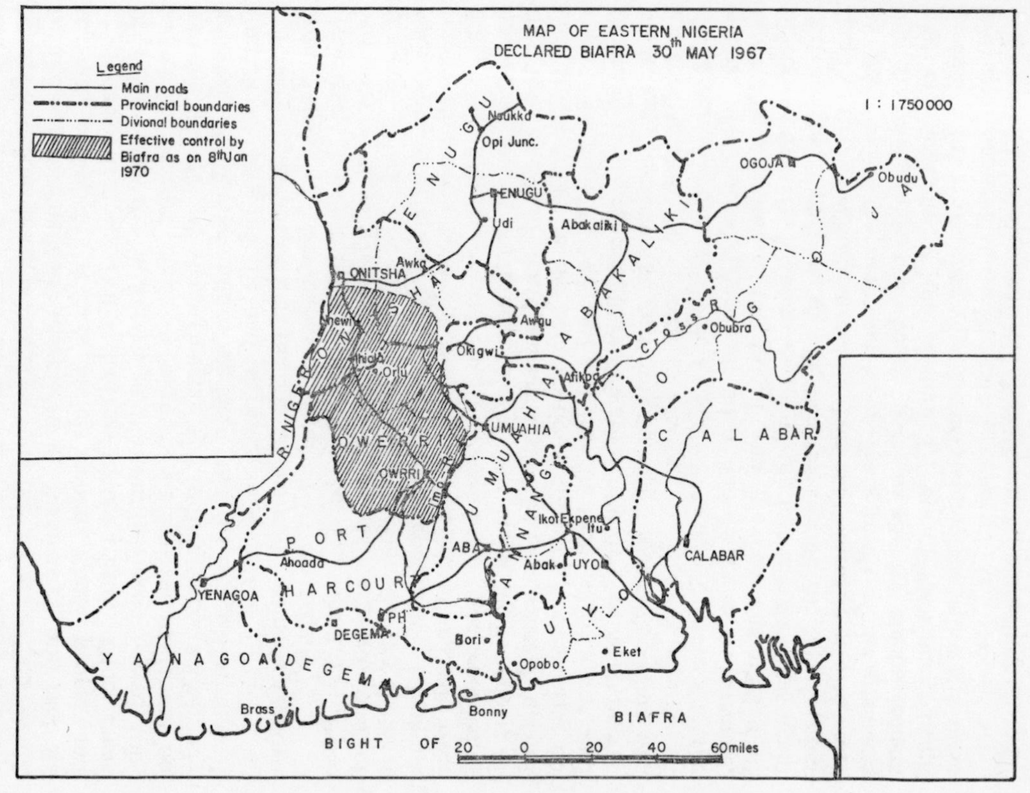
MAP OF EASTERN NIGERIA
DECLARED BIAFRA 30th MAY 1967
1 : 1750000
Legend
Main roads
Provincial boundaries
Divional boundaries
Effective control by Biafra as on 8th Jan 1970
ENUGU
Nsukka
Opi Junc.
ENUGU
Udi
Abakaliki
ABAKALIKI
OGOJA
Obudu
OGOJA
ONITSHA
Awka
ONITSHA
Nnewi
Ihiala
Oru
Awgu
Okigwi
Afikpo
Cross R
Obubra
R. NIGER
OWERRI
OWERRI
UMUAHIA
UMUAHIA
Imo R
CALABAR
PORT HARCOURT
Ahoada
YENAGOA
PH
DEGEMA
ABA
ANNANG
Ikot Ekpene
Itu
Abak
UYO
CALABAR
UYO
Bori
Opobo
Eket
YANAGOA
DEGEMA
Brass
Bonny
BIAFRA
BIGHT OF
20 0 20 40 60miles

executive committee not present was the Attorney-General, Dr. Graham-Douglas, who had either gone into hiding or left Enugu as a result of the mounting tension. Also attending this meeting were some outsiders who were neither members of the executive committee nor government officials. Mounted on the table was a microphone linked to tape-recording machines. Representatives of N.B.C. and E.N.B.C. were waiting outside. It was clear that something was going to be recorded.

After we had all assembled, the Governor pulled out a lengthy prepared statement. With some signs of excitement he read through the document from beginning to end. It was a declaration of secession of Eastern Nigeria from the rest of Nigeria to form the "Republic of Biafra"! After a brief pause, there were general murmurings of approval and nodding of heads. The Governor asked if anyone had anything to say—I had. I criticised the form and language of the statement and warned against consequences. I made a point about the Governor's earlier reported statements that he would never recognise the leadership of Col. Gowon since he was not the next senior officer in the army hierarchy. My point was that, if what happened on January 15th was not regarded as a coup, the event of July 29th, must be accepted as one. Once that was so, then whoever was accepted as the leader of that coup was the head of the Military Government. If, therefore, the statement read out to us was to be made and the steps mentioned therein taken, there was every probability that the Northern troops still in the Enugu barracks would be ordered by the new head of the Military Government to take action and put down what would be rightly regarded as a rebellion. I asked whether assurance had been received from Col. David Ogunewe, the O/C of Enugu garrison, and Chief P. I. Okeke, the Commissioner of Police, that they would be able and willing to cope with such a situation involving the Federal forces. I pointed out that the step proposed was a very grave one and that the people of Eastern Nigeria should first of all be consulted. I pointed out that our people of the former Calabar Province might not be in favour.

The Governor listened to me attentively. He called in the army and police leaders in turn. Col. David Ogunewe, who came in first, regretted that he could not support the move. His oath of loyalty was to the Federal Government, and if the Governor went ahead with his intention, he (Ogunewe) would be ordered by Lagos to arrest the Governor and if, for sentimental reasons of friendship he should hesitate to do so, he would be disposed of and another officer would carry out the orders. The

Commissioner of Police (Chief Patrick Okeke), who was also called in, adopted the same attitude as Col. Ogunewe had done: his loyalty lay with Lagos and he could not do anything without first consulting the Inspector General of Police. (Both Col. Ogunewe and Chief Patrick Okeke are Ibos.) Two of his closest advisers then accompanied the Governor into an adjacent room, where the Governor kept his bed, and held consultations, joined later by one or two others. On their return to the room where we were all waiting, the Governor announced that he was no longer proceeding with his proposed statement and the action contained therein. In my view, it was not so much the objections raised by me and others as the non-support of the army and the police leaders, which made the Governor and his advisers shelve the idea of secession at that stage. As later events showed, I was never again to be trusted about anything connected with their plans and Okeke was never acknowledged for his sound advice.

Meanwhile the representatives of chiefs and organisations had been assembled. I later discovered that the plan had been for the Governor to record his secession speech, and then go to them to obtain their support or mandate before the statement was broadcast. The statement in fact did talk of consultation with chiefs, leaders and organisations. It was that statement which was later updated, so I believe, for the broadcast of the morning of May 30th, 1967. With the original plans now shelved, albeit for the time being, the immediate problem was what the Governor should tell the chiefs and others who had been assembled. He met them that evening and spoke to them. I cannot say whether he spoke ex-tempore or from a prepared text, as I was not present at the meeting.

As I was to learn to my cost a few months later, the protagonists of secession were bent on this policy, while the world was assured to the contrary. But anyone now reading between the lines of the speeches of the military Governor can discover hints of secession all along. For instance, in his speech to the consultative assembly on August 31st, 1966, the Governor said, "there has been no breakdown of law and order in these provinces. I have therefore informed Gowon that any movement of troops into any part of the East would be regarded as an act of aggression which would be resisted with all the forces at our command. . . We now have our back to the wall. One more push and we either have to fight back or else be crushed. . . . Right now we are faced with a common danger, a danger which does not discriminate between us. I can hardly emphasise that at no time has there been a greater need for us in the East to remain united as now".

That meeting, which had been called to give the Eastern delegation a mandate for the Ad Hoc Constitutional Conference due to start on September 12th, 1966 in Lagos, passed the following among four resolutions:

> "In view of the grave threat to our survival as a unit in the Republic of Nigeria, we hereby urge/empower/advise him (the Military Governor) to take all such actions that might be necessary to protect the integrity of Eastern Nigeria and the lives and property of its inhabitants."

That resolution not only gave the Military Governor carte blanche but also presaged that states should not be created within Eastern Nigeria, a fact underlined by Resolution 4 which stated: "In view of the gravity of the present situation, we affirm complete faith in and urge the need for solidarity, of Eastern Nigeria as a unit."

Memoranda had to be prepared for the conference and it was during the preparation of these that I raised my first alarm. All my notes were completely discarded, and the notes prepared by those who undertook that responsibility envisaged something worse than a confederation. Innocently, I tried to show that the attitude of the memoranda we were preparing meant a break-up of the country. It soon became obvious to me that I was regarded as an intruder, and finding my views of no effect, I left them to carry on without me. We have already dealt with this matter of the Ad Hoc Constitutional Conference elsewhere, on p. 43.

With the outbreak of large-scale disturbances and killings of Eastern Nigerian civilians—men, women and children—in Northern Nigeria which began on September 29th, 1966 and the adjournment of that conference, things began to happen fast. Nightly meetings were held in State House. Eastern Nigerians in other parts of Nigeria were induced to return, while Nigerians who were not natives of Eastern Nigeria were expelled from the Region. People were sent out to look for arms and all restrictions on private ownership of dangerous weapons were openly overlooked. Demonstrations were inspired and encouraged on ever-increasing scales. People became worried. Lagos raised an alarm. Official denials of intentions to secede followed every alarm and questioning.

Addressing the meeting of the consultative assembly on October 4th, 1966, the Governor reassured the country and the world with these words: "Following wild and mischievous accusations and allegations about this Region's imaginary intention to secede, I recently called in the British and American diplomatic representatives and explained to them the position of Eastern Nigeria.[1] I left them in no doubt that 'we do not here in the East wish for, neither have we worked for, secession!' If, however, circumstances place us outside what is now known as Nigeria, you may be certain then that we shall have been forced out."

"If we leave Nigeria, it will be because we have been forced out." At what stage would Eastern Nigeria consider herself forced out of the Nigerian Federation? This was a question asked by everyone—diplomats, journalists and all. There were ready answers for them. "We shall consider ourselves forced out of Nigeria if any of the following things take place:

(i) If the Federal Government fails to implement the Aburi agreements.

(ii) If the Federal Government imposed an economic blockade of Eastern Nigeria.

(iii) If the Federal Government uses, or threatens to use, force against Eastern Nigeria.

(iv) If there is any interference with the territorial integrity of Eastern Nigeria.

Those were the conditions given, but we did nothing on our part to help. Those bent on secession were also bent upon seeing that the Federal Government was provoked into creating the above conditions. We have seen in a previous chapter how decree No. 8 which implemented the Aburi agreements was rejected, even though those agreements were first recognised as in effect making Eastern Nigeria a separate entity, and providing the most solid means of a total break whenever desired. The reason was that with arms now in our hands people were spoiling both for secession and a fight.

1. The British and American diplomats referred to were the British High Commissioner in Nigeria, Sir Francis Cumming-Bruce, and the American Ambassador to Nigeria, Mr. Elbert Mathews, who had both travelled from Lagos to see the Military Governor of Eastern Nigeria on September 22nd, 1966. Replying on behalf of the two visiting diplomats, Sir Francis said, among other things, "I have myself noted that you have in the past stated that the East has no wish to secede and I drew the attention of my Government to this. Your statement this morning about the East not having any intention of secession does not in any way come as a surprise.... Thank you very much for making this statement to us. I would like to say that I am very glad that you are going to publish this. I have been troubled about the degree of misunderstanding and suspicion that there has recently been in the country and I believe that your statement will go a long way to remove some of the basic misunderstandings and suspicions."

It was the rejection of decree No. 8 which convinced me that I was all along being hoodwinked, that I was not being told the truth or allowed to discover the truth. I had expressly opposed the so-called constitutional lawyers in their rejection of the Aburi agreements, arguing, point by point in writing, against their objections. All I had for my efforts were sarcastic "congratulations" from the Governor for my "courage in opposing constitutional lawyers"! My paper was not discussed at the meeting which had been called sometime about the middle of March 1967 to consider the new decree. The meeting was not even continued. Outside, I confronted one of the constitutional lawyers, who was honest enough to tell me that they had not in fact any answer to my points. All they wanted to do was to reject the decree. "We must fight with those people who have shed Ibo blood," he said. I immediately went back to the Governor and told him about my conversation with the lawyer. He said, "I know you don't like any idea of a fight. Let me tell you this. You'd better reconcile your Christian reservations with the fact that we shall have to fight with the North. They can't shed Ibo blood as they have done and get away with it." Then, when the Governor observed my consternation, and perhaps feeling that he had said too much, he quickly added, "It does not mean that we are going to fight today or tomorrow, this year or next. But we shall fight."

Later we heard that the Benin meeting of the Supreme Military Council had approved the decree which was to be promulgated without delay. I made one final effort by minuting to the Military Governor as follows:

"Y.E.,

It has been announced that the decree is being promulgated today. I don't know what the Law Officers have advised, but my own view is that the promulgation of the decree should be received by us with studied silence for the following reasons:

(i) It has implemented the Aburi decisions by restoring the Regions to their positions before the advent of the military regime.

(ii) The regions exercised their powers before the military regime within the limits and safeguards provided for in the Nigerian Constitution. Those sections of the Federal Constitution mentioned in the draft decree are those sections which provided the checks and limitations on the powers of the Regions. One can well imagine the Federal Government arguing that failure to restore these sections would be contrary to the

Aburi decisions, in that it would enable the Regions to have more powers than they were enjoying before the advent of the military regime.

(iii) Even that section of the decree dealing with the Emergency Powers can be argued to be part of the checks provided in the Constitution against secession by a Region. All we can perhaps do here is, maybe, to get our newspapers to make fun of this particular provision, pointing out that the present circumstances of the country with a regionalised army, make the provision unrealistic. I made this point clearly in Benin at the meeting of officials when the Federal Government representatives were insisting on this particular provision. It was meaningful when we had a unified and disciplined army under a unified command. With the army regionalised, the enforcement of this section would mean civil war. I also made the point that what was needed was the creation of conditions which would make it unnecessary for any part of the Federation to think of secession.

(iv) There are two features in the decree which are not strictly within the Aburi agreements, namely:

(*a*) The power of the Head of the Federal Military Government to concur in decisions affecting the whole country. Even though the Aburi decisions did not provide for this, it might be argued that the regional Governors were given these powers of concurrence by virtue of their being heads of governments, and so the Head of the Federal Government should also have similar powers. I do not, myself, think we should make a fuss about this point since I do not see how the Head of the Federal Government can use that power against any Region whose Governor has equal powers of veto.

(*b*) The establishment of the Federal Executive Council is superfluous. It would have made more sense to establish an Executive Council for the Federal Territory (of Lagos) since all the powers that used to be exercised by the Houses of Parliament and Council of Ministers are now vested in the Supreme Military Council.

My point is that we should make the best of the powers now restored to the Regions and prepare ourselves coolly for the vital battle of 'finance' which lies ahead.

Here I respectfully repeat the plea contained in my note covering my views of the 4th of March on the law officers' comments on the 'second' draft decree.

The above minute was dated March 17th, 1967. My plea of March 4th read as follows:

"Y.E.,

I very deeply implore you to study my comments enclosed in this file. I make them not only as your 'Chief' Secretary but as a man who sincerely and most honestly desires that you succeed as an objective administrator and soldier-statesman both within this country and beyond, and in posterity. I am not writing as a pacifist, or a person who wants to avoid trouble. I write as a realist, and as someone who is proud of the honour of being your administrative chief adviser.

The final decision in this matter is Your Excellency's. The responsibility for such decisions will be borne by you, and placed at your door, not at anybody else's including even your official advisers. In my position I owe you the bound and dedicated duty of saying exactly and honestly what I see. My views may not be right, but should be carefully considered before their rejection. Your Excellency is a soldier-statesman, and that is what I and Your Excellency's admirers would like the world and history to see you as. Your stature both nationally and internationally has been growing, and must be kept so."

The whole of this minute was a warning against the influence of those who were exercising powers without responsibility. I have reproduced in Chapter Four, (*d*) the full minutes to which the above minute was a covering note. It was a minute opposing the negative views of the law officers on the draft decree to implement the Aburi decisions—the minute which earned me the sarcastic "congratulations" from the Military Governor which I have already mentioned.

But things continued to move at an alarming speed. Demonstrations were intensified. "Civil defenders" brandishing weapons were menacing people, particularly those who could not speak Ibo. The activities of these people became out of hand when they started beating up policemen. A young Ibibio man was shot dead in his house as he was having his meal. The Governor had to take firm measures. Stern warnings went out; the person who had shot and killed the Ibibio man was himself publicly shot.

Then came the provocative edicts, called "survival" edicts by the Military Governor. These edicts had all been drafted in camera and were later sent to me for publication in the Regional *Gazette*. "The Revenue Collection Edict", was published on March 31st 1967; "The Legal Education Edict" on April 17th; "The Court of Appeal Edict" on April 18th; and the "Marketing

Board Edict" on April 19th. Before these edicts, I had been worried by the general tempo and trend of events. I therefore prepared a memorandum for consideration by the so-called strategic committee. I entitled it "The Fateful Decision", and its most important part contained the following:

Introduction

The majority of the people of this Region have been geared to the choice of secession or separate existence. Before that choice is finally and irrevocably exercised this Committee must satisfy itself that, taking a long term view, this is the best thing for *OUR PEOPLE.* I emphasise the words *OUR PEOPLE,* because in this present struggle for survival, even the Christian principle of selflessness must be forgotten, and our Fate and Destiny as a people made paramount.

Our Potentialities

God has endowed this Region with natural blessings unsurpassed and hardly equalled in any part of Black Africa. We have all the natural resources that can make a people great. We are endowed with people of impressive intelligence, initiative, enterprise and spirit of adventure. It is those which have sent our people to other parts of Nigeria and Africa. For these we have been envied by those with the will and ability to work and get on, and hated by those without those qualities. Nigeria as it is, has been too small to contain and satisfy our impulse and spirit for enterprise and adventure—hence our presence in all parts of West Africa.

Is A SEPARATE EXISTENCE the best answer for our future and those of our children endowed with the type of qualities and natural trait mentioned above? My clear answer is *No*. . . .

Now to my reasons for feeling that secession is not the best answer now:

(*a*) The Economic Adviser has promised to submit a paper on economic considerations. Those are real, and I shall reserve my views on them until we come to discuss the paper.

(*b*) We have suffered and lost a lot as a result of the events of 1966. But these sufferings and losses are not new. They only took on larger, crueller and more total proportions than before. Through past sufferings and losses we have built Nigeria. To throw away the fruits of our labours so lightly could turn out to be a sign of defeatism, which is alien in our nature.

(*c*) We have good cause to "hate" the North. But hate is a consuming and evil passion, which, once released, must continue to consume. If it does not consume outwards, it can consume inwards. This may sound philosophical or platitudinous. But it is a truism that generally holds. Our hate is now directed to the North. When the North is removed, are we sure that it will not spend its force on us internally? In any case, nothing based on hate can be right and lasting.

(*d*) The generality of the people of this Region want secession and will be "disappointed" if it does not come. But they do not understand the implications, and are hardly prepared for the initial difficulties it will entail. They look upon "secession" as a gateway to Canaan. The actual realities may cause problems and disappointment which it may be difficult to contain. We may find the Israelites turning against their Moses in the face of difficulties on their way to Canaan.

My experience during the introduction of the Richards and Macpherson Constitutions is a lesson of the absolute need for educating the people down to the village and even family level. That is not possible during a military regime but it is vital. Radio, mass resolutions and the "Outlook" do not provide the answer.

(*e*) Our mission to the people of this Region is to make it a coherent and mutually understanding Region. Secession will not allow time for this to be done and will sow seeds of real difficulties for a civilian regime when people will be free to organise and agitate. We must allow ourselves time to nurse the new provincial administration system to fructuation. I personally consider the welding of the people of this Region to a coherent whole of brotherhood to be overriding. Secession will introduce a chain of reaction bordering on the amoebic. The propaganda of the North and of "sons-abroad" from the minority areas is that the Ibos want secession because they do not want to be dominated by the North, and should not others in the East similarly resist domination by the Ibos? We need time to destroy and cremate the basis of that propaganda.

(*f*) The motive of the January 1966 coup was the preservation of Nigeria as one. Are we sure that the leaders of that event have changed their philosophy?

(*g*) Our people have lost their homes, wealth and property in the North. But they still have these in abundance in Lagos, the West and Mid-West. Must we, because of our losses in the North, deny them the chance of retaining these things in the South in freedom and confidence, under the umbrella of a common citizenship? Without secession, our people can yet retrieve part of their losses in the North, at least through some arrangements for compensation.

I then went on to say that confederation, which in fact was what the Aburi agreements gave, was to be preferred to secession. I showed the advantages of this in many different ways. In my efforts to use all available arguments, I even mentioned that with the army regionalised, as it had been done under decree No. 8, no people of any Region of the Federation (or confederation) would dare kill people of other Regions as happened in 1966, for fear of retaliation.

The Governor made no secret of the fact that he did not like my paper and actually said—perhaps as a joke—that I deserved detention for it. Two days later I sent another note to him in my own handwriting. I did this because of what I said in that note. I did not want it typed and did not keep a copy so as to convince the Governor that I intended it to be between him and me. In that note I appealed to him in the name of God and humanity to throw away all idea of secession, which was bound to bring war. I expressed my views and feelings about the dreadful consequences of civil war. I heard nothing further about that note.

Meanwhile, in answer to the provocative edicts passed in the East, the Federal Government decided to react strongly. The measures to be taken by the Federal Government were contained in a memorandum to be submitted to the Supreme Military Council. This prompted our Military Governor to summon diplomatic representatives in Enugu on April 24th, 1967 to make the position of the "East" clear. He addressed them for a while, recounting all that the Federal Government had done to make things difficult for the people of Eastern Nigeria. He then dwelt on the contents of the proposed memorandum for the Supreme Military Council and declared, "If Lagos carries out its proposal, it will mean they no longer accept the East as part of Nigeria. The path open to us, in that event is clear, and I shall have no alternative but to take it. . . . I want to leave you and everybody else in no doubt that if that vicious memorandum of aggression against the East is accepted by those now meeting in Lagos and even a single step is taken to carry its terms out, that will be the certain end. . . . I repeat again that anything done to carry out any of the proposals in Lieutenant Colonel Gowon's memorandum will mark the certain end for us as part of Nigeria."

I did not see the actual memorandum. I was not normally allowed to see such things, particularly if obtained through our intelligence agents in Lagos. However, the Governor himself outlined to the diplomatic representatives the proposals contained in "that vicious memorandum of aggression against the East" in these words:

> "That statement is a so-called programme before the return to civil government. The programme includes the creation of states, the drawing up of a new constitution, economic reconstruction, including restoration of economic links, a new development plan, purging of corrupt elements and restoration of ill-gotten gains, and the supervision of election for a civilian regime. The programme then sets out in detail various dates, beginning from April 30th this year and extending to March 20th, 1969, by which date the various stages must be completed."

Apart from possibly the question of creation of states, there is hardly anything in the programme which did not conform to the original intentions of the military regime, or which could be regarded as inimical to the East.

Considering how sincerely anxious the Head of the Federal Government was to avoid a bloody confrontation, and all that he was doing to appease the East—attitudes and acts we foolishly interpreted as signs of weakness and lack of resolution—it is not altogether unlikely that he could have agreed to suspend the creation of states even at that late hour, if we had shown signs of compromise and cooperation. Only a few days before he had announced the lifting of the Federal economic and communications blockade against the East and called for some reciprocation on our part. (The Federal Government's retaliatory measures took place in April 1967. For example, flights by Nigerian airways to Eastern Nigeria were suspended on April 4th, 1967. On April 10th the Federal Government closed Calabar and Port Harcourt as customs airports, leaving only Lagos and Kano. Postal and money order transactions between Eastern Nigeria and the rest of Nigeria were suspended by the Federal Government on April 29th, 1967. The source of this information is the Federal Government's publication entitled "Nigeria—A Diary of Independence 1960-1970".)

The announcement was made on May 21st, 1967 and was immediately greeted with inspired demonstrations all over the Region condemning it as insincere. A placard by a group of demonstrating workers read: "Gowon is putting the cart before the horse, if your purported lift of your blockade is not a propaganda stunt, Gowon, pay us our salaries." One would have thought that the lifting of the blockade would facilitate this demand for pay. Other demonstrators called upon the Military Governor to "go ahead and not look back".

In the midst of his address of May 26th, 1967 to the consultative assembly and council of chiefs, the Military Governor read a telegram containing a last minute appeal from General Gowon:

> "Following my telex of May 20th. I have just received your letter PG/0897/11 of May 16th, 1967. As you are aware, economic measures complained of were lifted in response to recommendations of National Conciliation Committee with effect from May 23rd. Therefore deeply disappointed that you have not responded positively. It is not too late to commence measures to resolve crisis without bloodshed and keep the country together.
>
> It is desirable you declare your agreement with political and administrative programme recently proclaimed by the Supreme Military Council. This, you will recall, requires the urgent creation of states simultaneously all over the country to remove threat of domination, preparation of new constitution on their basis. New

> constitution can provide all safeguards considered necessary for states' Governments. Also programme envisages immediate appointment of a revenue allocation commission to find new formula on basis of principle of derivation and need to provide adequate funds for essential central government functions. Programme will ensure fair play and justice for all sections of the country.
>
> Therefore I earnestly appeal to you to cooperate to arrest further drift into disintegration. On the basis of the foregoing representatives of all governments can meet without further delay to plan for smooth implementation of the political and administrative programme adopted by all your colleagues of the Supreme Military Council. Most immediate."

The cynical and contemptuous way in which the telegram was read in effect told the assembly not to take it seriously.

It is now clear that the meeting of members of consultative assembly and council of chiefs and elders was convened for May 26th, 1967 in order to anticipate, with a resolution of secession by Eastern Nigeria, the Federal Government's intention to create states. The speech delivered by the Governor left those attending with no other alternative but to adopt a resolution of secession which must have been prepared in advance. (We have discussed elsewhere the working and manipulation of the consultative assembly and the council of chiefs and elders.)

On Saturday, May 27th, 1967, the Head of the Federal Government announced the revocation of decree No. 8, the creation of states and other measures. There was a dance at the Hotel Presidential in Enugu in aid of the refugees. I remember one of the powers behind the throne walking up to me and cynically saying: "Congratulations. Are you going to be the governor or premier of your state?" It was the first hint I had of what had happened.

All the provincial administrators were then in Enugu, having come for the meeting of the assembly. The following day, Sunday, May 28th, they were all assembled at the State House. Although I was Chief Secretary, nobody invited me to the meeting although a number of my officers were summoned. At this meeting, I subsequently learnt, the Governor told of his intention to declare secession by midnight, Monday, 29th May, in "accordance with the mandate now given" him. He distributed to the provincial administrators the "Biafran flag", played to them the tune of the Biafran national anthem and ordered them to return to their provinces for the fateful occasion. I saw the Governor as a matter of routine that evening, but he did not give me so much as a hint. I tried to discuss the Lagos announcement of the previous night, and all the Governor said was, "We shall see."

I met the Governor several times on Monday, May 29th. He looked expectant and rather excited. I expected him to tell me something, but he did not. All he asked me to do was to prepare a draft statement, based on points he gave me, on the Lagos announcement of Saturday. The statement was broadcast at 8 p.m. that day. I did in fact ask the Governor if he was going to do something about the Lagos announcement; he replied "We shall see." Knowing that the creation of states was the last of the four conditions which would make the East secede (the other three had in fact previously occurred), I asked the Governor outright whether we were going to secede. "Who tells you we are going to secede," he replied. "We shall see. Make sure that the statement goes out today. It could be the last we have to make before something happens."

During the night of Monday, 29th May, I was awakened by the ringing of my telephone at 11.45 p.m. "What are you doing?" asked a friend's voice. "I am in bed," I replied. "Why?" the friend asked in a surprised voice. "Everybody is here at the State House. Didn't you know that the Governor was going to announce secession?" I could not believe my ears. I had suspected that something was in the air, but why had I not been informed? I jumped out of bed, put on casual dress and drove to the State House at Independence Layout. Before leaving, I telephoned Sir Francis Ibiam, the Adviser to the Military Governor, and discovered that he too had not been informed, neither had Sir Louis Mbanefo, the Chief Justice. At the State House I found everyone formally dressed. I saw for the first time the "Biafran flag" draping the large table, behind which hung "Biafran emblems and standards". I had never before even suspected that we had these things, nor even that we had been arranging for them.

It was now midnight—or slightly past that hour. Someone must have told the Governor, who was upstairs, that I had arrived. He sent for me and then asked me to go and tell "them" that if they were not ready he was going to call off the whole affair. What he meant by "affair" I could now imagine; but who did he mean by "them"? The Governor told me he meant those who were working on his speech. "Where are they?" I asked. They were in the Parliament buildings. I went straight there. I knew the rooms, and so went straight in. I saw them and delivered the Governor's message. After that, I asked them why I had not been brought into the matter. At first there was no reply, then someone told me that they did not consider it fair to involve me since they knew I had never been in favour of secession. The speech was concluded and taken to the Governor. With the Governor's approval I booked telephone calls to Benin, Lagos and Ibadan to apprise them of what was happening. I succeeded in getting through to Ibadan and Benin and informed my counterpart there. I got through to Lagos, but received no reply.

The Governor made his speech in front of television cameras and recording machines. The "sovereignty and independence of Biafra" was declared. It was the early hours of Tuesday, May 30th, 1967.

The declaration threw the youth, women and children into the streets in wild and hysterical excitement and jubilation. Many of these demonstrations had been arranged well in advance. But on the whole the announcement took most people by surprise. Not even the Adviser to the Military Governor or the Chief Justice had been given prior notice. Many public leaders heard the news only on the radio and some of them who were on tour, like some church dignitaries who were then in the most remote parts of the Rivers Province, had to curtail their tours and rush home. I know of one bishop who left on tour only two days previously, after the Military Governor had assured him that such a serious step as secession, though highly probable, could not be taken without giving people like himself prior information.

By noon that day crowds of people and public dignitaries began to assemble on the premises of the Parliament Building (Houses of Assembly and of Chiefs) in anticipation of the ceremonies to mark Biafra's sovereignty. The ceremonies were to include the swearing-in of the Governor as the first Head of State of the new republic, the administration of oaths of loyalty to high-ranking public functionaries and members of the armed forces, the inspection of a joint guard of honour mounted by the army, the air force, navy and the police. After that a ceremonial parade was to take place.

The ceremonies were due to start at 1 p.m., but the Governor did not arrive until three hours later, even though his residence was only a stone's throw from the Parliament Building grounds. He appeared glum, unsmiling, and responded to the cheers and hand waves from the crowds without enthusiasm and humour. He showed no signs of sympathy or respect for the feelings of the people, including the very important personalities, who had baked in the sun for more than three hours waiting for him. "Why does the Governor look so melancholy?" my wife whispered in my ear. "He did not sleep the whole night, and must be quite exhausted", I explained, without believing myself. I was also wondering what was making the Governor look so depressed and diffident.

Less than six hours after the declaration of secession, the Eastern Nigeria Broadcasting Corporation announced that a large number of countries had accorded the new republic diplomatic recognition! The news was, of course, totally unfounded, and caused a lot of embarrassment to the countries actually mentioned. It was the first fatal mistake of the ill-fated Republic of Biafra.

Far less serious offences or mistakes than this had earned many people detention or worse because they were considered acts of sabotage—a term which had come into common usage since about October of the previous year, and which constituted grounds for severe treatment of people. My initial feeling was that whoever had been responsible for such a terrible "act of sabotage" was certain to face a firing squad on the direct orders of the Governor. The radio functionaries had already revealed on whose authority they had made the announcement.

But when we met the Governor his attitude was quite different from what many of us had expected. All he said was that he would look into the matter later. We were taken aback and openly embarrassed. Nothing happened. Later I was to learn from the official concerned that the Governor knew about the announcement. Why on earth did the Governor do such a thing? We wondered. There is no doubt that that announcement actually prevented even those who would possibly have considered recognising Biafra from doing so.

After the ceremonies, the Governor assembled many people in his residence and announced his intention to send trusted people out to explain our position and seek recognition from other countries. Col. George Kurubo was one of those sent out, but Kurubo's aim was different—to return to Nigeria!

Driving back to my house late that afternoon, I saw throngs of placard-carrying crowds dancing in the streets. One of the placards read, "Akpan is Great". Which Akpan? Why me? I wondered. That evening a group of young men called on us and in the course of drinks congratulated me and then said that my God was a great Being. "Why?" I asked. "Do you know that we had all along been told that you were the only obstacle to secession? For that reason some people had contemplated disposing of you." My shock was undisguised. I thanked them for the information, although somewhat late, and then explained to them that nobody had ever told me we were going to secede.

At 5.30 that afternoon the Governor took a triumphal ride round Enugu township, at the end of which we all repaired to the

State House for champagne to celebrate the occasion. "I feel quite relieved, now that the whole thing is over. No one knew how it had been with me until now," the Governor said. And one could see the relief in his eyes and face, relief of one who has been carrying a very heavy load for a long time and over a long distance, and suddenly finds himself relieved of the burden.

SECTION III

THE PERIOD OF CIVIL WAR

7 The War Rages

Secession, of course, made civil war in Nigeria inevitable. Both sides knew this and were duly prepared for it. General Gowon would have done himself and his office dishonour and Africa disservice if he had not made even an attempt to put down a rebellion which was bound ultimately to cause a total disintegration of the country, and probably set a dangerous pattern and precedent for other countries of the African continent, all of which, without exception, are heterogeneous in character and sensitive in politics and internal relationships.

A fight with the North was, as we saw in the Introduction of this book, what the vast majority of the Ibos wanted. Secession, regarded as an end in itself, was also intended by those in control to provoke a military confrontation with the Hausas (i.e. Northerners)—for they were the ones who had made themselves enemies of the East by killing Easterners. For a long time the East had been doing its utmost to stress the distinction. Indeed, when the war started it was regarded mainly as a confrontation between the North and East.

Thus, in the early hours of July 6th, 1967 the Federal troops crossed into the East from three points in the North. The strategy of the East had succeeded. The Federal Government had started the war, and the East was doing no more than defending itself: a natural reaction. I have described in the Introduction the joy and excitement with which the news of the Federal invasion was received and welcomed everywhere. To the Biafrans, this was their moment. Boys left their schools and the university in large numbers for enlistment in the army, women offered to abandon their occupations in order to cook for the army, and so on. All those who had offered to fight and avenge the killings of 1966 were regarded as heroes, whose names would be immortalised in the history of Biafra.

One thing, however, was clear from the start of the tragic conflict—each side grossly under-rated the ability and determination of the other. The Federal Government regarded the affair as a matter for police action, a quick surgical operation, which would last only a short time. A leading Federal military man predicted that all would be over in forty-eight hours—but it was nearly that long before the Federal Government even announced that military action had started. Later, the Federal assessment was that the operation would last two weeks.

The Easterners, on the other hand, believed that they would win. They did not think that the Northerners would have much stomach for a fight and might not even know why they were fighting. The idea of Nigerian unity would not fire the imagination of the Northerners who had never really believed in such a concept. After all, was it not because of attempts to unite the country that they had unleashed the "pogrom"? As for the Easterners, they had everything to stimulate their will to fight. They were fighting because they had been intolerably wronged; they were fighting to sustain their independence; they were fighting for survival. The assessment of the Eastern Military Governor was that the war would last three months, and this alarmed many who considered such a period too long. None of those who had been urging a fight knew what a modern war involved. They were reckoning in terms of old tribunal or group war lasting at most four days, beginning each day in the morning and ending in the evening, and in which achievement would be assessed by the number of those counted dead in the field from the other side.

Within the first few days the Federal troops had overrun Ogoja, which was the first shock. But that was war; they would soon be cleared of the place. According to reports, the Federal troops had not been able to cross the border north of Nsukka—on the contrary, Biafran troops had actually made some gains. But these, if they were actually made at all, did not last. The Federal troops introduced Ferrets and armoured vehicles, and made lightning crossings into Nsukka. Against these weapons of war the Biafrans had no answer. No anti-tank weapons were included in the arms which had been received and were still arriving. This was the first demoralising disappointment to the Biafran officers who had all along been assured by governor Ojukwu that everything was there.

The one advantage which the Biafrans had over the Federal troops was the lone B.26 bomber and half a dozen helicopters. Although these helped to slow down Federal advance, they had no effect on the Ferrets and armoured vehicles. Efforts were directed to the destruction of these Ferrets and armoured vehicles which were proving such a scourge to the Biafran troops, practically all of whom were raw and inexperienced except for the group who had taken part in the January 1966 coup. These had been incarcerated by the first Military Government. It had been part of Col. Ojukwu's calculating strategy that the Federal Government had been induced to keep as many of them as possible in prisons in the East, so that later he might have them released and fêted as heroes. There were a few Yorubas among them, including Lt. Col. Banjo, who had the preferential treatment of being invited to live in the State House with the Governor. All of these were thrown into battle, although the suspicious Ojukwu was at first very wary; Major Nzeogwu for instance was not given a command.

As the situation worsened on the Nsukka front, both Nzeogwu and Banjo were allowed to help, but their duty was to lead raids at night against the Federal troops with the principal aim of blowing up the vicious and all-menacing Ferrets and Saladins. It had now been accepted that the Biafran soldiers could not withstand the Federal troops with conventional methods of warfare. The enemy was on our soil and we ought to know the geography of our land better than strangers. We ignored, as was often the case during the tragedy, obvious facts. The Nsukka area had been a training ground for Nigerian troops resident in Enugu. It was here that most of their exercises and practice took place. Most of these troops were Northerners who naturally were amongst those now leading the offensive. Night forays and sniping were for some time the principal tactics of the Biafran troops, not without some successes and effects. It was during one of those forays and incursions that Nzeogwu and Christopher Okigbo, along with Ojukwu's own brother, were killed.

The Federal troops had by this time occupied the University of Nigeria, Nsukka, which, with its buildings and vantage position, provided an impregnable barrier to Biafran military activities whether by night or day. But this the Biafran Commander-in-Chief would not readily admit, although he knew it to be a fact. "Blow up the whole place. Saladins and Ferrets are blind at night; so what you need is sufficient courage and will to approach them at night and with molotov cocktails or hand grenades blow them up." With what could the Biafran troops blow up the buildings at Nsukka? At that time they did not even have mortars and mortar bombs. Saladins and Ferrets are blind at night. Agreed. But all that this meant was that they could not operate at night. Was it to be believed that they would be left unprotected and undefended by the Federal troops at night, to enable our troops go close enough to blow them up with molotov cocktails, or maybe stones, and come back alive? Though not a military man, I knew that the troops did not at that time have more than a few hand grenades. But the Governor would not accept valid reasons for not doing what he wanted done. He charged the officers with cowardice and worse.

Eventually the Federal troops started to move out of Nsukka

towards Enugu. Within twenty-four hours of that move they had captured the strategic Opi junction, almost regarded at the time by the Biafrans as the "Maginot line". It was the greatest disaster so far. For the previous few days, impressions had been given, and hopes had risen, that the Biafran troops were about to clear the enemy from Nsukka and advance into the North. The tragedy was made worse by the fact that, only a few days before, we had received for the first time a few armoured French-made vehicles. A number of these had been put into the Opi operations, and were virtually all captured or destroyed. Scapegoats had to be found for the disaster, because everything had been so sure about the recapture of Nsukka. It could not be anything else but sabotage, and what better and more credible evidence could be found for this than that the person who commanded the Biafran troops in the Opi area was a non-Ibo, a Col. Okon. That explained it. "We have always known that these people are not with us." "Why on earth did anyone consider him fit to be given charge of such a vital junction?" Many were heard saying this. "He should be shot. I am prepared to do the shooting myself, if men will not," a woman said to my face, with the clear insinuative reminder that the culprit was my brother by ethnicity. Poor Okon. What happened in fact was that the Biafran soldiers, at the sight of the advancing Federal troops, threw away their arms and ran, abandoning their commander who was nearly captured.

Whether Col. Ojukwu accepted the explanation given by Col. Okon, who had been arrested and brought down to Enugu, one cannot say. But Okon was not shot for sabotage, most likely because the Governor did not want to offend the Ibibios so soon after the shooting and killing in cold blood of a young Ibibio by an Ibo civil defender, as has earlier been mentioned. The suspicion turned to those in the group who had taken part in the January 15th coup. No one was convinced that these men had abandoned their faith in one Nigeria, with what was now the Biafra part of it. All of them were punished and a few shot, for sabotage. Before going on, let me say something about the term sabotage in the context of Biafra.

It came into current use after the Governor had called in November 1966 for intensive vigilance against infiltrators, traitors, agents of the Federal Government (this was before secession), and even those who were indifferent. It was during that time that my telephone was tapped. People were asked to obtain new number plates for their cars, prefaced with the letter VIG, for twenty-five pounds, the proceeds of which were to go to the Rehabilitation Commission for the aid of refugees. This immediately set off a chain of witch-hunting activities by irresponsible elements against the non-Ibos, whose loyalties and movements were always suspected. But not even all the Ibos escaped the net. Many of them were in fact arrested as saboteurs, and dealt with even more severely than the non-Ibos—their punishment was made that much more severe because they were considered the real traitors to their fatherland. The witch-hunting increased after the start of the civil war. One's words, one's movements, one's moods, one's house—everything was watched. Anything could be judged sabotage, and one could even be executed without an opportunity to explain. Every success of the enemy was nothing but the work of saboteurs. For this, all those who came from, or were connected with, the area overrun by the Federal troops were practical or potential saboteurs, and were treated accordingly. In the same way, the officers and troops whose position or sector was overrun by the Federal troops were treated as saboteurs. In this the mob had the sway, and often the right to judge and punish.

In the case of Col. Okon, the Governor while deferring to the wishes of the people (and these included very responsible personalities), did not agree that he should be shot. He was, however, reduced to the rank of major and removed from the army, though, as the war went against Biafra, he was several months later returned to the army, but largely in administrative positions. Before then I had been instructed to find him a civilian appointment, and I recommended that he be sent to the Transport Directorate.

The fall of Opi took the Governor for the first time to the front. As was to be his regular practice subsequently, he took me and other top civilians with him. It was my first experience of being at the front. Some six miles or more from Opi we saw our soldiers moving back or clustering aimlessly along the road. The Governor stopped, asked what had happened, and ordered them to return to the front, leaving behind an officer from his entourage to ensure that the order was carried out. We proceeded and began to see the lorries, which had carried the troops, loaded and turned in the direction of Enugu. "That's the gun! that's the gun!" the Governor shouted almost in a panic as a vehicle with something mounted on it and covered came racing by. It was the artillery men retreating. The artillery gun had been acquired only a few days before and had just seen its first action. The vehicle was stopped, and the explanation was given that they had to move back to a more advantageous position. I could see from his expression that the Governor was worried.

Then we saw the refugees. We had started seeing the throngs

twelve miles from Enugu. Women and children, old men and old women, with fowls, cats, goats and whatever personal belongings they could carry, moving aimlessly to uncertain destinations. We saw a few lying dead, or nearly so, from hunger and fatigue. They were among those who had been trekking for days from the most remote parts of the Nsukka Division—those who did not remain behind or take to the bush. It was a very tragic and distressing spectacle.

Eventually we reached the front and the battalion headquarters. What we saw was not at all reassuring. Troops were milling about, confused and exhausted. The commander appeared to have lost all sense of mental and physical direction. Our visit was a surprise to him. He was poring over a map, almost as tired and confused as the troops around him. He came to us and explained what had happened and his plans to counter the situation. That he was confused and unsure of what he was saying was clear from his swallowing and coughing. An attack had been arranged to start in thirty minutes' time. Another officer was attacking—or going to attack—at the same time from the left flank. The Governor said he would wait to see the start of the attack. We moved into a room in a nearby school compound, the operational headquarters, I think. A few minutes later the officer whom we had been told was going to attack from the left flank walked in. He was no less confused and tired than the other officer on the main axis. What was more, he had not yet completed arrangements for the attack due in ten minutes' time. He had come to collect some arms and ammunition—which in fact were not there. We heard firing and the sounds of machine guns, five minutes before the planned attack from our side. The Federal troops had started ahead of us.

"Were you happy with what we saw?" the Governor asked us we drove back, and added, "I wasn't." Back in Enugu he sent out word to the administrative divisions to produce and send a thousand able-bodied men each to Enugu. They were all to come with anything they could lay hands on, which might kill or wound—dane guns, matchets, clubs, stones, knives. Those in the neighbouring divisions like Awgu and Udi were to arrive before the following morning, while others should be in Enugu not later than noon. The Ibo warriors from Abam Ohafia, Aba and other places had also to be organised and sent down.

A day before, he had asked for volunteers of able-bodied men. These had come in that evening and numbered some two thousand. Boxes of double-barrelled shotguns had also arrived by train. These were taken to the army garrison and opened, whilst those skilled in the task were cleaning off the grease and fixing the guns.

The two thousand men formed a queue outside in the open field. Lorries were waiting on the road. Each man was issued with a gun and four cartridges, shown how to fire and pushed to the waiting lorries. In my observation hardly any of those issued with the guns had seen that type of gun before, let alone known how to use it. Each lorry drove off as it was filled with some forty to fifty men. They were going to the Nsukka front to fight the Hausas.

It was this exercise which convinced me of the hopelessness of the situation. I actually went aside and wept for those innocent men, huddled in the lorries and driven to certain death. A number of officers had come down from Nsukka to collect anti-tank weapons which the Governor had told them had arrived and were being brought to Enugu that evening. None of the packages opened contained such things. Two of the officers called me aside to say that they were very disappointed. They had been given the impression that everything was there in the armoury with which to carry on the war. Now that it was clear that we were so deficient, some other means should be found to settle the crisis. I asked him what other means, and he told me he was thinking of political and diplomatic means. I caught his message. The army could not hold out, and its leaders would like us to approach the Federal Government for peace talks. Back at the State House I put the matter to the Governor as carefully and tactfully as I could. He wanted to know which of the officers had approached me and suggested surrender. I could not tell him, because I did not know their names, and could not even recollect their faces because it was dark when we spoke. And if I had known, I would not have told the Governor for fear of what might befall the officers concerned, whose principal interest, I was sure, was to save lives.

The following day the human levies started to arrive in Enugu and were accommodated at the Enugu University campus. The Federal troops had now advanced towards Ukehe. The Governor appointed what he called a strategic committee, made up largely of civilians. "It was Churchill who said that war was too serious a matter to be entrusted into the hands of commanders", one member of the "strategic Committee" said with elation as he took his seat and thanked the Governor for the honour accorded him and others. The first task of this committee was to harness the efforts of the civilians in the war.

"It has all along been my conviction that it is the civilians who will fight and win this war and not the soldiers. From all that has happened already, it would be foolish to expect the soldiers to satisfy the aspirations of this new Republic." Those were the words of the Governor to his strategic committee. "Nothing can frighten professional soldiers more than the sight of civilian masses confronting them. They will kill them, no doubt, but will soon be tired. That is the tactics adopted in the Asiatic countries, China for instance. I have got brought down to Enugu thousands of civilians from all over the republic. The aim is to throw them in in waves against the enemy who would thereby be confused and frightened by the prospect of mowing down thousands of civilians and incurring world condemnation."

So that was the aim of the Governor, I said to myself. He did not care; human lives did not matter, so long as it suited his objectives. I shuddered and grieved inwardly. Some people were given the charge of deploying the masses of civilians now assembled in the fields of the Enugu university campus. I later visited the scene and saw a first cousin of mine among them. He did not know, and none of them had been told, why they had been brought down to Enugu. It was not at all easy to organise the movement of such enormous crowds. Most of them had been without food for at least twenty-four hours. Some of them had been fed, but none were full. In the end the idea of feeding them proved impossible. They were loaded into lorries, given a pound each and told that they would have to kill, reap and eat wherever they might find themselves. Even the distribution of money soon became quite unmanageable. Those who did not receive the money were told to proceed and that they would be paid at the front.

It was while we were standing in the fields that the first mortar bomb exploded on top of Milliken Hill. "Oh, never mind, it is just our people testing weapons," was the explanation. Nothing much was heard of the hordes of people sent out. But very few of them got near the front where the Federal troops were—the rest deserted on the way. As for those who had been sent the previous night with shotguns, many perished, but the majority fled home with the valuable weapons.

As far as I was concerned, the very idea of sending unarmed and innocent civilians to be slaughtered was heinous and considerably destroyed my respect for the Governor as a human being and a leader. I do not normally keep diaries, but this was one thing I had to record along with my personal judgements. Unfortunately, the diary was one of the things taken by the Federal troops when my village house was completely looted and later destroyed as belonging to a rebel supporter!

It was during this time too that the Governor ordered that members of the police be sent to the front to fight, particularly those of them who were in the mobile police force. The Commissioner of Police did not like the idea at all, but he had no choice. I recall his distress when he heard that some of his men had been killed or wounded. He wept for several days and would not be consoled. Already under a cloud, he could only protest or plead that his men be trained at least before being sent to the front.

This desperate period also saw a number of important developments. The first of these was the establishment of what the Governor described as the "S" (i.e. Special) Brigade. This he intended as his own personal brigade. The officers comprised university undergraduates, secondary school boys and so on. Their training took place under his personal supervision. They were given a special uniform and accorded preferential treatment in the matter of weapons and food. They were taught to owe loyalty only to the Governor, and indeed to regard themselves as a privileged species, looking down on the ordinary soldiers. They lived apart from the common soldiers, were regularly visited by the Governor, and their officers could have access to the Governor at any time. They reminded one of the Nazi "S.S." but they were not exactly like that corps.

The establishment of this "S" Brigade naturally caused considerable resentment among members of the regular army. It was later to cause serious difficulties of command and control when it became necessary, after the fall of Enugu, for the "S" Brigade to fight side by side with the other soldiers. The Governor had personally to intervene and in the end to fuse the "S" Brigade with the regular army. But even here the relationship was not smooth. The elements of the "S" Brigade still considered themselves as the elite, while the regular soldiers did not think much of their fighting ability or tactics. A situation similar in practically every respect later repeated itself with the establishment of the Commando Brigade under the mercenary soldier Steiner.

The original motive behind the establishment of the "S" Brigade was the Governor's own personal protection from the regular army, which he had come increasingly to distrust and to suspect. He was never really sure of the army and had, right through the whole period of the war, to devise means under different guises for his own personal protection.

Another development was the establishment of the militia. The officers were largely recruited from amongst university lecturers, members of the professions and other highly educated elements of society, including junior civil servants. This was thought the easiest way of involving these classes of people in the actual fighting, since they would not be happy nor willing to join the regular army and be commanded and controlled by people of lower intelligence and education than they. They were separately equipped, and given their own head who was a holder of the rank of brigadier in the Biafran army. Members of the militia continued to draw their salaries from their original places of employment, except for those who did not have such regular or salaried employments. Among the militia were people who fought out of conviction. It was these people who fought most on the Nsukka front, and they formed the bulk of the guerrilla forces in the area. At first the militia operated independently of the regular army but were later, after the fall of Aba and Owerri, merged with the regular army, except for those who were still unwilling to be commanded and controlled by officers of the regular army. These people joined the Biafran Organisation of Freedom Fighters (B.O.F.F.). Among the most famous of the Biafran army commanders were those who started as members of the militia. Achuzia was one of them, and there were a number of others not so well publicised.

The third development was the establishment of what were known as directorates. The directorates were designed to take over the functions of Government ministries and departments who could not be trusted because of their insistence on red-tape and for other reasons. It was significant that of the twelve or so directorates, only four were headed by civil servants. The rest were all headed by people outside the civil service, with civil servants, including permanent secretaries, being made to serve under them. This naturally caused much resentment among civil servants who saw in it a lack of confidence in them. Ministries and departments continued, however, to run and function, though scarcely more than nominally. The directorates were those of food supply, fuel, transport, clothing, housing, medical supplies, civil defence, requisition and supply, militia, propaganda and food production.

The heads of these directorates were considered to be personally responsible to the Governor and Commander-in-Chief. At first they met daily under my chairmanship until the fall of Enugu, but minutes of the meeting were submitted to the Governor for his personal approval of any recommendations and/or the issue of instructions to the different directorates. Assisting him was the strategic committee. The directorates were given absolute powers over the expenditure of money or the employment of staff. They had no estimates, but could incur any expenditure. All the nonsense about General Orders, Financial Instructions, Procedures—those instruments of "red-tape and indolence"—was swept aside. It was only towards the end that it was realised and accepted that, given the sort of latitude and freedom accorded to the directorates, things could have been done far more efficiently and economically by civil servants through the normal civil service machinery. After the fall of Enugu, the Governor delegated his control and supervision of the directorates to the Executive Committee of Supply.

The original purpose of founding the directorates was to ensure that regular supplies reached the fighting forces. The food-producing areas of Ogoja and Nsukka had been lost and others were threatened. It was therefore necessary to establish an effective organisation, unhampered by regular civil service procedures, to acquire and stock-pile food. There had been complaints and reports that troops in the trenches were not having regular supplies of food and that members of the Supplies and Transport[1] units were purchasing food items at inflated prices and diverting some of them for other purposes. Similar reports and complaints were received in respect of other items like clothing and fuel. Apart from checking the reported abuses within the armed forces, and ensuring that supplies reached them regularly and promptly, there was also the consideration that as many personnel in uniform as possible should be released to engage in the actual fighting.

The arrangements did not, of course, work as precisely as originally intended. For one thing, rival women's voluntary organisations sprang up, all wanting to cater for the troops. A number of the women and young girls actually went to the fronts to cook and assist the soldiers in other ways. The S and T units for their part did not take kindly to what appeared to be a lack of confidence in their organisation and integrity. They placed some difficulties in the way of the food and clothing directorates, until occasionally the Governor himself had to intervene.

The consideration of conserving available resources as well as rationalising their uses motivated the founding of the other directorates. The Federal troops had taken Bonny, which meant that ships could no longer bring in materials to Port Harcourt. Drugs, spare parts, clothing materials and other items had to be bought by the appropriate directorates and conserved. At that time the idea of building make-shift refineries had not been mooted. The Port Harcourt refinery was still there, and there were people who could operate it, as well as extract crude oil for it. All the same, the refinery might be destroyed, even though the capture of Port Harcourt could be ruled out. Such was the confidence of keeping Port Harcourt against Federal attempts and onslaughts that one ran the risk of being branded a saboteur to think, let alone openly suggest, that it could ever be taken by Federal troops. With the fast and frequent movements of persons, civil and military, in the face of advancing Federal troops, the directorate for housing had for its

1. Supplies and Transport units of the armed forces were responsible for catering for the needs of the armed forces.

part to ensure the rational use of available buildings whether public or private.

There was also the directorate of military intelligence, whose designation was a cover for other activities. It was not regarded in the same way as the other directorates, but operated under the direct control and supervision of the Governor, to whom it was responsible in every way.

The invasion of the Mid-West

A fourth development before the fall of Enugu was the invasion of the Mid-West by Biafran troops on August 9th, 1967. It was a special operation organised and engineered by the Governor himself, with the support of some persons across the Niger.

"My men should be in Benin by now," the Governor said with cool elation and expectancy, glancing at his watch. I did not understand the allusion, and my countenance must have told the Governor so. "Yes we crossed into the Mid-West this morning. If things move as they have done already, then God bless Gowon and those in Ibadan." I was still at the State House (now the former Premier's Lodge, where the Governor had moved barely a week before the declaration of secession), when a message came through that Biafran forces had captured Benin and were already advancing towards Ore. There was general joy mingled with surprise amongst those of us who did not even know that a movement into the Mid-West had ever been contemplated. "I had to keep everything to myself," the Governor said in the tone of a superior individual addressing a mystified but adoring audience.

From letters written that night to Col. Banjo, who was in charge of the operations, the immediate aim of the adventure would seem to have been to relieve the mounting pressure from the Federal troops approaching Enugu from Nsukka. For this purpose our troops were to cross at a point in the North, cut off the main supply route of the Federal troops, and fight towards Nsukka. The troops already advancing to Ore (by the evening they had already arrived there), were to fan out in two directions—to Lagos and Ibadan. As far as the Governor was concerned, Banjo was already the foremost hero of the war. The Governor turned to those who had been warning him about Banjo, and said, "Don't you see how wrong you all have been about Banjo, and how right I am—as always." But the honeymoon was short lived.

That evening Banjo broadcast over the Benin radio. The text of his speech had not been cleared with the Governor as the Governor expected. What was more, the speech took a form which the Governor did not like. Banjo declared himself in control of the

Mid-West, explained the aims and purpose of the January 15th coup, and the part he had played or not played, and he spoke about the unity of Nigeria. At first the Governor could not believe his ears, and then became mad with fury and suspicion. He took up the telephone and asked Banjo to report at once to him at Enugu. Banjo agreed, and before his arrival a letter was ready for him setting out his role and personal position and what he was expected to do. Another letter was written appointing Col. Ochei the Military Administrator of the Mid-West, and the relationship between Banjo and the Administrator was clearly defined. Before the expedition, Banjo had been told that his brigade, which was given a special name, was completely independent of the main Biafran army. (As a matter of fact, the army commander, the Biafran Brigadier Hilary Njoku, had not been taken into confidence about the Mid-West operations.)

Prior to Banjo's arrival, the Governor's agents reported that Banjo had ordered the troops to remove the Biafran emblems from their uniforms as soon as they had crossed the Niger, and also that Banjo had been saying uncomplimentary and disloyal things about the Governor. Anybody who knew the Governor can imagine his reaction to the information about uncomplimentary and disloyal remarks about him. But he did not show it. Incidentally, the persons with whom Banjo was alleged to have passed these remarks were Ifeajuna and Alale. Ifeajuna was one of the leaders of the January 1966 coup. He had been released, along with others, by Ojukwu from the detention into which they had been placed by the Federal Government in 1966, and was in the Biafran army. Alale was an extreme leftist, already mentioned and discussed on page 66.

Banjo arrived that evening accompanied by Alale. The Governor received them after a while in his office where he held a long conference with the two, and then with them separately. In the end Banjo and Alale were kept in Enugu and not allowed to return to the Mid-West. While Banjo was in Enugu, arms arrived by ships through Calabar and also by air.

Banjo must have been planning and thinking hard. It was later alleged that it was during this time that he and others decided and planned to overthrow the Governor. A few days later, Banjo went and apologised to the Governor, promised never again to do anything to offend him, and pledged unquestioning loyalty to him. It was precisely the sort of thing the Governor liked, and by which he could be appeased. He forgave Banjo and sent him back to the Mid-West with Alale and Ifeajuna, satisfied that he had vindicated his authority and brought them to their senses. But Banjo knew what he was doing. Before leaving, he asked for and received the bulk of the weapons and ammunition, and also armoured vehicles, which had just arrived. As it turned out, Banjo did not take away the arms in order to fight in the Mid-West and to Lagos and Ibadan, but to ensure that Biafra did not have them. According to reports brought by Biafran soldiers returning from the Mid-West, the arms subsequently all fell into Federal hands!

There was one unfortunate aspect of the Mid-West operations which nearly involved me in serious trouble. A day or two after the capture of Benin, the Governor asked me if I had seen my opposite number from the Mid-West. I looked up enquiringly. He told me that the Secretary to the Mid-West Government had been brought to Enugu and was at the Hotel Presidential. When I left him I went to the hotel, where I met not just Mr. Imoukuede but also Mr. Adeola, the Commissioner of Police, and one or two others. I bought them drinks and started to console and reassure them that they must have been brought there for their own safety. I knew I did not sound convincing, even to myself. I could not understand on what grounds they had been brought to Enugu. Was it as hostages or what?

I told the Governor that I had seen them, and asked the reason behind their capture—I used the word "capture" deliberately. But before the Governor explained, I made my feelings known that it was unfortunate that civil servants carrying out only their normal duties, should be treated in this way. What business had civil servants in matters of war? Why should the head of the civil service of the Mid-West, and for that matter, even the Commissioner of Police, be so humiliated? What had happened to their families left behind? The Governor did not like my impertinence, and said so in undisguised words, at the same time putting me in my place. I never saw those unfortunate people again, for they were removed from the hotel to a private residence.

Trial and execution of Banjo and Co.

The Governor held a meeting of his "strategic committee" on September 20th, 1967. But it was an unusual meeting of its kind, for a few persons of standing who were not members also attended. The Governor listed a whole lot of complaints against the army and its leadership. He was going to hold his usual military meeting that evening and wanted some members of the strategic committee to wait behind and speak to the officers, whose interest was "waning in the struggle". He accused the army commander of a number of commissions and omissions, including his reluctance to accept orders from him in matters affecting operations. I left, and did not wait to attend the meeting of military officers.

About midnight, I got out of bed and telephoned the State House and was told that the meeting was still on. I was surprised, got up and dressed and went to the State House. I found Njoku alone with Sir Francis and others. The Governor was in a room in the annexe to the house. I went there and saw him consulting with a few people. He invited me in. What in fact he was saying was that it must be either Njoku or him, and those with him were pleading that now was not the time for a show-down with the army commander. But the Governor was adamant. The meeting continued until the early hours of the morning, when Njoku was forced to sign a resignation paper prepared by the Governor, after he had already received a letter from the Governor asking him to resign. That completed, the Governor ordered that Njoku be taken out of Enugu that morning. We left the State House at 6 a.m. but were told to return by eight.

When I arrived home my wife told me of telephone calls after 1 a.m. asking if I had returned. She suspected the voice to be Alale's. I did not understand the implications of those telephone calls until I went back to the State House as previously instructed.

More people, including some army officers, appeared for the meeting of eight o'clock. Among the army officers was Col. Madiebo. The Governor opened the meeting by announcing that a plot to overthrow him and make peace with Nigeria had been discovered. The coup was to have taken place the previous night. The leaders of the plot were Col. Banjo and Col. Ifeajuna. But there were others. It then dawned on us that that was the reason why the Governor had brought the elites of Enugu to keep vigil with him the whole night at the State House. It also explained the reasons for the repeated telephone calls to my house in the night. The ringleaders wanted to know if the meeting had ended in order to enable those assigned the duty of carrying out the coup to strike, which they could not do in the presence of so many people without killing more than was necessary.

The Governor turned to Col. Madiebo and said, "Congratulations, Brigadier and our new army commander!" Madiebo was obviously surprised. He then called on Madiebo to tell the gathering what had happened, but when Col. Madiebo showed some hesitation—he still had not recovered from the surprise of being promoted a Brigadier and Commander of the Biafran army—the Governor took over. The coup was to have taken place the previous night. Col. Madiebo had been approached to cooperate, and had been offered the post of army commander. (Col. Madiebo's unit was at that time the star of the Biafran army, holding down the Federal troops at Nkalagu.) It was Col. Ifeajuna who had approached him. Col. Madiebo, as a disciplined soldier, had decided that morning to come to Enugu and tell Col. Njoku, the army commander, what Ifeajuna had told him. While on his way to Enugu he met Mojekwu and others who had been sent to ask him to come and take over as army commander.

What the Governor did not tell us—maybe he did not know at the time—was that Col. Madiebo had told Ifeajuna that he would support their proposal only if the leaders of Biafra supported it. Ifeajuna had asked him who those leaders were, and Col. Madiebo had mentioned names which Ifeajuna took down and put in his pocket. The list was later found in Col. Ifeajuna's pocket when he was arrested, but was used by the Governor to convince us that all of us were included in the list of those to be killed if the coup had been carried through. It was part of his tactics to get everyone "committed". This type of blackmail and intimidation of members of the Executive Council and leading members of the public was common right through the war.

It is not certain or even very likely that Brigadier Hilary Njoku was involved in the plot to overthrow the Governor and make peace with the Federal Government. What is certain is that he was a victim of Alale's propaganda, the sole aim of which was to discredit him as an army commander. All the reverses suffered in Nsukka and other fronts were blamed on Njoku, who was publicly accused of ineptitude, lack of interest and worse. One story which was widely told at the time, and by those who had knowledge of what was going on, was that the plan had been for supporters of Banjo and Ifeajuna to arrest Njoku and take him to the Governor to demand his dismissal or punishment for all the reverses which had befallen Biafran troops in the field. The Governor would be expected to come out and meet the crowd bringing Njoku and, in the course of pretending to make complaints and representations to the Governor, the latter would himself be arrested or killed. The story did not quite say what would have been the fate of Njoku after that. The reason for adopting that method of decoy, it was explained, was in order to avoid the loss of lives other than those of the targets.

Banjo and company were arrested that day and thrown into the Enugu prison. A special tribunal was instituted for their trial. They were all court-martialled and condemned on September 23rd, 1967 and executed soon afterwards. The execution took place in public, and those who saw the accused and condemned men said they remained unrepentant to the end. About a week after their execution, Enugu fell.

The fall of Enugu

As in all other such occasions during the war this took the

general public by surprise, not because the signs were not there all along, but because people refused to believe in realities or accept the inevitable. "No matter what they do with me, the Federal troops will be here any moment from now, maybe tonight," Banjo was reported as saying as he was being pushed into the Enugu prison. His assessment was correct, except that Enugu did not fall that night.

For over a week shells had been falling in the Enugu township, killing people and damaging buildings. But both in official and public circles nobody would accept that they were coming from the enemy. They blamed saboteurs for them, and spent time and effort looking for the imaginary traitors, suspected to be everywhere—in the Iva Valley coal mines, on top of Milliken Hill, behind the police mess, in the bushes and thickets around, or mingling, with their lethal instruments in their pockets, among the people in market places and perhaps churches as well. The unfortunate thing was that many innocent people, including women, were murdered by the over-zealous defenders looking for saboteurs. Anyone found in the bush, for whatever reason, was automatically suspected of being responsible for the explosions or associated with those responsible for them. If they were lucky they were allowed to go after some beating; if not, they were killed. Foreign nationals resident in Enugu and who were knowledgeable about such matters warned that these mortar bombs falling in the town were being fired some three or four miles away. They had, however, to be careful to whom they made the statement or would themselves be suspected and treated like others.

On the day Banjo, Ifeajuna, Alale and Agbam were executed the Federal troops were less than ten miles from Enugu, stationed on the normal highways, and even nearer on the many bush paths, about four miles or less as the crow flies. But nobody would believe that fact, and to emphasise it meant that you were a saboteur or an "enemy collaborator". Then news reached the State House that the Federal troops were occupying the radio transmitting station just off the Nine-Mile Corner, along the Nsukka road. The Governor himself could clearly see movements and persons with his telescope, but would not be convinced by what he saw—and if he was, he never told anybody so.

By four o'clock on September 29th we heard small arms fire very clearly, no matter where one was in Enugu. By the evening there was heavy firing on top of Milliken Hill, which was only three miles from the Enugu post office. The Governor was frightened, and sent people to find out. They returned to report that the firing was by our troops. "Elements believed to be former followers of

Ifeajuna had refused to carry out orders and when the officer tried to disarm them they resisted, hence the firing." The brigade headquarters had already been removed to the centre of Enugu, and this the Governor knew for the first time from those he had sent to Milliken Hill. By eight o'clock the Governor sent for those he could contact, directed that the American Consul and the British Deputy High Commissioner should be advised to leave Enugu that night (I understand the message never reached them), and told those of us who had gone to the State House to leave Enugu as soon as possible that night. He too would be leaving and would be staying at Awgu, some thirty-six miles from Enugu. Government departments would be headquartered in Aba.

And so that night, on the verge of collapse to the Federal troops, Enugu started to move. But although the Federal troops had completely surrounded the town, they did not take full possession of it until two or three days later.

It had been expected that the fall of Enugu would mark the end of the war. That was the belief not only on the Federal side but also in Biafra. But the war lingered on for more than another two years. Why this was so is the concern of the next chapter.

8 Why Did the War Last so Long?

It has been difficult for those outside the secessionist enclave, or who never visited it during the war, to understand why it was that the war lasted so long—why it was that Biafra did not surrender earlier, or that the Federal forces with their overwhelming preponderance did not overrun Biafra much sooner. Others have wondered why the Governor, regarded as the architect of the tragedy and so responsible for all the suffering brought on his people, was not overthrown by force. As one expatriate told me in London, those questions have been the real puzzles of the tragedy. The purpose of this chapter is to try to find the answers to them.

If the Governor had ever lacked support or incurred unpopularity before the war, all that ended when the war started. We have already seen how determined and enthusiastic the people had been about the war. Apart from regarding it as a means of avenging the killings of Easterners in 1966, they saw the war as the only means of saving their lives. For if the Hausas could kill them when the country was not at war, a war was the only way to protect themselves and enable them to fight back. The Biafran propaganda, and the experience of those who faced the actual killings in the North, had firmly entrenched in the minds of the people that the aim of their warring opponents was the total annihilation of the Ibo race, or at least of the leadership of that race. Nothing on earth could convince them to the contrary. The reported activities of the Federal troops, in the first fifteen months of the war, supported and intensified these fears. It was these reports which led to the appointment of the now famous international observer team, which stayed in the country from the later part of 1968 till after the end of the war.

One of the things which hardened the Easterners' determination to fight to the last man, if necessary, was the Federal side's use of air raids. Nothing had contributed more to the prolongation of the war than the indiscriminate activities of the Federal air force for the greater part of the civil war. It was not until the last few months of the war that they relented somewhat in the bombing of civilian populations and concentrated on the war fronts and military targets.

I am convinced, from what I have seen of official attitudes since the end of the war, that the pilots who conducted those raids into the war areas never reported the truth. Those pilots never went near military targets, but acted out the views of a commentator on the Kaduna radio, who said that everything in Biafra, including the grass, was a military target, because Ojukwu had said that even the grass would fight! I am sure that if anyone in authority on the Federal side had visited the area during the time, or had known half of what was actually happening, and the feelings it engendered among the people, he would have considered it in the Federal side's own interest to suspend the use of the air force if more civilised pilots could not be found.

As a matter of fact, while all the reports of the bombings in the foreign press were true, they had not reported all. Markets, schools, churches, hospitals, refugee camps—wherever the pilots could discern any large concentration of people—were the targets for the Federal war planes. It was these indiscriminate and mass killings of helpless people, women and children, the sick and the maimed, that made the majority of the people come to accept the propaganda of "genocide", which no assurances from the Federal side could mitigate. Because of the raids, mothers decided to send their sons to fight, and girls to help in whatever ways they could. Those with money surrendered as much as they could, whether in local or foreign currency (and some had funds overseas) for the Government to use in buying aircraft and weapons. It was the activities of the Federal planes which won most sympathy and support in the world for Biafra. It was those activities which brought in Count von Rosen, a humanitarian pilot flying in relief into the secessionist area.

I can well remember the day the Count decided to seek military assistance for Biafra. He had come to offer his good offices in search of peace, to find out exactly what the Biafrans wanted, and to go to Ethiopia to talk to the Emperor whom he described as a good friend. (Count von Rosen had helped Ethiopia in the war with Italy in the 1930s.) While von Rosen was discussing with one of the officials in Umuahia, the Federal planes attacked. Von Rosen had taken shelter with others, but after the end of the raid he went to the bombed sites and the hospital where scores of civilians were lying dead and mutilated—some of them beyond recognition. He had watched the planes fly in before taking cover, and as a pilot was convinced that there had been no question of mistaken targets. From that day his attitude and plans changed. He abandoned relief flights and devoted his time to devising means of helping Biafra to acquire its own war planes. Von Rosen's experience is representative of the majority of people who came to Biafra and returned to their countries as ardent sympathisers of the Biafran plight. By some sort of fortuitous coincidence, the worst raids always took place when influential overseas visitors were in Biafra. And, of course, even when there were no actual raids, the sites and ruins of previous raids were always there for them to see.

Then came the effects of the blockade. Like air raids, the total blockade had a paradoxical effect upon the people and their morale. It brought the effects of the war to every single individual resident in Biafra. It was used to convince the people that the aim was to kill everyone without exception—a belief intensified when the Federal Government tried to stop relief flights into Biafra.

One should not, of course, forget the Biafran propaganda, which earned world fame. It had been influential before the outbreak of hostilities, but that influence considerably increased during the war. The best literary talents and intellect were found in the propaganda directorate and the Ministry of Information. They were drawn from the universities, the professions and the civil service. They were among the hardest workers, were very dedicated and derived much satisfaction from their work. They had about fifty specialist groups all concerned with different fields and aspects of propaganda.

Even more effective than the literary output and programmes were the emotional songs composed by the many talented musicians discovered in the country since the war began. There were dramatists, artists, actors and actresses devoted to touring the fronts, towns and villages, nooks and corners, to inspire the people. There were public enlightenment groups also, supplementing the effects of other efforts. And there were, of course, the long emotional speeches of the Governor.

Not long after the start of the war, Biafra had virtually exhausted its stocks of ammunition. But the scientists and engineers had been working for months in anticipation of such a situation. Through their research, they had invented mass killing weapons such as that known as "ogbuniwe", meaning "mass destroyer". They had built guns and manufactured ammunition to suit their own purposes, and even copied some of the imported ones. After the fall of Port Harcourt they designed make-shift refineries which provided fuel for vehicles. Towards the end of the war, they had almost had a break-through into the production of engine oils, brake-fluids and so on. Different types of alcoholic drinks were manufactured to replace whisky, gin, schnapps, liqueurs; just as soap and other toilet articles and drugs were produced. It would be difficult to exhaust the list of contrivances produced by the ingenuity and resourcefulness of scientists and engineers in order to sustain the war.

There was the question of luck which came to the aid of the

Biafran soldiers on several occasions. Many things happened by accident rather than design to provide a respite for the hard-pressed Biafran troops. By some sort of happy coincidence (for the Biafrans) the Federal Forces, apart from fighting at predictable intervals, always reduced their pressures or activities when the Biafran resources were at the lowest, and resumed them again when supplies had been received. Several instances could be cited to illustrate this luck, but the following will be sufficient.

When the Federal troops suffered their heaviest losses in vehicles, equipment and men in the Abagana-Awka area in 1968, it was as a result of a lone mortar bomb claimed to be the very last left in the whole of the Biafran stock—intuitively fired, without orders, by one of the troops. The bomb landed on a fuel tanker in the middle of a convoy of more than one hundred vehicles and set the whole convoy ablaze. That incident completely disorganised all Federal plans for the capture of Onitsha and Nnewi. Had that convoy with all the equipment succeeded in getting to Onitsha, the war would have ended in that month, for according to experts both in Biafra and from overseas, nothing could have stopped the Federal troops from moving with ease to Nnewi, then to Uli, Owerri and Orlu. The capture of Uli airport would, of course, have sealed Biafra's fate in so far as relief and military supplies were concerned.

The Biafran forces had been totally routed and virtually destroyed when Aba and Owerri fell in September 1968. One Federal platoon marching to Umuahia either from Owerri or Aba would have captured the place without any difficulty. But the Federal troops did not attempt such a move until the Biafran troops had been reorganised, reinforcements had been moved in from elsewhere, and new supplies had been received. Similar things might have happened, although not as easily, if the Federal troops had moved to Umuahia when Ikot Ekpene and Okigwe fell to them.

Even though the Federal troops made no move towards Umuahia, the last but at that time totally undefended stronghold and headquarters of Biafra, all hopes of further resistance had been lost. The Governor convened a meeting of selected members of the Executive Council and told them that the war had been lost. There was no longer any real hope of continued formal resistance. Genuinely fearing that the intelligensia of the East would all be massacred by the victorious Federal troops, he suggested that immediate arrangements be made to save as many of them as possible by flying them out to Gabon and other African countries. As for himself, he was going to take to the bush and organise guerrilla resistance. Meanwhile, in order to save lives, the resolution of the O.A.U. at the Algiers meeting should be accepted even if only to put world pressure on the Federal Government to stop the war.

The only thing which delayed action was the need to consult, or rather inform, the four African countries which had recognised Biafra, of the situation and what he proposed to do, unless immediate military aid in a massive scale was given to Biafra. Delegates were flown out that night from Uturu airstrip with instructions to come back the following night. (By the time they returned Uturu airstrip had fallen and they had to land at Uli.) They came back with assurances of an immediate supply of arms and ammunition which could be dropped from the air if necessary. Two planes arrived that night bringing the returning envoys and large quantities of arms and ammunition. With the receipt of those arms and equipment the Biafran troops were able to face and check the Federal advances on all fronts. As far as I know, it was from this time on that Biafra started receiving military aid from outside countries. Hitherto they had depended on what they could capture from Federal troops, what the scientists and engineers could devise, and on irregular purchases overseas.

The war was also prolonged as a result of the duplicity of some African countries. It now appears that these countries were actually playing to both sides. They encouraged the Biafran side through Biafran envoys by telling them that their cause was right and would eventually receive their support, including diplomatic recognition. They would give one reason or another why they could not come out immediately in support of Biafra. If these African countries had played fair and clearly told the Biafran envoys that their action was wrong and could not be supported, the optimistic expectations which sustained morale might have been removed.

Biafra also enjoyed much sympathy from countries outside Africa, thanks to journalists and relief workers shocked by the indiscriminate bombings of the Federal air force. This sympathy, particularly among the people of Britain, France, United States, West Germany and the Scandinavian countries encouraged the Biafran leaders to believe that sooner or later, so long as there was no total military collapse, public opinion in these countries would force their Governments to take positive action in favour of Biafra. Some countries outside Africa did in fact give indirect assistance to Biafra in one form or another.

There was, finally, the Governor's personal leadership. He was adept at manipulating the minds and feelings of people. Able to remain unruffled even at the worst moments, he always inspired confidence even where and when he deliberately told his audience inaccuracies or things without foundation. He alone, along with the very few in authority spending most of their time abroad, knew the sources of arms and foreign exchange. If anything happened to him, that would be the end of the war, since it would have been impossible for any other person to continue where he left off. Since the people strongly believed that their survival depended upon continued military resistance, the personal existence of the Governor was considered imperative and virtually sacred. It was mainly for this reason that most people were prepared and willing to do what they were told by the Governor.

The army and other military personnel never knew much, if anything, about the position and expectations of military supplies. They had to use whatever the Governor provided. They were not always told the truth, and even when everything had been exhausted, with perhaps no sure hope of any immediate or future supplies, the Governor would ask them to plan operations, assuring them that everything necessary would be made available when the time came for the operations planned to take place.

Even when as happened at certain stages, people felt that a halt should be called to the war, nobody dared say so openly. The intelligence network was complex and interwoven. Fear of sabotage and saboteurs was always present, particularly when the area controlled by Biafra had become so small and the Federal troops were so near. On the occasions when certain people tried to speak out more freely, cries were raised that such people were planning to stage a coup. Behind it all was the menacing presence of the directorate of military intelligence and the special tribunal!

We saw in the last chapter how the Military Governor seemed already to have no confidence in the regular armed forces, and how he told the civilian leaders that the war would be fought and won by civilians. Soon after the fall of Enugu, during the first week of October 1967, the Governor convened a huge meeting of members of the consultative assembly and council of chiefs, along with many others. The Governor spoke at length and with great emotion to the large assembly, first from prepared notes, and then impromptu, explaining why we had lost Enugu. It was nothing but the work of saboteurs still abounding in our midst. The execution of those known to be the arch-saboteurs—Banjo, Ifeajuna, Alale and Agbam—had not deterred their followers and other leaders not yet discovered. He had come to the people in order to receive their mandate as to whether to continue the struggle or surrender to the enemy. He listed the terrible consequences of surrender—the North would usurp our land and everything we owned, close down our educational institutions to ensure that the progressive people of the East were brought down to their own "primitive" levels, and in order to ensure this, every single person of education, wealth or social standing would be destroyed, without exception. The sum total of it all was that the Easterners would for ever lose their identify and become slaves to the North, paying regular tribute to them as war reparations. Surrender would mean the end of Christianity for the East, along with all that went with Christianity. As for him, he saw no other alternative than to carry on the war, even if it meant that he had to fight alone to the death.

He promised that, with the resolute support of the people in every way, he would bring victory to Biafra within six months. The immediate necessity was to look for the enemies in our midst, saboteurs, traitors and agents of the enemy; the code word for Biafra's existence—Vigilance—must henceforth be given a new force and meaning. That was the duty of every individual in our "young and promising republic". He had a few uncomplimentary words for members of the public services, with obvious insinuations against the police. His speech ended, the Governor received deafening applause and a long ovation. He walked out of the hall making signs of victory to the large audience.

The usual debate started, with everyone pledging absolute support for the war. There could be no question of giving up. As must have been pre-arranged, a few people spoke scathingly of the police force, with particular reference to its leadership, and asked for immediate steps to be taken to purge that "corrupt, inefficient, ignorant and not very loyal establishment". In the end one of the resolutions passed was a vote of no confidence in the leadership of the police force, and the Governor was called upon to cause immediate steps to be taken to reform the establishment.

The Governor's speech had had the desired effect. Witch-hunting increased, leading to the "discovery" of many saboteurs who immediately found themselves bundled into detention in official prisons or in improvised camps, where those in authority over them meted out the worst possible treatment and insults, considering them worse enemies than those shooting from the other side. In this way, innocent persons were thrown into detention, or sent to the special tribunal where they faced the probability of a death sentence. Evil and malicious men and women used this charge to undo those with whom they had some axe to grind. No complaint or report about a saboteur was irrelevant or ignored. As far as the Governor was concerned, it was always better to err on the side of caution. When the numbers of those detained began to grow too large, presenting problems of accommodation, he set up what he called an "executive Council Committee on security" with the declared function, among other things, of periodically reviewing the cases of those detained. But it was sheer window-dressing and a sham. Not a single case of a detainee ever came before the committee. And even in the case of the other functions supposed to have been assigned to the committee, nothing was ever really referred to it. In disgust and frustration, the committee went into voluntary dissolution without achieving a single thing.

It has been a source of surprise and amusement for me to read statements and writings in the press by those who, for some selfish reasons, want to show how much they stood up to Ojukwu, opposed the war or demanded that it be stopped. There were times when people felt very discouraged about the war, particularly after the fall of Port Harcourt, Aba and Owerri, coming after the defeat of Enugu, Onitsha, Awka, Calabar and virtually the whole of Ibibio/Efik areas. But not a single one of those people dared speak his mind without serious consequences to his liberty and maybe even his life. The intelligence organisation was such that one could not know who might be an informant and who not, and judging from the kinds of things the Governor knew about the private lives of individuals, the organisation was very effective and efficient. Much as it would have given me pleasure and satisfaction to describe the workings of the Biafran intelligence service, with its many ramifications, I am not in a position to do so, because I was never allowed to know anything about it. In any case, I was myself a target of that "intelligence service".

When the Governor in those days spoke of the people's war, he was not exaggerating. Everyone was involved, thanks largely to the Federal air force as we have already mentioned. Contributions poured into the government in cash or kind. Anything belonging to anyone could be commandeered, provided this was done officially, for the war. Everything, including juju and magic, was employed; individuals were known to spend hundreds or thousands of pounds of their own to the juju and witch doctors, diviners, invokers or supernatural or spiritual powers. It was not the Government which encouraged this—if anything the Government would have preferred that the money so spent be given to it for more tangible uses.

Thus, returning to the question posed at the beginning of this chapter, namely why did the war last so long, we can summarise the reasons as follows:

(*a*) Although the people of the East had originally embraced the war as a means of avenging the deaths of those killed in the North in 1966, they later regarded it as their only means of survival. Even after they had lost all hope of victory, they were made to believe that the longer the war lasted, the more sympathy Biafra would have from the world. Such sympathy might bring more recognition, thus making it possible for Biafra to survive as an independent entity from the rest of Nigeria.

(*b*) The people had been taught to distrust and fear the Federal troops. They sincerely believed that the Federal forces would carry out an indiscriminate massacre, and commit total genocide, once they won the war. The activities of the Federal air force made these fears a reality.

(*c*) Even if that fear had not existed, there was no means of making felt the popular desire for peace. Not even the soldiers and their officers, who had for several months seen the futility of continuing the struggle, could express their opinions.

(*d*) The Governor's leadership and speeches with their apparatus of blackmail, terror, intimidation and a show of false confidence and unrealistic optimism also helped to prolong the war.

(*e*) There was, of course, the element of foreign assistance without which the war would have ended in September 1968.

(*f*) The duplicity of some African countries who, while condemning secession on the platform of the O.A.U., continued to give the secessionists the impression that their attitude at the O.A.U. was only temporary façade, kept up the hopes and morale of the Biafrans. To this must be added the sympathy and moral support of some countries outside Africa, particularly France.

(*g*) The dogged courage, ingenuity, endurance and the sacrifices of the people, particularly the engineers, scientists and the fighting troops, were easily the greatest and most effective sources for sustaining the war, particularly during the period when Biafran soldiers were fighting virtually with their bare hands.

(*h*) Luck was often on the side of Biafran forces, while the Federal side never really took advantage of their superior resources and missed many obvious opportunities of a quick victory.

(*i*) The personal position of Ojukwu could not be challenged by the people who were helpless before the military with their guns. The military, which had put him in power, dared not even contemplate his removal when they recalled what had happened to former army commander Brigadier Hilary Njoku and, much worse, the fate of Banjo, Ifeajuna, Alale and Agbam who, everybody believed, had been betrayed by Ojukwu's spies and agents in their midst. In any case, with the will to continue the fight still lingering, and it being known as a fact that without Ojukwu there would be no supplies to carry on the war, any idea of removing Ojukwu was ruled out by the majority of the people.

9 Internal Tensions and the Ahiara Declaration

We have already seen how certain extremist elements in Eastern Nigeria had exploited the crisis and the injured feelings of the people for ends other than those they professed. Among those extremists were intellectuals obsessed with their own personal ideological ideas and doctrines. The Governor had for his part exploited the enthusiasm and zeal of these elements to his own ends. In spite of the intelligence network, and the forces of fear, terror and intimidation operating within Biafra, the activities and aims of the extremists had not been destroyed. All that happened was a change of tactics and the adoption of different methods and guises. The behaviour and abuses by public functionaries and agents close to the Governor and the tension and simmering discontent which these and the strains of the war produced, were ready weapons in the hands of the activists.

Their basic tactic was the usual one of idealising and idolising an individual whom they would use as a front to achieve their ends, after which he could easily be disposed of. That individual, in the case of Biafra, was found in Governor Ojukwu, whose weaknesses and idiosyncracies they exploited to the full. They were mainly intellectuals and professionals, now unable to practise their respective professions, and devoting their talents and expertise to the war effort. A good number of these people were concentrated in the directorate of propaganda, which was later fused with the Ministry of Information but never really lost its separate identity. They could not have chosen a better base from which to operate. A good number of the leading elements in the "progressive" and "revolutionary" elite had been known agitators during the pre-independence period, or had been trained in communist countries, or were former associates of extremist or leftist movements at one time or another. They were not all concentrated in the directorate of propaganda, but could be found in other war effort establishments such as research and production, commonly known as R.A.P. or R. and P.; they could also be found in the ordinary establishments of Government, such as the civil service.

For a long time, particularly after August 1966, the Governor had leaned considerably upon the intellectuals and professionals who had wormed themselves into his confidence. These arrogant so-called intellectuals, now finding themselves respected and admired by the Governor, exhibited open contempt and undisguised hostility towards the civil service and other branches of the public services. Even though their ignorance and naïveté in their approach to public affairs and problems were often obvious and sometimes appalling, they paraded themselves as the repositories of all knowledge, as lexicons with answers to all human problems. They saw scarcely any good in the existing order of institutions of public administration—the civil service, the police, the judiciary—which they considered as either bad in themselves or badly organised and manned. Top civil servants were often openly insulted and despised, until it reached a stage when I had to intervene as the head of the civil service, remonstrate with them, but not until well after a year, when the Governor himself had begun to be disturbed.

The civil servants for their part reacted appropriately. Some of these new "messiahs" were still at school when the civil servants they were now insulting had graduated and joined the civil service; others had been their colleagues in the universities. In any case, the fact that some people had chosen, after graduating, to join the civil service or other forms of Government employment did not mean that they were intellectually inferior to, or more lacking in initiative and enterprise than those who had chosen to go into academic life.

There naturally developed definite signs of tension and hostility between the public servants and these outsiders who had come to hold sway over them. Out of evil, however, good often comes. So, I believe, has been the case in this matter. In the end mutual respect and cooperation began to develop between the two classes.

The revolutionaries or reformers did not relent in their efforts. I must say that a number of them acted in good faith, with conviction and objectivity. These people deserved and received respect even from those such as I, who did not always share their views and methods. Others were not so selfless and disinterested, but had their own political or other objectives. Skilled in the art of indoctrination and in the use of subtle methods, this latter group soon collected adherents. Under cover of attuning the minds and the attitude of the people to the "struggle" and preparing the people for the ideals of "Biafranism" as against those of "Nigerianism", they started "schools of political orientation" and conducted seminars for the purpose. They were also prominent in organisations of mass education and assemblies or meetings. They frequented and endeared themselves to the armed forces and exhibited the most ardent enthusiasm for the war efforts.

The Governor became apprehensive about the activities of these people, and ordered discreet inquiries to be made and the police to keep a cautious watch on them. But when the police started to uncover suspicious trends, the Governor appeared typically unworried and expressly showed doubts about the police assessments, particularly when they identified some of the people concerned as known "communists" and former "fellow-travellers". It is possible that the Governor did not completely ignore these facts, but either by word or action made those concerned have some idea of what the police were saying about them. After all, they were the people who were producing all the propaganda material for Biafra and were also responsible for the preparation and issue of most of the pamphlets and documents for which Biafra soon became famous.

The hostility of this group towards the public service establishment was, as we have seen, quite undisguised. But towards the police, whom they did everything in their power to discredit, their attitude was positively venomous. Soon this hostility became open and unrestrained. All public institutions were defamed and abused, being accused of corruption, indolence, inefficiency, ignorance, reactionary practices, and being out of line with the spirit and aspirations of revolutionary Biafra. As such they had to be completely overhauled, if not utterly swept away. All the heads of these establishments were reactionaries and should be replaced, along with all their experienced members. The recipe for reform was that every public servant above the age of thirty-five should be retired. Not even the church escaped the reformists' notice and attack.

They attacked the Governor and the happenings in the State House and the innumerable "scandals" with which those in or close to that establishment were associated. In more than indirect ways, they were attacking the State House for betraying, or attempting to betray, the cause of the revolution for which Biafra was fighting. Always alert to such situations, the Governor decided to take swift and dramatic action, not by taking open and direct action against them, but by openly identifying himself with their views. Using their platforms, the Governor spoke against the manifold evils in our society with a louder voice and greater force, backed by authority. He openly attacked, to the utter embarrassment of all concerned, the judiciary, the civil service, the police, the army and all other public organs and institutions. But he was no fool: his aim was to beat the activists at their own game.

Now that he had made himself leader of his own critics—the potential trouble-makers who had in effect been preaching anarchy and counter-revolution—he was able to draw them closer to himself in order to control them. He directed that their efforts, should be harnessed with a proper sense of direction towards specific goals. Accordingly, he decided to establish what was known as the "National Guidance Committee", which would work under his personal supervision. The establishment and running of such things like the school of political orientation would be under the umbrella of the N.G.C. By careful selection, the most vociferous and active of the "revolutionaries" were made members of that committee, counterbalanced by moderates and conservatives. A moderate and cool-headed leftist was appointed chairman of the National Guidance Committee by the Governor, while a dedicated leftist was made secretary. Meetings were to be held once a week in the Governor's presence and in the State House. The aim of the N.G.C. was to discuss and crystallise the aims and tenets of the Biafran revolution.

The meetings were held every Sunday (later changed to Monday) and could last any length of time. There were occasions when they lasted from ten o'clock in the morning to five in the evening. As the Chief Secretary, I was invited to attend, but not as a member, although I was free to participate in the discussions. After the first meeting it was decided that, in order to guide the N.G.C., the views of cross-sections of the Biafran community should be ascertained. Thus, every Wednesday or so, people were invited at random to come and express their views in what were described as "kitchen parliaments". Each group consisted of some thirty to fifty persons ranging from high court judges, bishops, heads of departments, etc, to clerks, domestic servants and labourers—in the "true spirit of the revolution". Nobody was told in advance why he had been invited, let alone what topic was going to be discussed. A number of the first batch invited were quite worried, for fear that they were being decoyed for arrest and detention. The topics to be discussed were usually chosen by the chairman in consultation with the Governor, and the chairman was always the chairman of the N.G.C.

The meetings, which were usually held late in the evenings for fear of air-raids, were invariably opened by the Governor, who spoke for about fifteen minutes about the aims and aspirations of the people, and ended by exhorting all present to express their views without fear or favour. Everything said would be taken down by the verbatim reporters, but no names would be mentioned. The sole purpose was to enable those whose responsibility it was to plan for the future to know exactly what the people wanted, and to proceed accordingly. After the introductory speech, the Governor would take a back seat, in the true spirit of "Biafranism" where the leader must appear the servant of the people! He would participate in the discussions on the basis of absolute equality with the other participants. At the end of each meeting beer and soft drinks would be served. The topic chosen for the first group was, "What sort of Biafra am I fighting for?"—or something like that. Each group had a different topic to discuss.

At the end of each meeting of the "kitchen parliament" the secretary of the N.G.C. would take over the verbatim reports and extract and summarise for the next meeting of the N.G.C. the salient points made by the different speakers. At the following meeting the members of the N.G.C. would not only briefly discuss the points summarised by the secretary but also draw a general assessment of the quality of the participants and of what they said. After that the topic for the day would be tackled. I recall that one of these topics, which occupied something like three or four meetings, concerned the ownership of land. It was a subject over which even the members of the N.G.C. held strong and divergent views. Eventually a member of the N.G.C., a judge of the high court, was commissioned to prepare a paper for consideration. When, after a few weeks, the paper came, there still could not be any agreement. It all started at the second meeting of the "kitchen parliament" when some invitees, mainly from the non-Ibo areas where the most fertile lands existed, strongly opposed the idea of vesting all the land in the state or community.

The meetings of the "kitchen parliament" and of the N.G.C. continued regularly until the fall of Umuahia to the Federal troops in April 1969. With that event and the scattering of the people all over what remained of Biafra, it was no longer possible to hold the "kitchen parliaments" (later re-christened "people's parliaments", to make it sound more impressive, by the Governor). Everything now appeared in a state of flux. But within a week things began to settle. Confidence began to return with the recapture of Owerri from the Federal troops. While Owerri township was being cleaned up, and repairs to the different buildings undertaken, I established the administrative headquarters in Nkwerre, near Orlu. The Governor stayed at a place called Madonna, a former educational institution, ten miles from Umuahia, and forty from Orlu. Within three weeks of its recapture from the Federal troops, Owerri was ready for the principal ministries and the administrative headquarters to be moved there. But Madonna remained the Governor's principal place of residence, though he had four other alternatives—in Owerri, Orlu, Ogwa and Oriagu.

The N.G.C. started meeting again regularly two weeks after the fall of Umuahia, but members had to travel to Madonna from distances averaging forty miles for the meetings. It was not possible to continue holding meetings of the "kitchen parliaments", which was a great disappointment to the Governor, who saw in it more a way of diverting public attention from the war disasters than of learning about public opinion.

The fall of Umuahia had brought the morale of the people to rock bottom. Although much was made of the recapture of Owerri, this did not easily off-set the general feelings of disappointment and loss of hope which the defeat of Umuahia, the last citadel of Biafra, had brought about. The fall of Umuahia meant that the Federal troops were now in control of practically all the territory lying east of Imo River, allowing only very precarious routes to the few food-producing areas of parts of Annang, Uyo and Bende areas. The only achievement which could really boost morale and completely off-set the loss of Umuahia would be either the recapture of Port Harcourt or Onitsha, and to this the military seriously directed their efforts. Any small success made in one or the other of these sectors was given the widest and most exaggerated publicity.

The arrival of six minicon aircraft on May 22nd, 1969, and their initial spectacular successes, together with the world publicity they received, went a long way to raise morale. On their way to Biafra the aircraft attacked Port Harcourt airport, causing considerable damage to buildings and destroying Federal aircraft on the ground. They attacked Benin airport on May 24th, Enugu airport on May 27th, and Ughelli power station in the Mid-West on May 29th. June 3rd saw another attack on Ughelli, whose power station supplies electricity to the whole of the Mid-West and a greater part of the Western States.

Several months before—indeed before the fall of Aba and Owerri to the Federal troops in 1968—in answer to the Governor's appeal, people had contributed thousands of pounds as gifts and loans, both in foreign and local money, towards the purchase of war planes with which to retaliate against the Federal side. Although the Governor had assured the people that the war planes were ready to be brought in once they were paid for, several months passed after the people had contributed enough to buy, at the price the Governor had intimated, at least three aircraft, but nothing was heard about the planes. This failure set people talking, and openly saying that they had been duped. Because of their great desire to have their own air force for the purpose of retaliation, the disappointment very considerably undermined the people's confidence in the Governor and his administration.

The Governor was well aware of this, and did everything to redeem his promise and honour, but even after the six small aircraft had arrived, people were heard openly to wonder whether they had cost all the money they had been made to contribute. At the same time fingers were pointed at the conduct and activities of the Governor's relatives as well as of members of his household, some of whom were known to be engaged in the "attack trade"—a name given to the trade carried out with people living in the areas controlled by the Federal side. Others were known to be travelling regularly on Government planes to buy essential commodities which they returned to sell at exorbitant prices, while those who did not travel could get their supplies regularly from planes owned or hired by the Government to bring in military supplies.

These were the kinds of abuses which the activists and "revolutionaries" were openly attacking before the formation of the N.G.C. It now fell to them to go round and conduct counter-propaganda, with doubtful effects. Everything had become very scarce, with prices rising more than a thousand times. Transport was scarce and distances for acquiring food very great. The "land army", whose main task it was to encourage people to cultivate land and produce food, but which had lost everything they had managed to achieve following the defeat of Umuahia, was given new impetus. But how could they be expected to squeeze water out of rocks? There was not much land left now to cultivate, and what was available was not fertile.

As we have said, the novel device of consulting the people in the "kitchen parliaments", though officially announced to be a means of ascertaining the wishes of the people for their future, was in reality a means of diverting the people's attention from the disasters of the war and the simmering social discontent, while the real purpose of establishing the national guidance committee was to bottle up and control the forces threatening to canalise the feelings of the people to ends that might prove fatal to the war effort, and even to the Governor himself. The Governor was worried and frightened by those dynamic forces. One effective way of stopping them was to compromise their position by "committing" them directly with the Government and making them feel responsible as the architects of the new Biafra. In this the Governor succeeded almost completely, particularly in the subtlety of his tactics, which hoodwinked those members of the N.G.C. concerned so that they did not even suspect his real motives and strategy.

As far as the war itself was concerned, people had become tired, enthusiasm was flagging, and confidence waning. The propaganda of the threat of imminent genocide was losing its force, and even if that were not so, there were people who showed signs of preferring a quick death by the bullet to the slow and painful one by starvation. In any case, why should some sections of the community be made to suffer while others were known to be still living in relative comfort? It was therefore urgent and imperative for the Governor to devise something that would revive the people's will to fight now that the force of all the previous reasons for fighting was wearing out.

The new approach was to make the people believe that the war had already virtually been won and the Biafran nation firmly established. Biafra promised all the fruits of Canaan and Utopia for the people. It would be a pity if, after having gone so far and with the Promised Land already in sight, the people should by default throw away all their gains and forfeit the future. With the war virtually won, it was now necessary to cleanse our society of all social evils, for which a new term, "Nigerianism", had been invented. The term itself was a propaganda of hatred and contempt for any idea of rejoining Nigeria. This new approach was forcefully brought out in that portion of the "Ahiara declaration"[1] which read:

> "Fellow countrymen, we pride ourselves on our honesty. Let us admit to ourselves that when we left Nigeria, some of us did not shake off every particle of Nigerianism. We say that Nigerians are corrupt and take bribes, but here in our country we have among us some members of the police and the judiciary who are corrupt and who "eat" bribes. We accuse Nigerians of inordinate love of money, ostentatious living and irresponsibility, but here, even while we are engaged in a war of national survival, even while the very life of our nation hangs in the balance, we see some public servants who throw huge parties to entertain their friends; who kill cows to christen their babies. We have members of the armed forces who carry on "attack" trade instead of fighting the enemy. We have traders who hoard essential goods and inflate prices, thereby increasing the people's hardship. We have "money-mongers" who aspire to build hundreds of plots on land as yet unreclaimed from the enemy; who plan to buy scores of lorries and buses and to become agents for those very foreign businessmen who have brought their country to grief. We have some civil servants who think of themselves as masters rather than servants of the people. We see doctors who stay idle in their villages while their countrymen and women suffer and die. When we see all these things, they remind us that not every Biafran has yet absorbed the spirit of the revolution. They tell us that we still have among us a number of people whose attitudes and outlooks are Nigerian. It is clear that if our Revolution is to succeed, we must reclaim these wayward Biafrans. We must Biafranise them. We must prepare all our people for the glorious roles which await them in the Revolution. If after we shall have

1. See Appendix below for the Concluding Parts of the Declaration.

tried to reclaim them we have failed, then they must be swept aside. The people's revolution must stride ahead and like a battering ram, clearing all obstacles in its path. Fortunately, the vast majority of Biafrans are prepared for these roles....

Every day of the struggle bears witness to actions by our countrymen and women which reveal high ideals of patriotic courage, service and sacrifice; actions which show the will and determination of our people to remain free and independent but also to create a new and better order of society for the benefit of all."

The above extract brings out a number of points. For one, we are now engaged in a *revolution*, not in a war with Nigeria, nor in a war of survival, nor in a war to avenge the deaths of our kith and kin "wantonly killed in the North in 1966". In the course of launching the Ahiara declaration, Governor Ojukwu said: "I stand before you tonight not to launch the Biafran Revolution, because it is already in existence; it came into being two years ago when we proclaimed to all the world that we had finally extricated ourselves from the sea of mud that was, and is, Nigeria. I stand before you to proclaim formally the commitment of the Biafran State to the Principles of the Revolution and to enunciate those Principles." With the war "virtually won", the main preoccupation now must be the "Revolution". Another thing which the extract shows is that, while acknowledging the ills and evil practices then existing in his administration, the Governor wanted to dissociate himself from them. Every institution in his administration—the police, the judiciary, the civil service, the armed forces was corrupt, except the governorship.

But the Governor was not the sole author of the "Ahiara declaration", which was in fact the work of the members of the N.G.C., though under his supervision. That declaration also defines the role of the "Leader", the title which the N.G.C. felt should be given to the Governor, in these terms:

"Those who aspire to lead must bear in mind the fact that they are servants and as such cannot ever be greater than the People, their masters. Every leader in the Biafran Revolution is the embodiment of the ideals of the Revolution. Part of his role as leader is to keep the revolutionary spirit alive, to be a friend of the People and protector of their Revolution. He should have right judgement both of people and of situations and the ability to attract to himself the right kind of lieutenants who can best further the interests of the People and of the Revolution. The leader must not only say but always demonstrate that the power he exercises is derived from the People. Therefore, like every other Biafran public servant, he is accountable to the People for the use he makes of their mandate. He must get out when the People tell him to get out. The more power the leader is given by the People, the less is his personal freedom and the greater his responsibility for the good of the People. He should never allow his high office to separate him from the People. He must be fanatical for their welfare.

A leader in the Biafran Revolution must at all times stand for justice in dealing with the People. He should be the symbol of justice which is the supreme guarantee of good government. He should be ready, if need be, to lay down his life in pursuit of this ideal. He must have physical and moral courage and must be able to inspire the People out of despondency.

He should never strive towards the perpetuation of his office, or devise means to cling to office beyond the clear mandate of the People. He should resist the temptation to erect memorials to himself in his lifetime, to have his head embossed on the coin, name streets and institutions after himself, or convert government into a family business. A leader who serves his people well will be enshrined in their hearts and minds. This is all the reward he can expect in his lifetime. He will be to the People the symbol of excellence, the quintessence of the Revolution. He will be BIAFRAMAN."

The message of this particular portion of the "Ahiara declaration" is clear. It had a triple purpose: to serve as a code of conduct for the Governor; to remind him that he had not been behaving and acting as expected, and to warn against certain obvious traits in the Governor for the future.

The term "Biaframan" was a tentative and original title for the Biafran head of state to take after the war, in place of more common ones such as President, Chairman, and so on.

The "Ahiara declaration" was also directed at Africa and the negro race as a whole, in a desperate bid to win more practical sympathy and support from them. The Biafran struggle was not just a fight for Biafra's existence, but a struggle against all the forces which had denied the negro race its rights—a struggle against imperialism, neo-imperialism, colonialism and neo-colonialism; a struggle against Arab-Muslim expansionism.

"Our struggle has far-reaching significance. It is the latest recrudescence in our time of the age-old struggle of the black man for his full stature as a man. We are the latest victims of a wicked collusion between the three traditional scourges of the black man—racism, Arab-Muslim expansionism, and white economic imperialism. Playing a subsidiary role is Bolshevik Russia seeking for a place in the African sun."[1]

1. Note the mild reference to Russia whose war planes and rockets were at that time believed to be wreaking havoc on the civilian populations. This was a result of the influence of the leftist members of the drafting panel.

Exactly one-third of the nearly three-hour long speech was devoted to the suffering, potential and aspirations of the negro race and to a nauseating attack on the white race, which was all the more embarrassing because of the large numbers of white men present when the declaration was made. I was shown the completed draft and I made certain suggestions which were completely and immediately ignored.

"The Ahiara declaration" (in which were laid out the principles of the Biafran Revolution) was launched at a small village called Ahiara, on the highroad linking Owerri to Umuahia, by "Emeka Ojukwu, General of the People's Army", on the night of Sunday, June 1st, 1969, in the large church building of that village. The meeting place and its grounds were packed to capacity with several hundred people, including at least thirty foreign visitors, among them Professor Clyde Ferguson of the U.S. Government's relief programme. The declaration is a fascinating document and is reproduced in part as an appendix to this book.

Instead of inspiring confidence, allaying fears and inducing "commitment" amongst the people, the declaration set off a chain of hostile reactions and misgivings. The most disturbing part of it was the one affecting ownership of property, which read as follows:

> "In the New Biafra, all property belongs to the Community. Every individual must consider all he has, whether in talent or material wealth, as belonging to the community for which he holds it in trust. This principle does not mean the abolition of personal property but it implies that the State, acting on behalf of the community, can intervene in the disposition of property to the greater advantage of all."

It provoked wide-spread alarm. Everyone wanted an explanation or clarification of that particular provision. The very wording of that section betrays a lack of unanimity among the members of the N.G.C. responsible for the document. The second sentence, which tried to allay obvious and anticipated fears, in fact only added to the confusion. For instance, people wanted to know what exactly the word "personal" meant, and why the more common and understandable term "private" was not used to avoid ambiguity. To add to the general concern, those responsible for the preparation of the document were not only known but were bragging about their achievement, and they included those whose political philosophy was, to say the least, egalitarian or very leftist.

The Governor immediately ordered that intensive seminars, discussions and talks be held to educate the people about the Ahiara declaration. Groups of people were brought to Owerri to spend at least a week discussing and studying the declaration. Seminars were also held among the armed and fighting forces, the police, and the civil service. The Governor personally attended many of the discussions and seminars, but his personal attempts to explain or elucidate the most controversial sections of the document often increased rather than diminished the confusion. The result was that those who had been brought to be educated went back more confounded than when they came. In an attempt to reassure those who were determined to oppose the declaration, the Governor tried to give the impression that it was not a final document but a basis for discussion which would lead to a final document. Because of this, some of those who had helped to prepare the document and had considered it the magna carta of Biafra, were disappointed and accused the Governor of trying to back-pedal, developing cold feet, and even "betraying the revolution". Eventually, the Governor virtually had to recant that section of the declaration in his last speech in Akokwa before the collapse of Biafra.

But the problem was not confined to the genuine fears and opposition arising from certain sections of the declaration. Many people openly ridiculed some sections, while others used them as grounds for hooliganism and indiscipline, even within the services. A person forcefully depriving another of his goods or property would cite as his authority either the section saying that "all property belongs to the community", or the section saying that every Biafran "must be his brother's keeper and must help all Biafrans in difficulty". In the same way, for open acts of indiscipline in offices, a sentence could always be found in the Ahiara declaration either in support or in extenuation. A case was once brought to me of an office messenger, without wife or family, demanding that he be given the same share of relief supplies as his boss, who not only had a wife and eight children but was also looking after some five refugees within his household! The messenger had demanded it as of right, and when the boss called him to order, he had retaliated with insults and abuse. He was disciplined, and so appealed to me. Having read his petition, which in effect admitted all the charges laid against him, but claimed at the same time that the charges were unjust and "illegal", I asked to see the office messenger. When he was brought to my office I tried to put him at ease by treating him genially.

"I was only demanding my rights, sir," he said in answer to a question.

"What rights?" I asked, staring him straight in the face.

"Ahiara, page 29, sir", he replied. I was amused, took out a copy of the document from my drawer and turned to the page. "Where, on page 29?", I asked.

"Every true Biafran must know and demand his civic rights," he began to quote. "But the truth often is that we allow ourselves to be bullied because we are not man enough to demand and stand up for our rights . . ."

It was part of the Ahiara declaration, certainly, but I had to show the unrepentant office messenger that "rights" also involved "justice". In the case in question, his boss had a family and several dependants, which the office messenger had not. He also had the right to be obeyed and respected by his subordinates. But the important fact was that he had committed a serious act of indiscipline, and was therefore liable to dismissal, which had already been recommended. But in view of the hard times, I directed that a strict warning be issued to him and that he be transferred to outdoor duties as a punishment. This true story shows to what extent people were misinterpreting and abusing the Ahiara declaration.

The apostles of the Ahiara declaration, on the other hand, were unrelenting in their arrogance, tenacity and drive. In spite of the Governor's repeated and express warnings that the N.G.C. was not the Government, or even an alternative to the Executive Council or Cabinet, some members of the N.G.C. were behaving as if they were superior to the Cabinet. One of them actually defined the role of the N.G.C. as that of determining policy for the Executive Council to execute! A number of them went out of their way to engage in activities in fact belonging to established government departments. A classic example of this was the organisation of women's cooperatives.

The scarcity of food and other basic necessities of life had reached its peak, and those who happened to be in possession of them were exacting exorbitant prices for them. A tiny pinch of snuff was costing at least five shillings, while a cigarette cup of salt could cost anything up to fifteen pounds. These are just examples. And yet those commodities were being brought into the enclave by government aircraft. They were paid for either by private businessmen and organisations who had foreign exchange facilities, or by the government. In order to ensure a fair distribution it was decided that every item of essential commodities, other than those brought in by the relief agencies which had their own independent machinery and method of distribution, should be taken over by the government and sold at controlled prices through cooperative societies, operating under the supervision of the government officials. The advisability of forming women's cooperatives had also been considered and accepted.

Always contemptuous of organisations with which civil servants were associated, some members of the N.G.C. began to organise women into cooperative societies, regardless of the procedures laid down in the cooperative law, and without enlisting the cooperation of government officers available. What was more, these women's cooperative societies were formed in opposition to the societies already in existence under the law. Indeed, as far as the organisers of these new cooperative societies were concerned, the existing cooperatives were too corrupt to be reckoned with! The women were promised exclusive rights in the distribution of the scarce commodities. Because the organisers assumed the authority and backing of the Governor (not of the government, because they considered themselves to be members of that!), the women embraced the proposal with their usual enthusiasm. Mass meetings of women were called to explain not just the working and aims of the new movement, but the tenets of the Ahiara declaration.

The administrative officers in charge of the divisions began to wonder what was happening. Why should meetings be held in their administrative divisions without even the courtesy of their being informed? And who were those who were trying to organise cooperative societies while there were government officials specialised in that task? They noticed and worried about the political contents of the speeches made at these meetings, and, as their duty and responsibility demanded, intervened. The organisers of the meetings were naturally up in arms. Who were the divisional officers that they should have the audacity to try to interfere in what was being done on the direct authority of the Governor? The divisional officers sought my protection and I strongly supported them. Political meetings had been banned since January 1966 and as far as I knew that ban still stood. It was true that the government favoured the formation of cooperative societies for the fair distribution, through sale, of scarce commodities. But the formation of such societies must be in accordance with the existing law and with those authorised under that law to undertake such a task. There was no question of establishing exclusive societies; while the sizes of the legal societies had to be of manageable proportions, not the kind of large masses reported and which comprised women from several villages, registered almost by compulsion.

As I had expected, I became the direct target of attack and vilification by those concerned. I did not in fact expect the Governor to support me, and was prepared for the usual embarrassments which were my lot in such circumstances. All the same,

I had done my duty. Even the administrative officers originally concerned were not all that hopeful of support by the Governor, who could issue counter-instructions directly to them if he did not like what I had done. I took the first opportunity to tell the Governor what was happening and what action I had taken. To my surprise and relief, he thought I had done right. I later learnt that he himself had been worried that the organisers of the so-called women's cooperatives might be using that as a front for something else. When therefore the matter was raised at the next meeting of N.G.C., the Governor told those concerned that his intention had all along been that the law and established procedures should be followed.

This stand by the Governor produced a chain reaction of its own. The women who had built high hopes on the proposed new organisations were very disappointed, and their anger was not necessarily directed against those who had given them wrong impressions but against the government, the popularity and reputation of which had considerably diminished. The self-appointed organisers of the women's cooperatives were also not only embarrassed but deeply disappointed by the "Leader"—their Governor. How could they tell the women that the societies which were being launched with so much fanfare were no longer to continue, and what about the contributions some of them had already made? They had paraded themselves as in authority, with the Governor as the Leader. The frustration of their efforts to form women's cooperatives knocked the bottom out of their claims to importance and influence. It was no secret that the government administrative officers, whom they had come to despise, had been opposed to the activities of these "leaders of the revolution", who on more than one occasion had told those "incompetent" administrative officers, in the presence of the women "cooperators", that they would be taught a lesson. After all had not a few of them been transferred in the past from their posts because the Governor had been so advised? The Governor's refusal to support these revolutionaries showed how completely unfounded were all their previous claims to authority and influence. It was about this time too that one of the leading revolutionaries was queried about statements he was alleged to have made while in London, to the effect that communists and socialists were now in control in Biafra, and that the Ahiara declaration had in fact been produced by them. This in itself had wounded the Governor's pride, and he had to take every opportunity to assert his personal responsibility for, and his faith in, "everything contained in the Ahiara declaration", which he claimed to be a "crystallisation of my own political philosophy"—which in fact was not very honest, except perhaps in so far as it could be a springboard to absolute and dictatorial powers for the "Leader".

Tensions continued to mount in various ways and for various reasons. Thefts at the airport increased, as did cases of soldiers seizing relief vehicles on their way to refugee camps or rehabilitation centres. There were rumours of a planned coup d'état. The Governor's fears and suspicions increased, particularly when in August 1969 Dr. Azikiwe began to complicate matters. Ojukwu's relations with the leader and members of the directorate of military intelligence had become strained. That amorphous organisation had become virtually uncontrollable. The Governor wanted to disband it, but had not the courage to do so openly. He therefore decided to set up a completely new intelligence and security organisation, and convened several meetings of representatives of the police, the armed forces, the administration, "the foreign ministry" and occasionally, but with reluctance, the directorate of military intelligence against whose continued existence the whole exercise was directed. But these meetings did not provide an immediate solution. The membership of the directorate of military intelligence had grown to several hundreds if not thousands. Not even the Governor, to whom they were supposed to be directly responsible, could give an accurate figure. To disband such a gigantic organisation suddenly might create and aggravate more problems than the action was intended to solve.

The Governor decided to bide his time, while increasing his personal vigilance and devising additional methods of personal protection and security. As history has shown to be a common feature of dictatorships, the Governor could no longer really trust the old faces around him. Not long before, he had openly humiliated and discharged a number of them, including a senior police officer. Under the guise of guarding against the rising tide of hooliganism and pilfering at the airport, particularly by members of the armed forces, and especially by those of the air force who were in control of the airport, the Governor began to form what he called "a third force".

The formation of this force between October and November 1969 was undertaken in a curious way. It was to be headed by the senior member of the mobile police force, and the Governor went ahead and made his selection without reference to his Inspector General of Police. The officer was in fact summoned to the State House, given instructions and warned not to inform the Inspector General of Police about it, since the officer was not, henceforth, to work under him, but to be directly responsible to the Governor himself. The embarrassed police officer did not know what to do, but did his duty—in spite of the Governor's instructions to the contrary—to his professional boss by telling him what the Governor had done. As for the other officers and men of the "third force", the Governor was to select at random those he liked—whether from the army, the air force, the navy, the police, the civil defenders, or even from amongst civilians. Because of the urgency attached to the whole affair, the Governor proceeded at once to withdraw the men he had selected from their respective commands in order to form this "third force". Naturally, this involved even the dislocation of military operations in some cases. Neither the police nor the armed forces were in favour, but were powerless to do anything. The very idea of establishing this third force meant that the Governor had lost confidence in them for his protection and safety.

Those were the types of tensions and the kinds of measures existing in Biafra when it collapsed. The examples given are not exhaustive, but they give a picture of the sort of situation obtaining in the secessionist regime just before its final collapse.

10 Attempts to End the War

"Never in history have a people lost a war of independence"—this was Governor Ojukwu's repeated propaganda which he intended the people of Biafra to accept as an article of faith, a magical axiom, of which the Biafran situation was a natural and automatic proof. "We are fighting a war of independence and Biafra cannot be the first to break this immutable law of history!"

It is for political historians to confirm or dispute that maxim. I myself never looked upon the Biafran resistance as a war of independence, but as a war of secession, a struggle to break away from the corporate whole of which the area then called Biafra had been an integral part. Thus, whenever the Governor endeavoured to draw analogies between the Biafran situation and the American War of Independence of the eighteenth century, I had always felt that a better analogy lay with the American Civil War of the nineteenth century. Similarly, the Algerian and other wars of independence fought in this century against foreign colonial powers could not accurately be compared with the Biafran war, which, if it had been successful, would probably have been unique in history! But nobody could openly contradict Governor Ojukwu without making himself suspect.

Where existing or former political unions were broken up, it had been as a result of negotiations or mutual agreements. The examples of Mali, and the Central African, Malaysian and West Indian federations are relevant. But even here one cannot accurately say that these federations were exactly like the Federation of Nigeria. The component parts had been distinctly separate and sovereign entities (albeit under colonial rule or tutelage) which had voluntarily—even if under persuasion—decided to join the union in the first instance, but later decided to resume their sovereignties. The case of the Balkans, though involving war—and some international involvements—may be seen to be nearer the positions of these dissolved federations than to the position of Biafra vis-à-vis the rest of Nigeria. It is possible that Governor Ojukwu sincerely believed that Biafra, under his leadership, was fighting a war of independence. He still spoke of "Biafra having resumed her sovereignty" until the very end.

Early in September 1967, Governor Ojukwu caused a

memorandum to be prepared, for the benefit of those travelling abroad to seek support for Biafra's sovereignty, defining "possible areas of future association between Biafra and the rest of the former Federation of Nigeria". An interesting aspect of that memorandum was the assumption that other parts of Nigeria would break up as the former Eastern Nigeria had done:

> "In this exercise, an over-all view of the rest of Nigeria breaking up into independent and sovereign units has been taken. *It is appreciated that in the scheme of things the nature of association between Biafra and the States will vary according to the political relationship.* It is expected therefore that the recommendations elaborated below might have to be modified accordingly. They, however, could form the basis of discussion at the Conference table."

The portion in italics (which are mine) implied the possibility of closer ties with the States which might emerge from the breakup in the South, than with those in the North.

The areas of cooperation included *Economic, Cultural, Diplomatic and Consular,* and *Citizenship Arrangements.* For the purpose of the type of cooperation envisaged, "an authority composed of the heads of governments of the member states is envisaged. It may be vested with legislative functions and the authority to determine policy, subject to individual state ratification". There might be "an executive board composed of two or more representatives from each member state. Each member of the board, in rotation, may be charged with responsibility for one or a group of related services. The executive board shall be responsible to the authority for the efficient performance of their duties. The executive board, acting collectively, shall be responsible for the recruitment of staff for the running of the various services."

This memorandum was intended to be a kind of olive branch offered to the Federal Government through indirect means. It was produced in August 1967. Biafran troops were then still in the Mid-West, but without much hope of holding the area, let alone going forward. But their presence was seen as providing Biafra with effective bargaining power. Soon, however, the Mid-West was retaken by the Federal troops. Enugu fell, followed within two weeks by Calabar. Port Harcourt later fell, not to mention all the important towns in the Efik/Ibibio/Annang areas as well as those of former Ogoja province.[1] The Kampala talks failed. But since

1. Enugu fell on October 4th, 1967, Calabar on October 18th, 1967, the whole of Ibibio area and the greater part of Annang area at the beginning of April 1968, Port Harcourt on May 19th, 1968. The whole of Ogoja Province, as well as Enugu, and the vital port of Bonny in the Rivers State, were all taken during July 1967.

"never in history have a people lost a war of independence", Governor Ojukwu still believed that Biafra would survive as a nation, independent and sovereign. Moves were being made, it was known, throughout the world, for negotiations to end the war. Suffering and deaths were mounting among the civilian population. Huge sums were being spent for Biafran envoys to conduct diplomatic offensives abroad.

In June 1968, Governor Ojukwu invited the international press to Aba, when there were definite signs that a conference to end the war might be held. Addressing the press, the Governor had this to say:

"The main obstacles to a peaceful settlement have come from the Nigerian attitude of belligerence, lack of faith in agreements mutually reached, and the backing of the British Government, which has claimed to be committed to the principle of founding a federal Nigeria. Wrong premises have been adduced to support the argument that the territorial integrity of Nigeria must be maintained, no matter the cost in human lives. The recent utterances by British government spokesmen, notably Lord Shepherd and Mr. Thompson, clearly indicate that the British government has still not altered its colonialist attitude, which places no premium on African lives if it means compromising its own selfish economic interests. They have stated that they will continue to support Nigeria so long as there is no unnecessary destruction of lives, and that they will stop supplying arms to Lagos only when there is a catastrophe.

Nigeria sees the pogrom, the expulsion of Biafrans from Nigeria, the economic blockade, sanctions and other hostile acts against Biafrans, as steps in the final military solution of the Ibo problem, that is, the extermination of 14,000,000 Biafrans. Thus the obstacles in the way of peace may be summarised as follows:

1. The British government's desire to maintain her economic dominance over the single Nigeria she had created and her open support and encouragement of Gowon by:

(*a*) continued supply of arms to Nigeria;
(*b*) economic, diplomatic, and propaganda offensives on behalf of Nigeria;
(*c*) dishonest representation of the facts to the British Parliament and public.

2. Nigeria's intransigence, which has resulted in:

(*a*) her refusal to agree to a cease-fire;
(*b*) her insistence that Biafra must renounce her sovereignty and accept a twelve-state structure created without consultation of the people or their representatives;
(*c*) her provocative request in the twelve-point plan at Kampala for virtual surrender:

(*d*) her continued rejection of all appeals and blackmailing of reasonable African heads of state, and international organisations.

3. Russia's ambition to establish a communist sphere of influence in West Africa. Consequently, Russia, Britain and the United States of America—countries with diametrically opposed ideologies—are competing to maintain an influence in Nigeria by supplying arms for the genocide of Biafrans.

4. The unrealistic attitude of the Organisation of African Unity. The O.A.U. had the unique opportunity of proving to the world and to the member states that African independent countries were capable not only of ruling themselves but also of solving African problems. The O.A.U. Mediation Committee failed because of its unrealistic approach of attempting to solve an African problem in an un-African manner. Until a couple of days ago they had not indicated their willingness to listen to both sides in the dispute.

5. The United Nations, which has turned a blind eye to evident genocide. The United Nations Organisation, whose charter on human rights empowers it to intercede in cases of genocide, refused to accept Biafra's application for intercession to halt Nigeria's genocidal war against Biafra."

The above passages indicate an open admission that the whole world was against Biafra. And yet, since "never in history have a people lost a war of independence", Biafra would go on fighting in spite of all these terrible and terrifying odds. We still hoped that peace would come on our own terms, and so the Governor proceeded to set out those conditions:

"In spite of all these obstacles to peace, Biafra has offered peace terms which, if accepted, would achieve a lasting peace in this part of Africa. These proposals are:

(i) immediate cessation of fighting on land, sea and air. We are prepared to discuss with Nigeria the terms rather than conditions for a cease-fire;

(ii) immediate removal of the economic blockade mounted by Nigeria against Biafra;

(iii) the withdrawal of troops to behind the pre-war boundaries to enable refugees to return to their homes.

With regard to (i), cessation of fighting, Biafra will agree to:

(*a*) the policing of the cease-fire line by an international force, the composition of which must be agreed to by both sides;

(*b*) a supervisory body, the composition and power of which are to be agreed, which will be stationed in the areas from which troops are withdrawn to ensure that the local population are not in any way victimised.

With regard to (ii), the removal of the blockade, we shall be

> ready, if it is agreed, to accept the supervision at points of entry into Nigeria and Biafra to ensure that there is no arms build-up by either side while talks on the arrangements for a permanent settlement continue. The aim should be to restore civilian life and administration back to normal in the war-ravaged areas as soon as possible. Biafra is still willing to discuss:
>
> (i) Maximum economic cooperation and common services with Nigeria;
>
> (ii) problems relating to the sharing of assets and liabilities (including the external public debt) of the former Federation of Nigeria;
>
> (iii) problems relating to the payment of compensation for the lives and property of Biafrans which were lost during the pogrom and as a result of the war;
>
> (iv) the holding of a plebiscite in the disputed areas inside and outside Biafra to determine the true wishes of the people"

They all sounded like the terms of a victor to the vanquished!

The above is quoted in full to illustrate the type of arrogant and rigid attitude adopted by the Governor towards peace negotiations. The Kampala talks had been held after preliminary talks in London. Sir Louis Mbanefo with, of course, Mr. C. C. Mojekwu, was the leading Biafran spokesman at these preliminary talks. I remember the frantic messages sent to Sir Louis in London, making sure that he took no initiative without instructions from home. Some of these messages were quite harsh to a man in his position. The preliminary talks were held under the auspices of the Secretary-General of the Commonwealth Secretariat, Mr. Arnold Smith. When eventually the talks started, the Biafran delegation was under strict instructions to be rigid, not to allow the talks to last too long, but to break up the discussions at the earliest opportunity.

By this time Biafra had received recognition from Tanzania, Gabon, the Ivory Coast and Zambia thanks to the efforts of Dr. Nnamdi Azikiwe and others known and respected by the leaders of those countries. The moves by the Commonwealth Secretariat were seen as nothing but a clever manoeuvre by Britain and the Federal Government of Nigeria to stop further recognition which indeed seemed likely. As long as the impression was given that talks were going on, no country would take action for fear of being accused of trying to undermine the success of the peace talks. Equally, once they knew that negotiations for talks were in progress or even possible, no action would be taken. Our strategy, then, was to do more to obtain additional diplomatic recognition than for successful peace negotiations. The more diplomatic recognition Biafra had, the surer the possibility of the world's accepting the fact of her international existence.

But any person with an informed and objective appraisal of the situation ought to have realised that Biafra ceased to exist the moment practically all the non-Ibo areas—namely, Calabar, virtually the whole of the Ibibio/Annang area, Port Harcourt and the other Rivers areas, following as they did the whole of Ogoja—were retaken by the Federal troops. It was therefore unrealistic and fatuous of Governor Ojukwu to talk of Federal troops withdrawing to the pre-war boundaries. The Israeli-Arab situation should have pointed a warning. In spite of all the world pressure, the United Nations resolutions and Security Council orders, Israel would not withdraw from the Arab territories occupied during the Six Day War of 1967. That was a clear case of one country occupying the territories of another country by force. Compared with it, Biafra had no moral or legal right to expect the Federal Government to withdraw from areas which were not foreign but its own territory *de jure* and *de facto*; areas they regarded as liberated from the rebels. Even in the absolutely unlikely situation of the Federal Government's being willing to consider such a preposterous demand, these areas were now in the newly created states, proud and determined to keep their identities, and the Federal troops could not withdraw except with their consent. Many of us were under no illusion about these, but dared not express it except in private and to the most intimate circles. Our main concern and prayers were for negotiations which would end the war and save lives.

With the utter failure of all subsequent attempts by the Commonwealth Secretariat to revive peace talks, the Organisation of African Unity decided to step in. This was hailed in Biafra as a major break-through. Preliminary talks were held in Niamey from July 20th to July 26th, 1968. Apart from the delegations attending from both sides, the O.A.U. had also invited the leaders of both sides—Major-General Gowon and Lt. Col. (as he then was) Ojukwu—to attend. The Governor had expected to confront General Gowon directly, but this did not turn out to be so. Both leaders arrived at different times and addressed the O.A.U. Committee separately, leaving the delegates to carry on.

The agenda for the Niamey talks adopted at the first meeting of the delegates included five items: (*a*) concrete proposals for the transportation of relief supplies to the victims of the war; (*b*) conditions for cessation of hostilities; (*c*) conditions for a permanent settlement; (*d*) procedure for the Addis Ababa meeting and (*e*) date of the Addis Ababa meeting.

Although the meeting of the delegates got off to a promising start, and remained very cordial to the end, it achieved practically nothing concrete except agreement on the agenda for the Addis Ababa meeting. Great importance had been attached to the matter of relief for the civilian victims of the war, and tied to this was the question of a temporary suspension of hostilities. In both these items the attitude of either side was influenced more by military considerations than by anything else. This whole question of relief, like many others about the tragedy, can and will form topics for different volumes, and will not be given detailed attention in this book. Suffice it to say that, compared with those who died as a result of the actual fighting, including air-raids, it would not be an exaggeration to say that fifty times as many died through starvation, disease and other viccisitudes arising from loss of homes and exposure to the physical forces of nature.

The Addis Ababa talks opened on August 5th, 1968. I went with Governor Ojukwu in an entourage which included Dr. Nnamdi Azikiwe, former President of Nigeria. It is not widely known that Governor Ojukwu was quite confident that the meeting would end the war. Before leaving, he had confided in us that once he met General Gowon in Addis Ababa, he would make concessions, including the acceptance of the idea of Nigerian unity. He would press for a confederation on the lines of the Aburi agreement.

Unfortunately, General Gowon did not attend, and the lengthy speech delivered by Governor Ojukwu did not betray signs of compromise. Besides, the speech was a breach of what the delegates of the two sides had agreed at Niamey, namely, that the opening speeches should be in camera. The Governor's speech, coupled with the public statements by the leader of the Federal delegation, Chief Anthony Enahoro, doomed the meeting to failure in advance.

While in Addis Ababa Governor Ojukwu, accompanied by a select few, held meetings with the Emperor twice. Not being among those who went, I cannot say what was discussed. He also met representatives of some countries. After very many wasted days, the conference broke up. Indeed the real collapse of the conference took place a few days after the opening, when the leader of the Federal delegation went home "for consultations" but never returned. The rest of the Federal delegation remained in Addis Ababa with the Biafran delegation under the leadership of Professor Eni Njoku. The only reason for staying on was the reluctance of each side to be blamed for breaking up the talks. Nothing worthwhile happened or was done. Eventually, with the O.A.U. meeting at Algiers only a few days off, and the Emperor, as the Chairman of the O.A.U. Consultative Committee on Nigeria preparing to leave, the meeting was formally closed.

The Governor and those of us in his personal entourage had returned home within ten days of our departure, stopping at Libreville for the Governor to report to President Bongo. Dr. Nnamdi Azikiwe, had gone to Europe en route for North Africa and America on a "special mission", but with the fall of Aba and Owerri he had considered further efforts futile, and so stayed on in Europe and then went to London, after sending a frantic telegram to the Governor urging in effect that the war be ended. In the hope that the O.A.U. meeting being held in Algiers would grant a hearing to the Biafran delegation returning from Addis Ababa, Professor Eni Njoku and his team proceeded to Europe, but were denied visas for Algeria.

The O.A.U. meeting heard the Emperor's report on the efforts to end the war and later passed a resolution similar to the one passed in Kinshasa the previous year, except for slight changes in wording and phraseology, calling for a ceasefire and discussions within the context of one Nigeria. Before the start of the O.A.U. meeting—indeed on September 4th, 1968, which marked the start of the meeting—Aba fell to the Federal troops, followed two days later by Owerri.

From November 1968 behind-the-scenes moves took place. Appeals went out from leading world personalities, for an end to hostilities—or at least for a truce during the Christmas and New Year period. At first, it appeared that both sides had accepted the call for a truce, but it never actually took place. These efforts continued and were intensified during 1969, following the meeting of Commonwealth Prime Ministers in London. Public opinion mounted in Britain against the continuing sale of arms to the Federal side; but the British Government remained adamant. Many delegations representing foreign governments, organisations and the church, as well as individuals, including British parliamentarians and American congressmen, visited Biafra and sometimes Nigeria as well, seeking ways towards peace.

During 1969 the O.A.U. Consultative Committee made another serious effort, by inviting the two sides to a meeting in Monrovia. Nothing came of it. Then came the efforts of the Prime Minister of Sierra Leone, who had shown open sympathy for the Biafran cause. With the quiet prodding of some big powers, it was agreed that both sides should meet in Addis Ababa under the chairmanship of His Imperial Majesty, the Emperor of Ethiopia. Since Biafra had insisted that it would not participate in any discussions under the auspices of the O.A.U. operating under the "unacceptable" resolutions, it was agreed that these latest negotiations should take place under the auspices of the Emperor himself. Optimistic that Sierra Leone and other countries might accord Biafra diplomatic recognition—and there were hopeful signs of this—Biafra was more interested in such recognitions than in the negotiations. Our delegates should attend, but they should not waste valuable time in Addis Ababa. As in the case of the Kampala talks, the moves by the Emperor were seen as an attempt to stop or delay further recognition being accorded to Biafra. The direct assurances from the President of the Ivory Coast that those latest moves were genuine, and that the Emperor's efforts had the support of some big powers, did not affect the Biafran attitude.

Just before the departure of the Biafran delegation, led this time by Dr. Pius Okigbo with two other officials, Governor Ojukwu issued a statement that the meeting was being held, not under the auspices of the O.A.U., but under those of the Emperor, acting independently of the O.A.U. That statement took the form of making Biafra appear as having won a major victory. The leader of the delegation was also instructed to make a similar statement on arrival at Addis Ababa. These statements had the effect of stopping the Federal delegation from even leaving for the meeting, and made the embarrassed Emperor issue his own statement affirming that he was acting under the auspices of the O.A.U. After waiting a day or two, the Biafran delegation left for home, in spite of the efforts of Biafran friends, including the President of the Ivory Coast, to keep them at Addis Ababa, to see if the Federal Government could be persuaded to send its delegation. It was Governor Ojukwu who ordered them back.

Early in January 1970, the Biafran representative in London transmitted a message from the British government suggesting that the Governor or his trusted representatives should meet the British government representatives due to attend the tenth anniversary celebrations of Cameroon's independence in Yaoundé to discuss how to bring the civil war to an end. I was thrilled by the message and rushed from Owerri to Madonna to suggest to the Governor that the invitation be accepted, and was surprised to find the Governor so cold about it. At that time the Federal forces had already linked up between Ikot Ekpene and Aba, and were threatening Mbawsi. A message had already in fact been transmitted to the Biafran representative in London before I arrived, spurning the invitation. The only explanation for the outright rejection was that if we were wanted in Yaoundé the invitation should come from the Cameroon government. In other words, the Governor wanted to be invited to Yaoundé as a head of state. As Cameroon had never recognised Biafra's existence (indeed President Ahidjo, a member of the O.A.U. Consultative Committee on Nigeria, was among the most hostile to Biafra's existence), I tried to reason with the Governor that, even if we did not want to treat with the British, the invitation would be a good excuse for him or his representatives to go to Cameroon, where most of the African heads of state and representatives of governments outside Africa were assembling for the celebrations. The Governor's only reply was to ask me to leave him to deal with the matter in his own way.

Before the start of Cameroon's tenth anniversary of independence celebrations, Biafra had collapsed.

11 Biafra and the British Government

"In modern times of international power politics, no great power can succumb to threats of intimidation." That was my warning in October 1966 to members of a committee set up to advise on the propaganda tactics of Eastern Nigeria in the light of the prevailing circumstances. The committee was in fact set up by the Military Governor on my own suggestion. My reason for approaching the Governor with the suggestion was my serious concern about the abusive and offensive tactics adopted by the government information media, particularly against foreign powers. I had been disturbed by the crude language used both in the Government newspaper and on the radio against individuals in Nigeria and against foreign powers.

When the meeting opened (we met at the old Government House) I put forward my points as forcefully and reasonably as possible. At the end of my remarks, others spoke as though I did not know what I was talking about. Some of the journalists present, who took my remarks as a criticism of their work, left me in no doubt that I was dabbling in matters outside my field. I replied that I would not personally have minded if the kind of inaccurate facts daily put out had been supplied by private information media. It was not to the government's credit that its own information media should spread wrong information aimed at misleading the public and deliberately annoying those affected. I asked if I could be told, for my own personal information, the basis of the information that the killings in May of that year had in fact been inspired by the British; and if it was true, as was then strongly believed, that some named British lectureres at the Ahmadu Bello University in Zaria were known to have organised or were actually seen inciting students there to go on a rampage against the Easterners in the North, would it not have been better to isolate those individuals for attack rather than to include the entire British people and their Government?

After one of the journalists was "kind" enough to recount to me what he knew about the British activities against Eastern Nigeria, including the "personal involvement" of some British diplomats, he told me that journalism was a specialised profession, the practice of which should be left to those specially trained and experienced in it. Aware of the implied disrespect to my person and office in the remarks, I reminded the meeting that I was the Chief Secretary to the Government, and as such, must be interested in what government functionaries and departments were doing. I had also been told that the policy was to attack the British relentlessly, and I wanted to know who had laid down the policy. At this point they all burst into pitying laughter—pitying me in my ignorance. It was at this point that I made the statement which opened this chapter.

The committee was not made up of journalists alone. It also contained some top government officials, including the Economic Adviser. When the idea of setting up the committee was first mooted I had thought that it should meet regularly—indeed, if possible, daily—to discuss happenings and settle propaganda tactics. I had also hoped that before the meetings, I should be able to obtain from the Military Governor his views, which I should then make available to the meeting. It was in anticipation of regular meetings of the committee that we decided to meet at the old government house, which had now been converted into a V.I.P. rest house, and had very good facilities with its many rooms. But my experience at this first meeting was not very encouraging. I had disagreed, standing alone against the rest of the committee. I left before the close of the meeting to go and report to the Governor what had happened.

I was surprised to see that he had been expecting me. So someone had already reported to him on the telephone! My suspicions notwithstanding, I recounted to the Governor as faithfully as I could what had happened at the meeting, and the stand I had taken. I told him that, in my view, any information given out by the government, whether directly in the form of a plain government statement or through government information media, should contain accurate facts, properly checked. I then took up the vicious attacks against the British which had been mounting at that time. I repeated what I had said at the meeting of the committee about the error of openly attacking or offending a big power.

The Governor, who had been half listening to me and half signing papers, replied that he agreed with the committee's attitude towards the British. He did not agree with me that even in attacks, decent and cultured language should be used. The English language which we were using, the Government argued, was not our language, and no matter how we tried we could never reach the finesse of those speaking their native language. On the question of decent and cultured language which I had mentioned, the Governor reminded me that, in terms of those things, the British had reached a stage of development and sophistication which we could not yet expect to reach. It was therefore futile to attempt to match the British in such matters; if we tried, we were bound to be beaten. "The only thing which can frighten the British is crudity. Here we can beat them, and it should be our tactics", the Governor emphasised to me. I then recalled the sarcastic laughter which had greeted my question about who had laid down the policy of attacking the British "relentlessly". I decided not to make a greater fool of myself and so dropped the discussion by raising a different topic altogether. I never returned to the committee and do not know how many more meetings, if any, they held. I later learnt that a special committee known as the "dirty language committee" had been set up in the Ministry of Information. The purpose of that committee was to operate a programme of abuse and vilification against individuals outside Eastern Nigeria. It was this committee which ran the programme called "Outlook" on the Biafran radio network. I was told that this was a concession to my strong views and feelings in the matter. Abuse, attacks and crude language would continue on our radio, but they would now be regarded as the work, not of the government or of the authorities in control of the information media, but of a committee which should accept responsibility for them.

The attitude of the people of Eastern Nigeria was that the British were always partial to the North and against the South. Much literature and evidence were later to be produced by the propaganda directorate and the Ministry of Information, as well as by historians and political scientists, to "prove" how the British had always opposed the South in general and the East in particular. From the time of Lord Lugard, every action, every move, every political and administrative arrangement made by the British had been in favour of the North against the South. It was at least with the approval if not the encouragement of the British that people from other parts of Nigeria were not allowed to mix with those of the North—even in Northern Nigeria where they were made to live in strangers' quarters known as sabon gari. It was a deliberate policy of the British administrators that the "south should not be allowed to pollute the purity of the north"—hence the system of making children from the South attend separate schools from those attended by Northern children. The catalogue of British acts of partiality was long, culminating in the independence constitution which ensured for the North "the perpetual domination of the rest of the country". It was the British who stopped the North from seceding after the coup July 29th, 1966, promising the North through General Gowon all necessary support, "moral, diplomatic and military". It was the British who advised the North to change their original position at the Ad Hoc Constitutional Conference, which was for a loose federation with a secession clause, and declare themselves in favour of a strong Central Government for Nigeria. The British were also blamed, as already mentioned, for inciting the North to the killings in May 1966. They were now also accused of at least knowing about the plans for the incidents of July 29th and after, and of the killings which took place from July 29th until October 1966. Finally came the failure of the Federal Government to implement the Aburi agreements, which was also blamed on the British through their High Commission in Lagos.

A number of the points raised about the British role in Nigeria before independence are historical facts. Other points, if true, could not be conclusively proved, while others were mere conjectures. For instance, the mere fact that the British High Commissioner visited the North just before the disturbances there was not proof that he had gone to incite the Northerners against the Easterners. While there was strong evidence pointing to the fact that the British High Commissioner (and the American Ambassador) might have persuaded General Gowon and others not to secede after the overthrow of the first military government, there was scarcely any conclusive evidence that the British High Commissioner had, at that time, namely about August 1st, 1966, promised them military support when nobody then considered the possibility of a civil war, or even envisaged the East's attempting to break away from the rest of the Federation.

My view was that, even in propaganda, facts, not fiction or fantasy, should be used, particularly where government propaganda was concerned. I accepted that I was not a journalist, nor could I ever be a good propagandist. All the same, propaganda, as the experience of Germany during the last world war has shown, can very seriously misfire or boomerang. It can prove quite effective and useful for the purposes of internal morale-boosting, but the world has become so small that no country or people can afford to be absolutely selfish in their actions and attitudes, particularly where others are or might be affected.

Mention was made in an earlier chapter of the visit to Enugu of Sir Francis Cumming-Bruce when, in the company of the American Ambassador, he came to persuade the Governor to work for a peaceful settlement of the country's crisis within the context of one Nigeria. Sir Francis Cumming-Bruce left Nigeria a few months after the visit—which in fact also had the flavour of a farewell. He was succeeded by Sir David Hunt. The appointment of Sir David led to a short moratorium on the anti-British propaganda. In the course of his familiarisation tour of the country, Sir David visited Enugu in March 1967, and had an audience with the Governor on March 14th. It was the general belief in Enugu and in the rest of the Region that Sir David would be more sympathetic towards the East than the previous British High Commissioner. He had already served in Nigeria, and had just left Cyprus, where conditions not unlike those then obtaining in Nigeria had existed. On the morning of his visit the Governor asked that a welcome memorandum be prepared, setting out the case of Eastern Nigeria and appealing for his understanding. Unfortunately, the memorandum was not ready until about thirty minutes before the arrival of Sir David at the State House, which did not give the Governor time to study and approve it.

This first meeting between the new British High Commissioner to Nigeria and the Military Governor of Eastern Nigeria did not turn out to be either very cordial or very successful. It was therefore just as well, in the view of the Governor, that the welcome memorandum had not been ready for delivery to a person who, as it turned out, did not deserve the honour. I did not know in detail what they had discussed, but I recall that the Governor was not happy about Sir David after the meeting. Sir David too did not seem to be very impressed with the Governor, and had occasion to tell some people in Eastern Nigeria so. With the failure of this first meeting the moratorium on anti-British propaganda was removed. Thenceforth Sir David was subjected to the most vicious radio attacks, some of which were quite shocking and embarrasingly crude and personal. Some of us wondered what we expected to gain by so openly antagonising the highest and most trusted British representative in the country. After all, the impersonality of their profession notwithstanding, diplomats are susceptible to natural human reactions. This might probably explain some of the harsh reports which, judging from British government statements in the House of Commons, Sir David must have been sending home.

Because of the strong anti-British propaganda, the British subjects in the East were targets for suspicion everywhere in the Region. Their houses were often searched for "private transmission sets" which they might be using to "send out information to Nigeria". The vehicles of British subjects were searched by civil defenders on the highways. Even the offices of the British Deputy High Commissioner were not immune to such embarrassments, and the reason for this, after secession, was that since the British government had not granted Biafra diplomatic recognition, the British diplomatic representatives could not expect diplomatic immunity from Biafra.

The recapture of the Mid-West by the Federal troops and the efforts of Col. Banjo and others to overthrow Governor Ojukwu were blamed on the British Deputy High Commissioner in Benin. The position was complicated by the fact that on the day that Banjo and the rest of his group were arrested, at least two of them, Ifeajuna and Agbam, were known to have visited the British Deputy High Commissioner. It is reported that a call by another of the group was also made to the American Consul. Claims were later made that Col. Ifeajuna was in fact arrested as he was leaving the British High Commission. From my own subsequent enquiries, it does not appear that the callers at these two offices told their hosts much about what they had in mind or intended to do. They only made vague soundings about the British and American attitudes regarding the war. This visit of Ifeajuna and Agbam to the offices of the British High Commission was used however as a reason for entering those offices and removing all the radio communications equipment.

About the middle of June 1967, the American Embassy sent instructions to the American Consul in Enugu to remove all American nationals from Nsukka to Enugu for safety, because of the impending military operations by the Federal Government. The American Consul must have mentioned it to his British counterpart, who sought guidance from Lagos and London. But the latter did not advise the evacuation of British subjects. Wives and children had already been sent out of the Region, and British subjects were told to carry on with their work and not to panic.

A classic example of tactless and self-defeating high-handedness towards the British was the Governor's dealings with Shell-B.P. whose Nigerian head at the time was a Mr. Gray. The Governor had been demanding that the company should no longer pay oil royalties to the Federal Government. Before secession, the Governor's approach was no doubt cautious, lest the cat should be let out of the bag about the planned secession. But after secession, he decided to adopt a tough attitude. He demanded that all royalties should be paid to the new republic of Biafra, and since it had been the practice all along to pay royalties in advance, Shell-B.P. should do the same. One evening I was shocked when the Governor hinted that he was going to detain Mr. Gray in Enugu until he produced the money. By this time the war had started. In my view, the very idea of detaining or even harassing Mr. Gray, was madness. I told the Governor that it would be a most unfortunate action, although I did not believe that he was serious. By that time Mr. Gray had agreed to pay an amount based on what was usually the share of Eastern Nigeria. But the Governor would not agree to this, particularly as the payment was to be made in arrears, not in advance.

As I was driving to my house that evening, it occurred to me that the Governor might be serious about detaining Mr. Gray. I therefore stopped at the house of the Chief Justice, Sir Louis Mbanefo and told him what the Governor had said. Sir Louis shared my disbelief about the seriousness of the Governor's intention. It was inconceivable that a man in the Governor's position could even contemplate such a thing. An antagonistic oil company could make things difficult for any government, to say the least. Sir Louis and I went back to the Governor to express our views and to advise him not to deal harshly with Mr. Gray.

Mr. Gray came the following day, and the Governor invited me and others to be present. I was there in order to write any necessary letters. He talked with Mr Gray for a long time, and not having his own way, had Mr. Gray placed under house arrest at the Hotel Presidential. Word was sent to London and a top man of Shell-B.P. (I have forgotten his name) flew out to see the Governor. Although he arrived early enough in the day, and had planned to return to Lagos with Mr. Gray that very day after seeing the Governor, Ojukwu refused to see him until well past midnight. It is difficult to describe the personal embarrassment of myself and people like Sir Louis Mbanefo, who was very well-known to Mr. Gray. Both of us, because of our official positions, were supposed to be among those who could influence the Governor. It was while he was at the Hotel Presidential that Mr. Gray instructed all his staff in Port Harcourt to leave, and the departure of the Shell-B.P. personnel, coupled with the shabby treatment meted out to Mr. Gray, appeared to be the last straw as far as the British were concerned. To me, such crudeness on the Governor's part was simply madness.

Here I must say a word (even if it means embarrassing them) about the personal comportment of both Mr. James Parker, the British Deputy High Commissioner, and Mr. Robert Barnard, the American Consul. The Americans, of course, were not subjected to the sort of abuse and provocation which were the lot of the British. Mr. Parker behaved like an ideal diplomat, out to serve the best interests of his country, by exhibiting extraordinary calmness in the face of the strongest provocation and insults. I was the most accessible person to them, and I was always impressed by their transparent sincerity and concern about all the unfortunate developments. Their desire was to help, through their respective countries, to avoid a tragedy. The proverbial diplomat's impartiality was fully exemplified in these two. It is a pity that they, like so many of us, did not succeed in their efforts. After the fall of Enugu, they tried to set up offices in Aba where the new administrative headquarters were to be sited, but were not allowed. In Port Harcourt they did not find things easy either, and they had to leave via Calabar, just before the fall of that town.

I have not reported all this to show that the British government was without blemish; indeed, far from it. On the contrary, it was the general belief amongst right-thinking persons, both in Biafra and outside, that the British government could have done much more to stop the war. It is true that, initially, the British government did not want to take sides in the conflict, but rather to play the part of mediator. It is said in some circles that it was the Biafran incursion into the Mid-West and the fear that Russia might supply the Federal side with weapons which made the British side with the Federal government.

I have mentioned in the previous chapter the efforts made by the British government to bring about talks leading to a settlement. One effort not mentioned there was the offer of a British warship on which the Biafran leader and General Gowon could meet. But Biafra would not even consider the proposal for fear that it might be a trap. Some people even thought that it might be a plan to kidnap the Biafran leader. The feelings of hatred against the British government were intense among the masses of the people in the secessionist enclave, to the extent that the most deadly disease (kwashiorkar) which took the heaviest toll of lives was nicknamed "Harold Wilson syndrome".

The name "Harold Wilson" became a curse among the people, both living and dying. I saw a dying child in hospital at Umuahia muttering words which I did not catch, and when I asked the nurse what the child was saying she told me that she was invoking God's vengeance on "Harold Wilson". Children were intimidated by the name. The Governor, who made sure that all his speeches contained at least a paragraph of abuse about Mr. Wilson, once called him "Harold Weaseling", while the Biafran radio commentators and others referred to him as "Herod Wilson".

Yet, incredibly, the rumours of a possible visit by the British Prime Minister to Umuahia in March 1969 were greeted with the keenest enthusiasm and expectation. Great receptions were prepared for him, and he would have received the highest possible courtesy and respect from all. This showed that, in spite of the bitterness towards the British government, many still felt that it alone was in a position to end the war. It is difficult to say what effect such a visit could have had on the Governor, who was always unpredicatable.

One of the things which badly disappointed even the greatest admirers of the British (including those who regretted the war) was the inaccurate statements which the British government spokesmen frequently put out in the House of Commons. Many of us had come to regard the British House of Commons as a place where nothing but truths were asserted. Those inaccurate statements undermined people's faith in the sincerity of the British desire to end the war.

I know that people will wish to know how I thought the British government could end the war, short of committing a complete volte face, which of course nobody could expect a big power to do. I honestly cannot give categorical answers or proposals. All I can say is that it would have been easier for the British government to stop the war during the first few months, before its open involvement by supporting one side. Nigeria was Britain's own creation, and Nigerians looked upon Britain as the Mother Country, and as such Britain should have played the role of an imperial parent. But this has not answered the question—how then could the British have done this, short of recognising the independence of Biafra, which it was their definite policy not to do? I cannot pretend to know the answer. Again, all I can say is that the British government is experienced in these matters and could have found a way to end the war without compromising their policy or offending the Federal government, if they had really wanted to.

12 The Minorities

The killings in the North in 1966, particularly those which occurred from the end of September, were indiscriminately directed against people from Eastern Nigeria, known in the North by the generic name of "Yameri". Thus, although the Northern wrath was supposed to have been directed against the Ibos of Eastern Nigeria, there was nothing to distinguish one Easterner from the other, whether of Ibo, Efik, Ibibio or Ijaw origin. They wore the same type of dress and, generally speaking, behaved in the same manner. Thus, every area in the East was affected, and those who fled the North were not only the Ibos but also others of Eastern Nigeria origin. The subsequent attempts in the North to distinguish between the Ibos and other peoples of Eastern Nigeria came too late to make any impression on the non-Ibo members of Eastern Nigeria, who now shared the same fears and dread of the North as the Ibos.

But the behaviour of the Ibos in the East soon disillusioned these people. The first evidence came when the East started to recruit young men into the army. Thousands from all over the Region turned up daily for the recruitment. While the Ibo candidates were regularly selected, scarcely any from non-Ibo areas were recruited. Many called on me to complain, but there was nothing I could do. Occasionally, in order to show the young men concerned that I cared, I gave them notes for the recruiting officers, but without any effect. Even those who were already in the army, and had fled to the East along with their Ibo colleagues, were not really made to feel that they belonged. Lt. Col. Philip Effiong who was staying with me at the time, following his return from the North, was concerned about the apparent discrimination. He too could do nothing. In the end the non-Ibos who had come to Enugu for recruitment returned home to tell others about their experiences. At that time nobody thought that there would be war. The youths who came for recruitment were those in need of employment, although there were others who were genuinely attracted to the army.

As the crisis developed, the ordinary Ibo men and women began to behave as though the East belonged to them alone, as though the others should be content with second place. There were occasional threats of massive attacks against the non-Ibos by the Ibos. These threats prompted leading personalities from the "Old Calabar Province, resident in Enugu" to address a direct petition, dated September 26th, 1966, to the Military Governor. It was short but representative, and read as follows:

> "We, the undersigned, representing the people of the Old Calabar Province (comprising the Ibibios, Efiks, Annangs, Ekois, etc.) resident in Enugu are constrained to write to you on a matter of utmost importance which we consider necessary to bring to your notice and attention.
>
> We are sorry that at a time like this when Your Excellency is being saddled with the heavy burden of state responsibilities these ugly rumours should necessitate this letter.
>
> We have heard strong rumours that there is a plan by the Ibos to attack our people resident in Enugu and other towns of the region any time from now.
>
> This rumour has so gained ground that we feel our lives and those of our families are in danger. We could have dismissed the rumours as trivial but for the unfortunate incidents in Enugu last Saturday and Sunday when one of those attacked and looted was a lady from the Old Calabar Province resident in the Artisan Quarters—Mrs. Aniode.
>
> Furthermore, it is also being alleged that the planned attack is based on the false hue and cry sometime in early September, 1966 at Uyo when the police invited certain personalities for questioning on allegation that there was a plan to attack the Ibos in the Old Calabar Provincial areas.
>
> We assure Your Excellency that there is a lot of panic amongst our people here in Enugu with the result that some people have started sending their families home.
>
> We should therefore be grateful if Your Excellency would grant representatives of our people an audience on this issue."

Apart from the above petition, representations had reached the Governor from many other sources. A statement had to be issued from the State House in October 1966 sternly warning the public against any acts or words that might cause disaffection among the people of Eastern Nigeria. Part of the statement read:

> "I particularly deplore any actions or words capable of inciting the people in this Region against one another, of undermining confidence and instilling fear among the different sections of this Region. No acts of intimidation or hooliganism will be tolerated. Here, I warn everyone that the police have been given firm instructions to be on the look-out and deal very sternly with any person or persons attempting

actions, or indulging in rumours, capable of causing fear and panic, and thereby threatening law and order."

Later, the Governor held meetings with representatives of the different ethnic areas in the Region. They all spoke quite frankly and strongly against acts of discrimination and molestation by "members of the majority ethnic group". The Governor assured them of his determination to ensure that all the ills of the past were cured, and that justice and fair play would in future be guaranteed for all. Addressing the second meeting of the Consultative Assembly held on October 4th, 1966, the Governor referred to his meetings with the different groups in these words:

> "...I arranged for and met in long sessions, and on separate occasions, representatives from the Old Calabar Province, the Old Rivers Province, and the representatives of the Old Ogoja Province. At these meetings the people spoke out their minds boldly, frankly and fearlessly. They complained that they lacked a sense of belonging, owing to the attitude of the majority group. They pointed to alleged injustices which they had suffered in the distribution of amenities, the siting of industries, and appointments to public offices, boards and corporations. They therefore felt that a separate state for them would cure all those ills.
>
> ...I was finally left with the impression, and this applied practically to all the groups with whom I had discussed, that all they wanted was to feel that they belong, on a perfect footing of equality, to the Eastern Nigerian community, where all vestiges and grounds of domination of one group by another are removed, where social amenities and other government benefits are fairly and justly distributed. I expressed an honest sympathy with, and understanding of, their feelings and assured them that it was precisely those types of things that the military government was here to put right."

The Governor then went on to declare that nobody in the Region was opposed to the creation of states for healthy objectives. But he was "loath to be party to any discussion about the creation of states on the poisoned principles of hate, fear and spite, because that means laying foundations for a worse country than anything we have so far known. It would be an open betrayal of the trust and pledges of the military government." It was his reply to the proposals made at the Ad Hoc Constitutional Conference for the creation of states, and the demand from the minority elements outside the Region who were agitating for this. The real truth was that, having set his mind and soul on secession, he could not agree to the creation of states within what he intended to be the future "Biafra". This in fact was evident, as we have seen, from the resolutions passed at the very first meeting of the consultative assembly held at the end of August 1966.

In place of states he wanted what was called the "Provincial Administration System" under which "executive and legislative powers would be devolved on the provinces". This was the issue over which I first openly clashed with the Governor and his "constitutional advisers". I saw nothing basically wrong in the principles of provincial administration as such. But I saw much that was wrong and sinister in the way the system was being evolved in the East. To start with, those of us who had had some experience in such matters, and who held official positions, were studiously excluded from playing a full part in planning for the system. Rather, a small extra-governmental committee (that is to say, a committee comprising people who held no official government positions) was entrusted with the task. Instead of open debates or even discussions in official circles, these people set about their task in a clandestine way, paying nocturnal visits to different parts and people in the minority areas. It is said, and I cannot confirm or deny it, that some leaders in these areas were induced with money to support the proposals.

In the end the committee came out with a proposal to establish fifteen provincial units on which "executive and legislative powers would be devolved". Such powers would in fact be virtually the same as those of the former regions. How could such units be viable? Where would they have the funds to run the services in order to ensure the aim of "even development" which the system was supposed to bring about? If the aim was ultimately to make them subsist on grants from the central regional government (I did not know then that there would be "Biafra"), then the whole exercise was a farce.

I felt so strongly on the matter that I submitted my views to the Governor in writing, and suggested that, for the system to make sense, the provinces should not be more than six at the outside. I suggested that ethnic considerations should not be the determining factor, but administrative convenience and considerations of viability. I went out of my way to canvass my views among those whom I thought were objective, only to be disillusioned, and this applied not just to the Ibos but to the non-Ibos as well. As a matter of fact, a close friend from my own area with whom I discussed the matter took my views straight back in a mischievous way to those against whom I was "fighting". It soon became clear that the real aim of the authors of the system was not to ensure peace and even development, but to weaken the solidarity of the different minority groups. For, whereas they were prepared to create as many new administrative divisions and as many provincial units as the unwary people of the minority areas wanted, they originally intended to leave things as they were in the Ibo areas. It was in the course of discussing the status of the different provinces, that it dawned on the authors of the new system that their scheming might misfire by placing the majority group at a disadvantage. For instance, if the provinces would send equal representatives to the central legislature, as they had openly said would be the case, then the minority areas would be in the overwhelming majority, just as they would receive more by way of central financial grants. It was then quickly decided to avoid such a situation, and so the number of the proposed new provinces was suddenly increased from fifteen to twenty, by the creation of more provinces in the Ibo areas. Additional administrative divisions were similarly created.

Meanwhile as the crisis deepened, the molestation of members of the minority groups increased. Non-Ibo-speaking people could not move freely, without insults and embarrassments, through the different checkpoints manned by civil defenders. My own family experienced serious difficulties when they were travelling home from Enugu to my village. If such was the experience of the family of the Chief Secretary to the Government at the time, then the position of others can be imagined. But I must say that these acts did not receive the approval of official or responsible circles, and did seriously embarrass responsible Ibo opinion.

As far as the Ibibios were concerned, nothing increased their doubts and suspicions so much as the Governor's address to the people in Uyo, which he visited for the first time early in 1967. As was usual on such occasions, advance copies of the addresses of welcome to be presented to the Governor had been received. As my duty demanded, I studied them and prepared a reply for the Governor. I saw the Governor glancing through my notes as we made the journey by helicopter. But when the time came for the Governor to respond to the addresses of welcome he completely ignored my notes and spoke impromptu. Advising the people on how to behave, he likened the Ibibios to wives while the Ibos were husbands, and this he said, was the principle by which the relationship between the two groups should be governed. I am sure that the effect which the speech actually produced was not what the Governor could have consciously intended. But it left the Ibibio people with the impression that the Ibos regarded them as inferiors, perhaps as chattels, which were what wives in certain areas of the region were supposed to be. My subsequent efforts to temper the effect of that speech never really succeeded.

Then came the war. Geographically, the minority areas lay in the periphery of what used to be Eastern Nigeria (which was declared

Biafra). It therefore followed that the Federal troops retook those areas first in their advance into what was now Biafra. Every Federal victory was ascribed to the work of saboteurs or lack of cooperation by the people of the areas concerned. We have already mentioned that not only were the refugees from such areas molested, but even those of their people already in Biafra and actively helping in the war effort were suspected and sometimes harrassed. The swift movements of the Federal troops from Oron to Ikot Ekpene within two days were blamed on the inhabitants of those areas, who must have either been hiding enemy troops in their houses, or leading them through bush paths. In this case, the suspicions were not without foundation in important respects. But the reactions of the Ibo people living along the borders of these areas were quite brutal. Whole villages were burnt and individuals murdered. The violence done by Ibo neighbours to these places was also motivated by old grudges and disputes over land. It was an opportunity to settle old disputes and resolve age-old enmities, and it was quite shocking to know those who were the actual leaders of the bloody and destructive rampage—professional men, university lecturers, and others. The Governor himself gave at least tacit approval to these acts of brigandage. His instructions were that once the Federal troops were known to be approaching an area, the first task of the Biafran troops and people was to move in there and bring out as many people as possible by force into the Biafran heartland. Those who would come out were friends, while others were to be regarded as enemies and treated as such. It was as a result of these incidents that representatives of the Old Calabar Province met the Governor in Umuahia to protest against the atrocities, only to be told to their face that, "in this present struggle, I can vouch that the Ibos are involved one hundred and fifty per cent, while the involvement of others (i.e. Non-Ibos) is at best fifty per cent. I still need to be told how it was that the enemy could cover a distance of over seventy miles in less than forty-eight hours!"

Port Harcourt was the last place whose fall led to the inhabitants being suspected as saboteurs, and so cruelly treated. I went to Igrita shortly after the fall of Port Harcourt and was terribly shocked by the number of bodies being carted into mass graves—bodies of persons killed not by bullets but by cruel handling, and not by soldiers but by frenzied and ill-motivated civilians. The attitude and excesses of the civilians were prompted by the widely held but erroneous belief among large sections of the people that the Federal troops could not enter a place without the assistance and cooperation of local saboteurs. Mortar bombs fired by the Federal troops some miles away were believed to be fired locally from the houses or the backyards of "saboteurs" or "enemy collaborators". Curiously enough some Biafran officers and men, including those fighting in the front, helped to fan and spread that belief. It was not until the Federal troops started capturing Ibo towns and villages that it was realised that they could in fact advance and capture places without the aid of sabotage.

13 The Relief Agencies

I do not intend, in this brief chapter, to do much more than put a case for the relief agencies, the motives of which had been grossly misunderstood on both sides of the conflict. Theirs was never at any time an enviable position. For, while they were accused by the Federal side of providing food for the enemy, they were suspected in Biafra as being spies for the Federal side. The awkwardness of the situation bears testimony to the impartiality of those agencies, who were motivated by no other consideration than the urge to bring relief.

Of all the relief agencies the most maligned had been the International Red Cross, whose dilemma was increased by the fact of their being sustained by contributions from some governments and at the same time being expected to act independently of those governments. The World Council of Churches had found itself hamstrung by the fact that it was the Nigerian, and not the Biafran, churches which were its legal members, despite the fact that one of its former vice-presidents was on the Biafran side. Its legalistic attitude had led to internal rebellion, with many of its member churches defying its authority to join other religious organisations, both Christian and Jewish, and forming the Joint Church Aid organisation for bringing relief to the innocent victims of the civil war on the secessionist side, without prejudice to the World Council of Churches, which continued to channel relief through the Federal side.

"All is fair in war, and starvation is one of the weapons of war", was a statement credited to Chief Awolowo, whose words were at once accepted by the world as the policy of the Federal Government. (His Excellency the Head of State and Commander-in-Chief later said it was not his own policy.) But similar statements were credited to other spokesmen of the Federal Government. This may sound incredible, but it is true that even Ojukwu was willing to accept that General Gowon could not himself be a party to a policy of using starvation as a weapon of war.

The civil war has now ended, and it is right and possible now to look at events in their true perspective. While it cannot be denied that the efforts of the relief agencies did in fact help to prolong the war, it cannot be denied—except by the totally ignorant and prejudiced—that, even if the war had been curtailed because of lack of relief supplies, far more innocent lives would have been lost had they not intervened. As far as I know, their main interest was with the innocent victims. Although some of them, out of emotion arising from their on-the-spot experiences, did come out openly in favour of Biafra and made statements against the Federal Government, the officials of these relief agencies did all they could to ensure that their relief materials went only to the innocent civilians. For a long time, civil servants and others in paid employment were excluded. I remember a stern letter sent to me by one of the relief agencies, drawing my attention to the fact that some civil servants had approached them for relief supplies, and threatening to stop operations if I did not, as head of the civil service, call a halt immediately to what was clearly contrary to their policy. It sounded like blackmail, but I had no alternative but to comply with their request.

It was not until the situation had become quite desperate and when they discovered that civil servants and others in regular paid employment were not just catering for themselves and their families, but for a host of other refugees who were obliged to go to them, that they began to modify their policy. For example, I found myself, after the fall of Aba, having to cater for nearly two hundred refugees who had arrived at Umuahia and, having nowhere else to go, had flocked into my premises. It was a Roman Catholic priest (I am Presbyterian) who discovered this and was appalled. He returned that evening with a truck-load of relief materials which he distributed to the refugees sprawling about in the open premises. Eventually the majority of them were removed to refugee camps. It is a fact that even after the relief agencies' policy had been relaxed, I, as Chief Secretary to the Government, never officially received supplies from the relief agencies. Whatever we got was from individuals attached to the relief agencies who happened to know our plight. What we had in our family was purchased overseas with the little royalties paid by my publishers.

The altruism and disinterestedness of the relief agencies, particularly those of the church, were absolutely transparent. I am sure that if even the Federal army field commanders had been able to enter Biafra as individuals and seen the enormous suffering of innocent people, they—unless they were inhuman—would have agreed that relief should be allowed in for the suffering and dying masses. I went to a refugee camp and, within the space of half an hour, at least fifty children and women collapsed and died in my presence. This is no exaggeration and no propaganda, even if such were necessary or relevant at this post-war stage.

> "A major aspect of this war, which everybody has talked about, is the question of starvation. There have been arguments for and against, whether or not it is a legitimate weapon of war. The fact is that with the contraction of the areas under our control, with the other difficulties of currency and movement, we have reached a stage where one does get apprehensive about the food supply problem in the Republic. *In fact the danger is greater along this line than along the line of enemy weapons*".

That was Ojukwu addressing an agricultural seminar in January 1969. The sentence in italics confirms what I said in an earlier chapter, namely that far more people died in the civil war through starvation than through military action, including the air raids.

While it is true that a number of the pilots flying in relief supplies were motivated by financial gain (it was costing something like twenty-five thousand dollars or more a flight, I understand), there were others, perhaps the majority of them, whose main consideration was humanitarian, and who were prepared to lay down their own lives in the course of saving the lives of others—and a good number of them did pay that supreme price without in the least deterring others. I am not an expert student of history, but I know enough to state that never in the history of this world have the church and other humanitarian organisations defied such extremely grim odds in order to save humanity. I had the privilege of meeting a number of leading representatives of the relief organisations. Some of them did not conceal their feelings against secession and the political stand of Biafra, but were all the same determined to ensure that the innocent victims of the war were catered for. The Biafran government, for its part, did not show outstanding appreciation of the efforts of these agencies. There were several occasions when many of their representatives travelled from Europe or America to see the Governor but were refused an audience. There was a time when they were even required to pay landing fees, in foreign exchange, for bringing in relief.

The proposal to charge relief agencies for landing rights on the Biafran air-strips evoked one of the strongest letters ever written by Dr. Akanu Ibiam to the Governor, condemning any such move. I believe a copy of the letter can be found in official files in Enugu, unless they have been lost. This shows the kind of complicated situation in which the relief agencies found themselves. I had all along been under the impression that no fees were charged to the relief agencies for landing on Biafran airstrips. But I have been surprised by what is considered to be incontrovertible evidence in the Federal hands that such fees were in fact charged. I still cannot personally confirm or deny these allegations.

Out of every evil can come good. The Christian church has often in the past been charged with indifference in their mission to humanity, particularly in areas of human suffering. If, as a result of the Nigerian civil war, a precedent has been set for Christian courage and conviction then not just Christianity but the world it is supposed to serve have stood to gain for the future. No matter what one's feelings in the past, the courage of the pilots who risked their lives to fly in relief supplies for the victims of the war in the beleaguered secessionist enclave, is something which history will always admire.

SECTION IV

THE COLLAPSE OF BIAFRA

14 The Flight

"All right. I shall go out in search of peace. I have decided that the Political Adviser and the Chief Secretary will accompany me. And we must leave tonight." Those firm and final words were uttered by General Ojukwu Head of the Biafran Regime and Commander-in-Chief of its armed forces. The time was two o'clock in the afternoon, on January 9th, 1970, and the place a small village called Ogwa, some thirteen miles from the Owerri township. The words ended discussions which had lasted three hours during the previous night at Owerri, and from 10 a.m. to 2 p.m. the following day at Ogwa, whither General Ojukwu had moved immediately after the previous night's meeting.

The Governor had arrived at Owerri on the evening of Thursday January 8th, in a hurried flight from Madonna, forty miles away, his permanent residence since the fall of Umuahia. It had been a confused and panic-ridden day for everybody. The Federal troops had crossed the Imo River at more than two points. And Imo River had always been regarded as the most effective natural barrier against the enemy. Shells were falling in Madonna. Early in the morning of the said January 8th, we had been told that the Federal troops were twenty-nine miles from Owerri along the Aba-Owerri road. By noon they were less than fifteen miles away. I phoned the Commanding Officer, Brigadier Kalu, who told me that the situation was now hopeless and advised that any contingency plans made should be put into immediate effect. Later that afternoon Major-General Philip Effiong (Chief of General Staff, Biafran Armed Forces) called to inform me that Major-General Madiebo, the G.O.C. of the Biafran army had told him that the army could no longer hold. It being a "purely military matter," I advised Effiong to go and tell the Governor. Both of us agreed that the end had come. At seven o'clock that evening I drove from Owerri towards Madonna, but met the Governor and entourage some twenty miles from Owerri and so turned back and followed them. At Owerri I told him what I knew of the situation, particularly what Effiong and Kalu had told me. Although he tried to conceal his feelings I knew that he was worried.

He told me to contact members of the Executive Council

resident in Owerri to come for a meeting at midnight. He mentioned, in particular, Sir Louis Mbanefo, the Chief Justice, Dr. M. I. Okpara, Political Adviser (who, incidentally had just arrived at Owerri that evening), Dr. Pius Okigbo, Chief Ekukinam Bassey and one or two others I cannot now remember. We met at midnight, and the meeting started with the Governor saying that he had fixed the meeting for eleven o'clock, and suggesting that we move to Ogwa now that we were so late—through the fault of the Chief Secretary. It was not that I had misheard the instructions but that the Governor did not consider Owerri safe. However, everyone else thought we should have the discussions there at Owerri.

The Governor opened by describing the military situation and then stressed the need for the "leadership of Biafra" to leave for safety. After that Dr. Okigbo tried to elaborate. But it was clear that what was being said in tortuous verbiage was that the Governor had decided to leave the country, and I said so, drawing some signs of embarrassment from the Governor. Nobody had any objection to the Governor's leaving immediately. To me, and I believe others as well, it was the easiest way of bringing the senseless war to an end. It was Sir Louis Mbanefo who suggested that it would be bad taste for the Governor to leave without giving some honourable reason to the people. He then suggested a broadcast saying that the Governor was going out in search of peace. The occasion was opportune, with the heads of African and some European States then assembling in Yaoundé for the tenth anniversary of the independence of Cameroun.

At this point the Governor insincerely wondered whether it was strictly necessary that he himself should go, or if he must go, whether he should leave alone. He was still speaking when his wife suddenly came in from Arondizuogu and the Governor went out to meet her. Those of us who were sitting close to the door overheard the Governor reassuring his wife in a low tone that nothing could stop him from leaving the country. Thus when he came back to continue "wondering" whether someone else should leave instead of him "in search of peace" nobody appeared to be impressed. As I now recall this incident, I wonder if this is perhaps the explanation of the surprise announcement the following day, that I and others should accompany him out "in search of peace".

Nobody commented on his last statements and expressions. It was now past two o'clock in the morning and the meeting had to be adjourned until eight o'clock at Ogwa as already mentioned. The Ogwa meeting was an enlarged one with many more people attending than the previous night's meeting. It was all a repetition of the previous night's meeting, save for the mentioning of those to go out with the Governor and other decisions which will be treated presently.

The Chief Secretary who was to accompany the Head of State out of the country in search of peace was myself and the announcement came to me as a shock. My reaction was immediate and spontaneous—a vehement protest, a passionate plea against having to leave the country at that stage. I put forward several reasons and arguments, such as that as head of the civil service I should stay behind to give the leadership expected of me; I honestly felt that I would be more useful remaining at home than travelling abroad at that time; my wife had been discharged from hospital barely four days before, and how could I leave her and my children in a strange village, among a people who did not know her and whose language she did not speak or even understand. I spoke with great emotion, which I could not control. There was silence when I stopped. I looked round at those present expecting support. None came. At last the Political Adviser spoke, but only to show the "wisdom" of the Governor's taking his Chief Secretary with him. I had lost. There was silence. Then someone whispered into the Governor's ear, and there was the additional announcement that the Army Commander, Major-General Madiebo, who was not present at the meeting, should join the team.

Then came a third announcement, an apparent concession to one of the points I had raised in my arguments against going. It was that the families of members of the delegation should leave that night—January 9th—along with the Governor's wife and children. The Governor and those accompanying him would now leave the following night, January 10th.

Much as I was relieved that at least I would not have to abandon my family in such dangerous circumstances, I still found my inclusion in the delegation quite incomprehensible. Only a few minutes before, Mr. C. C. Mojekwu, a man of the greatest influence on the Governor had intimated to me that the intention was to set up a "Presidential Commission" of about five to seven persons, which might include myself, to take charge of the government while the Governor was away. I looked at him for a while, and could not conceal my surprise and incomprehension. I then bluntly told him that I did not see the logic of the proposal. Were they trying to borrow from Ghana? But then Ghana had had a President which Biafra had not. I reminded Mr. Mojekwu that I was a civil servant and should not be included in such a Commission. He then asked me what I would suggest. I replied that I thought the Executive Council, as already constituted, should be allowed to continue with Major-General Philip Effiong or the Political Adviser, Dr. M. I. Okpara, as Chairman. He left me without any further comment and went into private conference with the Governor, who had been restlessly moving in and out of the conference room all the time, possibly to receive minute-to-minute briefing on the military situation.

While I was wondering why Mr. Mojekwu had left me without any comment on the views I had expressed, and while I was trying to whisper to Sir Louis Mbanefo who sat near me what had transpired between Mojekwu and me, the Governor came into the room accompanied by Mojekwu. There was silence while the Governor began to speak. He put forward the idea of a "Presidential Commission or Committee" to continue the war and keep the government going. He suggested a body of three persons, comprising the Chief Justice, Sir Louis Mbanefo, as Chairman, with Major-General Philip Effiong and Mr. Iheanacho as members. He called for views. It was the Chief Justice who spoke. He reminded the Governor that it was still a military regime incompatible with the sort of commission or committee he proposed to set up. Sir Louis therefore suggested that one person, a military man, should be given full and personal responsibility, particularly at that critical moment when everything hung upon military considerations. Mr. F. O. Iheanacho supported Sir Louis, and the Governor then named Major General Philip Effiong as the "Officer Administering the Government of Biafra" during "my absence abroad in search of peace".

It was four o'clock in the afternoon when I arrived at Nkwerre to inform my wife, whom I had not seen for the past three days, that she was to leave for the airport by six o'clock, that is, in two hours' time. She broke down, and with tears in her eyes asked where I was going to be. I briefly told her what had happened and she was relieved to hear that I would be joining her and the children the following day—but where, I had not the faintest idea.

We left Nkwerre at ten minutes past six that evening with only two portmanteaux containing not only her clothes but those of three children and a maid. She had no money with her. It eventually turned out that the two cases she managed to carry away did not even contain her essential needs. How could a housewife, just out of hospital, who had been anxious the whole day about the fate of a husband she had not seen for three days, be expected to sort out her belongings and pack essential things for herself and children within two hours, in order to travel to an unknown destination overseas?

We had been advised to go to a certain point along the road to the airstrip and wait there to join the entourage of the Governor's wife to the airport. We were to be at the spot not later than 7.30 that evening in order to reach the airport before 8 p.m. when the plane was scheduled to leave on time. We arrived at the spot precisely on time, but had to wait until near midnight before a stream of cars and lorries, which included the car carrying the Governor's wife, rolled by. We followed and arrived at the airport after midnight. I was completely taken aback to see the number of people—young and old, some in ill-health—with all sorts of luggage and personal belongings, waiting at the airport and scheduled to leave that night. I called Mr. Mojekwu aside, and remarked that this was contrary to what we had been told. I said that if I had known that such a large crowd of selected people were to leave that night, I would have left my wife behind (and that, of course, would have meant my remaining behind the following day) and damn the consequences. He professed that he knew nothing about any arrangement to send so many people out.

Just as my wife was about to board the plane, an exercise which involved the climbing of a very steep ladder, Mr. Mojekwu handed to her one hundred pounds in sterling for incidental expenses for herself, Mrs. Mojekwu, Mrs. Philip Effiong and Mrs. Chukwudima (all with their children) at Sao Tome. "Sao Tome?" I repeated, somewhat incredulously. Mr. Mojekwu confirmed the destination, and explained that Mrs. Ojukwu and the rest of the crowd were going to Abidjan while the four families he had mentioned when handing over the one hundred pounds sterling were going to be dropped in Sao Tome, from where they would subsequently be transported to Lisbon. I knew that when we came to leave the following day, we would not be going to Lisbon but to either Libreville or Abidjan, most probably the latter if that was where the Governor's family were going. While I was remonstrating with Mr. Mojekwu the engines of the Cargo Superconstellation started to roar. The runway was suddenly flooded with light and in less than two minutes the plane was airborne.

It was pitch dark. My car was parked far away from where we had been standing. It had rained earlier in the evening, and with big potholes all over the ground we stumbled here and there into them as we groped our way to the car. I could hear abuse and curses from the airport workers and soldiers on duty—all directed against those who had sent their families away, leaving them and others behind to die in a war which they had brought about. Names were mentioned. Most of the words were in Ibo and one did not need to understand the language to realise the amount of vehemence and contempt the words conveyed. One soldier was actually heard regretting not blowing the plane up with a hand grenade which he boasted was in his possession at the time. Curiously and significantly, no one mentioned Ojukwu's name among those they cursed. Indeed they were praising him—their hero—for having the courage to stay behind and not abandon them at the last hour. This frightened me. I feared what might happen when these very people came to know that in less than twenty-four hours from then, Ojukwu would be flying to safety from that very airport.

Finally we got to our car. The driver, totally exhausted, was understandably fast asleep. My police orderly, himself tired and famished—for none of us had eaten for two days—opened the door of the car and shook the driver out of his sleep. Dutifully, the awakened driver, having wiped his eyes with the back of his hand, put the key in the ignition and started the car.

It was nearly four o'clock in the morning of Saturday, January 10th when we got back to Nkwerre. Without bothering to undress, I threw myself into bed for a sleep which never came, on account of my wandering and frightened thoughts. I mulled over all the events and experiences of the previous evening—the long wait on the roadside before going to the airport; the departure of the Governor's relations, a move obviously long-planned, judging from the belongings they carried; the disappointed and disapproving utterances of people at the airport. I then thought about my family: had they arrived safely? Why were they not sent to Abidjan with the majority of the people with whom they had left? What game was Mojekwu playing with me? The streams of refugees we had passed on the road—the children, the pregnant women, the sick—all moving as though in a daze and aimlessly, without any sure idea of where they were going. Why did the Governor suddenly decide to take me out with him? There was no doubt that neither I nor my family had been included originally among those to go out. Many possible explanations came in and out of my mind.

By five-thirty I was up, bathed and planned for a day whose end would see me out of the country, at a destination still unknown. I could not do much by way of assembling my personal belongings. I managed however to pack some clothes into a suit case and asked my son to do the same. By seven o'clock people had started to come in to find out what was happening. They were mainly people of what is now the South Eastern State who had fled from other parts of Iboland to Nkwerre and its suburbs. I gave them what assurances and advice I could—pitiable, miserable and frightened fellows.

My main concern was, however, to meet the senior members of the civil service and give them my parting words. None of them could have known or even suspected that I was going, as it were, to desert them that evening. It was not easy or even possible to assemble all of them. I could not tell where most of them might have run to, after leaving Owerri in hopeless confusion and fright. Luckily, however, a number of them managed to make their way to Nkwerre, where I was staying. I tried to keep up their morale by being as cheerful as I could and serving them with what drinks and food I had found. I spoke to them and explained the circumstances of my departure. I emphasised the fact of my having been forced to leave against my will and promised to return in about three weeks' time. I went on to advise them on what to do and how to behave when the end finally came. I doubt whether in their state of mind all the things I tried to say actually penetrated. While they believed that I was being forced to leave the country (a fact confirmed to them by those who were present when it happened) none of them appeared to take me seriously when I promised to return in three weeks' time. Some might have thought that I was trying to deceive them as if they were children. It did not require much intelligence to know that in three weeks there would be no Uli Airport or Biafra to fly into. That apart, how could one expect them, unless out of their right senses, to believe that a person in my position would be so foolhardy as to contemplate returning to the country after being fortunate enough to get out. At that time nobody had heard or even suspected that the Head of State General Gowon would pronounce a general amnesty. The fear of wholesale killings by Federal troops was still widespread.

I was, however, very deeply impressed and touched by the apparent sympathy and understanding extended to me on that occasion. I am grateful to Providence that, contrary to the misgivings shown about my promise to return to the country, I was in fact able to keep my word. For it was exactly three weeks almost to the day that I reported to our High Commissioner in London and asked for a passage home.

At the Ogwa meeting of January 9th, the Governor had announced plans to keep the enemy out of Owerri. He did not tell anybody, although he must have known, that the Federal troops were already in control of Owerri. According to the Governor, plans had been completed for Col. Achuzia to move with two thousand troops to fight the Federal troops inside Owerri. No such plans, it is now known, had been made except in the Governor's own imagination. At that time Achuzia could not in fact boast of more troops than the few who had accompanied him to Ogwa.

Achuzia himself, though present and knowing the truth dared not contradict the Commander-in-Chief. If anything, he exhibited a great deal of confidence and left us with totally wrong impressions.

Thus, when I was talking to the few colleagues and others in Nkwerre whom I had managed to contact, none of us even suspected that the Federal troops were less than ten miles away from us, having overrun Owerri early the previous day, and were approaching Orlu from two directions. I came face to face with this reality when, travelling with Dr. Pius Okigbo, Mathew Mbu and T. C. M. Eneli to see the Governor at Ogwa, and hand to him the draft broadcast he was to make that evening before leaving, we met, less than five miles from Nkwerre, streams of panic-stricken Biafran troops both on foot and in vehicles, fleeing in disorder in the opposite direction. Pulling into a side bush-path we managed to learn, after considerable difficulty, what had happened. It was with equal difficulty that we managed to turn about and negotiate our way, through the throngs of civilians and soldiers, back towards Nkwerre. Anxious about the Governor's safety, we went through extremely rugged and narrow bush-paths towards Ogwa. But three miles from the place we were told by a lone Biafran soldier, who scarcely concealed the fact that he was a deserter, that Ojukwu was no longer at Ogwa. It was now three-thirty in the afternoon and by the time we got back to Nkwerre it was past four o'clock. We agreed that Dr. Okigbo should take the draft speech to the Governor at Nnewi while I gathered the few things I was to take out with me that evening. I could not take much—only two suitcases for myself and son—and had to leave everything, including important documents, behind.

I got to the Governor's house at Nnewi with my son at 7.30 p.m. on January 10th. The premises were full of people. The Governor was quite cheerful, serving drinks and food liberally. It was obvious that many more people from his clan were going to travel that night as well. The draft broadcast had got to him and he had heavily revised it. But the Ministry of Information people, who were expected to come and do the recording, did not turn up. The explanation given was that it had been impossible to assemble the necessary personnel and equipment for the recording. This could well have been true, for at the time everyone was principally interested in the safety of himself, his family and his dependants. Federal troops were closing in from many sides at once. By the time I left Nkwerre around 6 p.m., information had been received that Federal troops were about five miles from Uli/Ihiala road junction, which meant that the road to Nnewi could be closed or made impassable at any moment. When it became clear that

Federal troops were about to enter Owerri, government personnel and property had been evacuated to Umuaka, some fourteen miles from Owerri, as a staging point. The Ministry of Information had already been established there as their main centre of operation. But by four o'clock that day, January 10th, the place had been overrun by Federal troops. Thus it might well have been physically impossible for those concerned to come and do the recording. But there might also have been reluctance on their part, if, as was most likely, the news of the Governor's intended flight had got round. Those who had been instructed to come and do the recording might have regarded it as unseemly, and so deliberately refused to risk their persons in order to do the recording. I have since met a number of those concerned who are very embittered towards Ojukwu, whose sudden departure they consider despicable, cowardly and ignominious.

Ojukwu displayed a kind of fatalism by vowing not to leave without having his message recorded. His many aides were running here and there looking for the Ministry of Information officials who never came. It was now past ten o'clock the deadline for our scheduled departure to the airport for a flight due to take off at 11 p.m. Fortuitously, Dr. Ifegwu Eke arrived, carrying with him a small personal tape-recorder. The problems of recording the message appeared to be solved. The message was recorded for broadcast the following morning after Ojukwu had left.

The long motorcade, which extended for over a mile, was assembled. Except for despatch riders, the usual escorts were assembled in military and police vehicles. Ojukwu began to take leave of those remaining behind, and distributed largesse in Biafran currency to his personal servants, many of whom could not disguise their disappointment and displeasure at being left behind to be "slaughtered", as they had been taught to believe, by the Federal troops. The Governor's personal car, the white Mercedes, VIG 1 (VIG stood for Vigilant), flew both his personal standard, which bore the inscription "To Thyself be True", and the Biafran flag, and took the usual position prescribed by protocol in the entourage.

We started moving around midnight, but instead of turning towards Ihiala and Uli we went towards Akokwa and Uga. I did not understand, for I had not then learnt that someone had telephoned from Uli to say that the airstrip had been put out of action by Federal planes, which had bombed the runway. For that reason all flights, including the one which was to take us, had been diverted to Uga. We stopped several times on the road to Uga for unexplained reasons. A few miles from Uga we stopped for thirty minutes, with vehicles pulled into the roadside, and lights out. Again no explanation was given, but those of us following immediately behind could see a vehicle driven forward and so deduced, rightly or wrongly, that someone had been sent to check conditions at the airstrip. After some time the car returned. Then there was a sudden movement back in the direction from which we had come. We turned round and followed without knowing or asking why. It was then that we discovered that the Governor was not travelling in his flamboyant and flag-decked Mercedes, but incognito, though in full military uniform, in a Peugeot 404 station wagon. I now also noticed that the positions of the cars had been changed, which probably explained the occasional stops as we were moving along. It was after we had passed Nnewi that I knew definitely that we were after all making for the Uli airstrip. I never really ascertained whether the airstrip had in fact been hit in an air raid that evening, or whether the journey towards Uga was simply a manoeuvre to hoodwink possible hostile elements.

We finally reached the airstrip. The huge cargo plane was waiting in pitch darkness. Several people, apart from those who had travelled in the Governor's entourage, were already at the airstrip, ready to leave. The news of the number of people who had left the previous night from the Governor's own town of Nnewi had gone round, and people who could make it had travelled to the airstrip to leave or at least send out their families, if they could. The Governor had stopped somewhere outside the airstrip, while Mr. C. C. Mojekwu who had apparently travelled with him in the same car, came in to arrange things. He announced that only those in the "delegation" were to travel on the waiting plane, while others should go to another side of the airstrip and board a French Red Cross plane which was waiting there. A senior government official who had come to the airstrip with his family, intending to leave as well, was assigned the duty of separating the sheep from the goats—those in the delegation and those who were not. In the end everyone from Nnewi and a few favoured others boarded the plane with us members of the delegation, while all the rest, including the family of Col. Achuzia, were to travel in the Red Cross plane. We learnt on reaching Abidjan the following day that, as the result of a disagreement between Col. Achuzia and the pilot, the Red Cross plane took off leaving almost all the prospective passengers behind.

After we had all boarded the plane, the Governor came in accompanied by a European friend. There were only four seats in the entire huge plane. The Governor and his European friend took two of the seats; Dr. M. I. Okpara took another, and I shared one with Madiebo, with whom I also shared occasional sips of whisky handed to me, as I was about to board the plane, by an incoming passenger who had brought it along with other bottles as presents from a friend abroad. Mojekwu managed a place with one of the crew near the cockpit. All the other passengers sat either on their luggage or on the floor. My son sat close to me. It is not true that Ojukwu travelled disguised either as a priest or a nun, nor is it true that he took out a car, as was widely reported in the world press at the time.

The journey from Uli to Abidjan took five hours or so. We landed at a military airport at exactly six o'clock in the morning of Sunday, January 11th, 1970. General Ojukwu was completely calm and collected right through the journey, occasionally jesting and laughing. It would, however, be wrong and unfair to infer that he was indifferent to what had happened or to his own future. A natural actor, he had the enviable quality of controlling and concealing unpleasant emotions, a quality which he exploited to the full in inspiring false confidence even in the bleakest hours of the civil war.

As soon as our plane touched down, Mr. Mojekwu turned to General Ojukwu and said with elation and a broad smile, "We have made it." General Ojukwu made no reply.

15 Eleven Days in Abidjan

The military airport where we landed in Abidjan was far from the international airport. Awaiting our arrival were Dr. Kenneth Dike, the Biafran Representative and Mr. Peter Chigbo, the senior civil servant in charge of the Biafran office in Abidjan. No sooner had the plane landed than the Governor was whisked away in a waiting car. Dr. Kenneth Dike went with him while Mr. Chigbo remained behind to look after the rest of the passengers. There were no ceremonies of any kind, a telling contrast to Ojukwu's visit there in July 1968 on his way to Addis Ababa.

Mr. Chigbo was shocked and embarrassed by the number of people who had arrived. He could not hide his feelings and made it known that the crowd would not be allowed to stay in the Ivory Coast. He would not even allow anyone to leave the plane except the four of us who were said to be in the "official delegation", and it was left to Mojekwu to say who we were. After a long discussion between Mojekwu and Chigbo it was agreed that the passengers should be taken to Gabon where adequate provision had been made for them. But that did not immediately solve the problem. The pilot and crew of the plane would not go to Gabon except on additional payment. They also complained of hunger, fatigue and the need for sleep and rest. Eventually a fee for the plane's crew was settled by Mojekwu and Chigbo. The passengers could now alight but were not to leave the airport where they would be fed. The crew would also be fed and given a place to sleep for some hours before starting off for Libreville in Gabon. Mojekwu was going to take a commercial flight straight to Lisbon. He was well known in the Ivory Coast and it was probably thought that his appearance in Abidjan would compromise the secret of Ojukwu's arrival.

With all these details settled we, the members of the "delegation", were driven to Abidjan, a long and tedious journey for people who had had no sleep for two days. The four of us, Dr. Okpara, Madiebo, myself and my son were taken to a self-contained house next to Dr. Dike's residence and exactly opposite where Ojukwu and his family (who had arrived the previous day) were staying, in the same street.

The house was lavishly stocked with all kinds of drinks and food. We could call for drinks at any time—and it did not matter whether we wanted champagne, whisky, brandy, beer or anything. We did not know until the following day, Monday, when we wanted to visit the shops, that our presence in Abidjan was to be kept a strictly guarded secret, at least for some unspecified time. For this reason we could not move about freely, except across the street to see Ojukwu, or across the fence to Dr. Dike's residence. Considering the wild speculations about Ojukwu's whereabouts in the world press, speculations which included the sensational one that he had been assassinated in Biafra, the secrecy was most successful, in spite of the fact that Ojukwu stayed next door to the American Embassy, separated only by a fence. This, however, is not to claim that the American Intelligence was ignorant of our presence in Abidjan. Ojukwu had arrived with his A.D.C. and two or three others in Biafran military uniform, which they wore and openly displayed for nearly two hours before they were told to take them off and put on civilian dress. It is impossible to think that the staff of the American Embassy could have failed to notice them, or the fact that some strangers had arrived in the vicinity. To be a news agency is, of course, not part of diplomatic functions.

The French Government and Embassy, though perhaps not the French press, knew all about our presence in Abidjan. For one thing French officials served in the President's office. One of these officials paid Ojukwu a visit soon after our arrival. It was he who informed him that President Houphouet-Boigny, who was then in Yaoundé in connection with the celebrations of the tenth anniversary of Cameroun's independence, had been promptly informed of our arrival and had sent back word that he would be returning as soon as possible, and cutting short his stay in Yaoundé. It was a French official who saw to our security and comfort.

In Biafra President Houphouet-Boigny was known by the code and affectionate name of "Big Brother", normally abbreviated to "B.B.". In anticipation of a meeting between B.B. and General Ojukwu a short aide-memoire was prepared for B.B. to study in advance. This took the form of explaining the sudden collapse of Biafra, and contained suggestions about what should be done to save the lives, leadership and talents of the "heroic people" of Biafra, concern for whom Ojukwu expressed in the following words:

> "The whole purpose of resisting Nigeria's aggression was to ensure the survival of our people. The position now is that unless something is done immediately the whole leadership and talent of our heroic people in Biafra will be destroyed within the next forty-eight hours

or so. This will be done without the world knowing, for our only links with the outside world, namely the airport and the radio stations, will have been taken by the enemy. The fact that Nigeria has untypically not made fanfare of their lightning military movements of recent weeks can only mean that they want to complete their genocide by the destruction of the talent and leadership of Biafra".

Earlier, I had discussed the whole military situation and our presence in the Ivory Coast with Dr. Okpara and suggested that in order to give credibility to the Governor's announcement that we had come in search of peace, a statement should immediately be issued by him ordering Biafran troops to stop fighting and surrender. Dr. Okpara agreed with me and went to discuss my suggestion with Dr. Dike, who also agreed. The three of us and Madiebo then went to Ojukwu and put forward the suggestion. I took the opportunity to tell him that, for all I knew, Major General Philip Effiong or some other person would announce surrender the following day. General Ojukwu did not disapprove of the idea but counselled that it would be improper to make such a statement on host soil without the prior approval of B.B. We all saw the point. It was not normally part of Ojukwu's nature to accept advice readily and we were impressed that he did so on this occasion. His aide-memoire to the President contained the following step, *inter alia*, which he proposed to take immediately.

"(i) I should order our troops to stop fighting and for all refugees to return to their homes. This will not necessarily stop Nigeria continuing and hastening their genocidal intentions, but should at least draw world sympathy to our desire to stop the carnage. . . ."

For my part I took the opportunity of this first meeting to repeat my desire to return home or at least to go and meet my family, wherever they were. I had asked that enquiries be made about the whereabouts of my family and was still awaiting a reply. General Ojukwu merely looked at me without comment, but I could not discern his thoughts through the look.

"Big Brother" returned to Abidjan on Monday, January 12th, 1970. We were told later in the evening of that day that he would be seeing us in his private residence at eight o'clock or thereabouts. We arrived there at the appointed time and found him slumped helplessly on his couch. He was a completely distraught and broken man. His face lacked the lustre, his voice the power, and his handshake the warmth for which I had noted and admired him when we met him in July 1968 on our way to Addis Ababa. On that occasion he had been full of confidence, zeal and words, displaying a generous and knowledgeable mind. All these were absent on this occasion—and understandably. We hardly looked each other in the face. After we had taken our seats, Ojukwu began to speak along the lines of his aide-memoire. He had scarcely finished introducing his first point when B.B. cut in and, holding a document in his hand, asked if we had heard of Effiong's broadcast. The document he was holding contained the text of the broadcast, which he had no doubt obtained through the French Embassy, and he was obviously quite distressed, disappointed and hurt by it. He took particular exception to that portion of the broadcast which said that the people were now "disillusioned", and asked if any one could explain that statement. "Why should a person feel disillusioned about fighting for independence and survival?", he asked with emotion. He had very unkind words for Effiong, whom he likened to some treacherous generals of history. He expressed astonishment that Sir Louis Mbanefo, for whom he had the highest respect, should be a party to the statement. His mood was such that the discussion could not be continued. After assuring Ojukwu of his country's hospitality, and hinting that he would be given political asylum if he wished, he released us. With the President was his Minister of Defence who had come to Biafra twice to negotiate the release of the Italian oilmen.

President Houphouet-Boigny was by far the most sincere, dedicated, practical and active foreign supporter of the Biafran cause. I knew this when I met and heard him in the company of General Ojukwu, Dr. Nnamdi Azikiwe and others on our way to Addis Ababa in July 1968. He had the highest admiration for the Biafran people, whom he considered the heroes of Africa. His support of Biafra had a kind of religious zeal and ring about it. A very wealthy and conservative man as well as an ardent Roman Catholic, he feared and hated communism and pan-Arabism as the twin forces really fighting against Biafra. He regretted that the Western Powers, particularly Britain and the United States, had not, for neo-colonialist, economic and other reasons, been able to see the grim threat of these twin evils and enemies of Black Africa. He had sent delegations to the United States (the two Commonwealth countries of Tanzania and Zambia were to deal with Britain) to make them see the realities of the situation. He had very strong arguments at his finger tips for supporting Biafra as a means of saving Black Africa from spiritual, moral, economic and political domination by the Communist-Muslim forces.

It was largely through the efforts of President Houphouet-Boigny that Biafra had gained so much outside support, particularly from France. It was through his efforts that Biafra had, as from

September 1968, received foreign assistance in arms. He spent much of his own income on the Biafran cause, and must have personally guaranteed a number of loans contracted by Biafra to buy arms. For our 1968 journey to Addis Ababa, he had personally hired and placed at our disposal a DC 8 aircraft and provided a good deal of money for expenses.

He had great contempt for the Organisation of African Unity as an Arab-Muslim dominated organisation, particularly in so far as the Biafran case was concerned. He did not in the slightest trust the O.A.U. Committee's objectivity, and therefore believed that the real solution would come not from Africa but from Europe and America, and he was strenuously working towards this.

It is necessary to emphasise these points here in order to understand the shattering grief which overwhelmed President Houphouet-Boigny when he heard the news of the Biafran collapse. As my intention is to be as fair and objective as possible, I must say that I recognised the altruism of President Houphouet-Boigny's motives. I do not believe that his aim was to destroy Nigeria, but rather to serve humanity and Black Africa as he saw it. No doubt he was totally ignorant of many things about internal conditions in Nigeria, particularly the fact that the majority of people in the former Eastern Nigeria, including the Ibos, did not initially support secession, and would have rejected the whole idea if they had been freely and fairly consulted. He had been influenced in his belief and convictions by the fact that people like Dr. Azikiwe, for whom he had the highest respect as a leader of Black Africa, and other men of political, diplomatic and academic fame were supporters of Biafra. It was these people whom he had met, and who had convinced him of the justness of the Biafran cause. He had, of course, been fully taken in by the propaganda issuing both from Biafra and the international press. As a humanist, his approach was also humanitarian.

He took to General Ojukwu at first sight, and treated him as his own heroic son, symbolising the aspirations of the youth of Black Africa. One could see this in his fatherly demeanour towards Ojukwu during discussions. Vivacious and oratorical himself, he admired Ojukwu's oratory, wit and logical arguments. It would be interesting to know what impressions he now has of Ojukwu's character, now that they are staying so close.

Apart from President Bongo of Gabon, who appeared to me a faithful satellite of President Houphouet-Boigny, I never had an opportunity of meeting the Heads of State of the other two African countries—Tanzania and Zambia—which had openly supported

Biafra. And thus I may be excused for not saying much about them in this book.

The B.B.C. and V.O.A. had given advance warnings that Major-General Philip Effiong would be making an important broadcast at noon on Monday, January 12th. Although we had a fair idea of what the broadcast would be, we awaited it with interest. The broadcast came much later than twelve noon, and was tape-recorded by the Biafran Office and played to us at six p.m. The part which came to my particular notice and that of others was the portion which said that those who had been obstructing peace had "voluntarily removed themselves from our midst." "That is unfair to you, N.U." General Ojukwu said to me later. "Everyone knows you have always stood for peace. I must issue a statement to the world that it was I who took you and others out." I must say that I considered these remarks of Ojukwu most thoughtful and considerate, and I respected him for them. He then asked me to put up a draft for him, which I did without real mental composure. Understandably, he did not accept my draft and with the help of others, not members of the "delegations" but close relations who were with him, prepared his own draft. He did not show this to anyone until he had cleared it with President Houphouet-Boigny. When he gave me the draft at about eleven o'clock that night he told me to look for flaws in syntax and construction but not to disturb the contents.

The speech was to be recorded either that night or early in the morning of the following day for Mr. F. C. Nwokedi to take out for release in Europe on or about January 14th, as was later done. On January 15th, coinciding with the date of the first military coup in January 1966, Biafran leaders were reported to have signed unconditional surrender terms in Lagos. I think it was on this date, or before, that Ojukwu told me that he had given instructions for the family of Major-General Philip Effiong to be brought down from Lisbon to the Ivory Coast as hostages, a reprisal for what Philip Effiong had done. I considered such an action mean and vindictive, but made no comments, checking myself with difficulty.

Ojukwu had a number of meetings with the President, sometimes in the company of Dr. Dike but never of any of us in the so-called delegation. On the morning of Thursday, January 15th, we were told to get ready to move out of Abidjan to a place in the country where we would have freedom of movement. The place was Yamoussokro, the country home and farm of the President. The real reason of our departure that day was the impending visit to Abidjan of U Thant, the United Nations Secretary-General. Apart from the fact that our presence might be compromised as a result of the number of people, including members of the world press, visiting with U Thant, our accommodation in Abidjan was probably required for the visitors.

We called and saw the President that evening before leaving. He now felt much more relaxed. Warmth and life had returned to his face. He now appeared more understanding and sympathetic towards Major-General Effiong and Chief Justice Mbanefo. He appeared fully appreciative of the fact that there was nothing else they could have done in the situation. After handing what were obviously parcels of money to Mrs. Ojukwu and chocolates to the children, we took leave of him on our journey to Yamoussokro which took nearly six hours of fast driving, and we reached Yamoussokro after midnight. We learnt before leaving Abidjan that the President would be coming to Yamoussokro the following Sunday to meet the "delegation" and would return to Abidjan on Tuesday, January 20th.

Yamoussokro is a very pleasant country town. The President's land is dotted with many pleasantly constructed and furnished houses, all belonging to him personally. In terms of food, drink and care we were treated as in Abidjan. As in Abidjan also our movements were restricted—or at least until I left the place on Tuesday, January 20th. There is an artificial lake, but whether or not the lake contains crocodiles as the world press later reported, I had no means of knowing, since I was not allowed to go out and examine it, although it was only a few yards away.

I continued to show my unhappiness and resentment about staying in the Ivory Coast. I persisted in this until Dr. Okpara saw my point and told General Ojukwu that I should be allowed to go. Dr. Dike also did the same on my behalf. On Sunday January 18th, Ojukwu agreed that I should meet my wife, after going to Switzerland to ask Dr. Ibiam to come to Abidjan and discuss finances with Ojukwu. After that I should return to Abidjan. I merely smiled at the latter suggestion, but told Ojukwu that I did not think Dr. Ibiam would come to Abidjan. "Then if he refuses to come, we shall have something on record," Ojukwu replied, still apparently regarding himself and acting as the "Head of State and Commander-in-Chief of the Republic of Biafra".

President Houphouet-Boigny came, as he had said, on Sunday, January 18th. He had a long meeting with General Ojukwu in the latter's residence. But Ojukwu did not bring any member of the "delegation" into the discussions. We later learnt that the President had said that there should be another meeting the following day, and had specifically said that Ojukwu should have at least one of his aides with him. For his part, the President was going to send for one or two of his aides from Abidjan.

On Monday the meeting was held in the President's own residence, some three hundred yards from where we were staying. Ojukwu went alone. Dr. Okpara, who had been told that he would go with Ojukwu, waited the whole day to be sent for; but no such message came. He was very hurt and felt insulted. It became clear that we had been brought out purely to serve as a cover for Ojukwu's flight. The meeting ended, and Ojukwu returned, and told us individually as we went to see him what had transpired. I had gone to tell him that I was leaving the following day, and took that opportunity to ask him about his meeting with the President. He told me that the President had decided to announce, on Friday January 25th, that Ojukwu was in Abidjan and had been granted political asylum. He would be free to move about, to live anywhere in the Ivory Coast, and to engage in any business, but he must refrain from all political activity and political statements. Ojukwu said he did not quite like these last conditions and had told the President so, but the President was adamant.

I told him that I had decided to leave the following day and would be taking my son with me. I reminded him that it was winter in Europe, and from all reports it was the severest for several years. I therefore needed money to buy warm clothing both for myself and my son. All I had with me were the few dollars I had brought out of Biafra and the little amount he gave us as spending money. General Ojukwu countered that he had no money to give me. I knew he had asked Mojekwu to come with money, but the latter had not appeared. It was for this reason that he wanted me to ask Dr. Ibiam to come to the Ivory Coast. He suggested I should approach Dr. Dike and see what he could do for me, and assured me that things would be all right by the time I came back from my trip to Europe. I later approached Dr. Dike who, after great arguments and much pleading, on my part, promised to give me two hundred dollars, which I should collect from Mr. Chigbo when I reached Abidjan. I was openly disappointed. The following day I left with my son for Abidjan, leaving no one in any doubt that I was going to return to Nigeria and never come back to the Ivory Coast. (Dr. Okpara, I understand, left less than twenty-four hours after me and went to Europe.)

I spent the whole of Wednesday morning and afternoon trying to buy scanty warm clothing for my son and also to obtain his travelling documents. For myself, I bought only a mackintosh. At eight o'clock that evening we left Abidjan airport and arrived in Paris the following morning at 6 a.m. Because of some difficulties over our travel documents we missed the first plane to Lisbon that morning but managed to leave later in the evening arriving in Lisbon, again, near midnight.

The very first information I received at the airport was that my family had been booked to travel to Abidjan the following morning! My immediate reaction was undisguised amazement. They had known at Lisbon that I was coming, so why did they decide to send my family to Abidjan? They were to travel on the same plane as the family of Philip Effiong.

I asked to be driven straight to where Mr. Mojekwu was staying, and there asked him why my family, if my information was true, was being sent to Abidjan. Was it for the same reasons that Mrs. Effiong and her children were going? Mojekwu explained that the action had been taken at the request of my wife. But even so, why the hurry when it was known that I was coming?

I met my wife later and she confirmed that it was she who had asked to be sent to Abidjan, or wherever I was, to join me. Since the day she and our children and Mrs. Effiong and her children had been dumped in the hotel, no one from the Biafran office in Lisbon had shown any interest in them. The families of Mojekwu and Chukwudima who had arrived in Lisbon with them were staying elsewhere in private flats or villas. Only two rooms had been booked in the hotel for our two families, comprising ten persons! Nobody had paid them a visit or even telephoned them until the very day before my arrival, when Mojekwu went to tell them about travelling to Abidjan the following day.

To cut this part of my experience short, I later discovered from Mojekwu himself that he had been angry both about Major-General Effiong's broadcast and General Ojukwu's statement, which did not mention himself as one of those on the "delegation in search of peace". Mojekwu believed the omission of his name from Ojukwu's statement to be my doing, since he thought that it was I who had drafted the statement. After explaining to him how the speech was written and that I had not had much to do with it, I began to wonder if this could be the reason for the utter indifference towards my family and that of Philip Effiong. None of them could speak Portuguese and Mrs. Effiong was about to have a baby at any time.

Two days later I went to Switzerland and saw Dr. Ibiam who, as I had anticipated, would not go to Abidjan. He had many reasons for being displeased and angry with everybody.

All along I had been wondering where to keep my family in Europe while I returned to Nigeria. I sought Dr. Ibiam's assistance in Switzerland but that was not possible. Thus I was very relieved and grateful when, on returning to Lisbon (I spent only two nights in Switzerland) I learnt that friends in Britain had completed arrangements for us to go there. We left Lisbon on Monday, February 2nd for London. Pastor Khul of the German Church in Lisbon had undertaken to meet all our hotel expenses from his refugee vote—that is, a vote set aside by his organisation for the aid of those compelled to flee their country. On Tuesday, February 3rd, 1970 I reported to the office of our High Commission in London and asked for a passage home. I was highly impressed by the courtesy and kindness of the High Commission, which undertook to contact Lagos at once. They expected a reply in ten days and I used the time to arrange for my family's stay in Edinburgh. I eventually left London on the night of Wednesday, February 18th and arrived at Lagos airport on the morning of Thursday, February 19th, 1970.

16 The Dramatic End to Secession

Ojukwu's departure from the scene, selfish and ungallant though it was, shortened the war by at least a few days if not weeks, and so saved the lives and suffering of thousands of helpless and innocent people. But this could hardly have been the intention of General Ojukwu, who clearly wanted the futile struggle to continue regardless of consequences to his people, whom he had decided to leave without warning at the last moment. This was clearly borne out not only by his departing instructions to Col. Achuzia in Ogwa, and to Major-General Effiong and other army officers at the airport, but also by his farewell broadcast and subsequent statements. He simply could not bear the grim but obvious fact that Biafra must cease to exist. He regarded Major-General Effiong's broadcast as treacherous, hence his decision to bring Effiong's family from Lisbon to the Ivory Coast, where they were to be held as hostages—whatever he meant by that, since it is difficult to see what he expected from Effiong in exchange for them. His recorded statement of January 14th, released in Europe to the world press, ended with the following self-deceptive words: "Biafra lives; the struggle continues; long live the Republic of Biafra."

There was something farcical, but revealing about General Ojukwu's confused state of mind at the time, in his statement that his departure from Biafra to safety would keep not only the concept but also the struggle of Biafra alive. Explaining, somewhat inaccurately, how he came to flee the country, Ojukwu explained again in his statement of January 14th as follows: "I decided personally to lead any delegation in order to give it maximum effect and to speed up matters in order to save the lives of our people and preserve the concept of Biafra. *I did this knowing that while I live Biafra lives. If I am no more it would be only a matter of time for the noble concept to be swept into oblivion.*" I have already mentioned how the delegation was treated and how it worked.

Ojukwu in fact could not have done more to kill Biafra and sweep its concept into oblivion than by leaving in the way he did. He could not have done more to destroy his personal image and embarrass all those at home and abroad who had helped to build up that image. He could not have done more to disenchant and disillusion his followers. And he could not have done more to discredit himself and everything he had professed to stand for. He had repeatedly stated that, as far as he personally was concerned, he had put everything—his wealth, his life, his family—into the struggle, and if everybody else should fail or falter he would stand alone, if necessary, fighting for Biafra on Biafran soil.

Speaking to a seminar in Umuahia on February 16th, 1969 General Ojukwu had this to say about a good leader:

> "To be a good leader, you must serve the people. The day a leader becomes a slave to the people (God bless them) he is not worthy of the leadership. He must stand uncompromisingly for right and justice at the expense of losing his leadership. This is what I call true greatness . . .
>
> If what you are doing is right, it should bear complete light of day. Your actions and motives should be searched by anybody who wants to. If you are not found wanting, you will emerge more confident. I really do have that confidence. Call it naïve. I like it that way. Some do talk about martyrdom for everybody. Martyrdom for everybody? No. A leader should have a pronounced streak of martyrdom.
>
> If a leader accepts himself as already dead to society, there will be no reason for cowardice in his leadership. One thing that frightens leaders and leads them to a number of excesses is usually the fear of death. *No. A leader should accept the fact that from the moment of leadership you are sacrificed to death. Each subsequent day becomes a bonus for the preparation of one's memorial. This is my own idea of leadership.*"

(My italics.) Moving, dedicated and self-sacrificing expressions!

The struggle would probably have continued, certainly longer than it did, and sympathy for the concept of Biafra would have been kept alive *if he had remained in Biafra to the end and, if necessary, died a martyr*. History amply bears out this fact and, as a student of history, Ojukwu should have known this. The loss of his own life would not have been more costly than those of others who had fought and perished or were yet to perish, fighting under his personal inspiration and leadership. However, enough lives had been lost and, no matter how ironic it may seem, Ojukwu did his people and country a favour by leaving them when he did. It might have been better still if he had done it much earlier. Leadership is not worth its salt if the leader is not prepared to pay the price of that leadership, and this is the lesson which the new generation of African leadership must learn if Africa is to expect and enjoy the respect which it deserves in the world.

I have had the privilege of meeting and talking to a large number of the most ardent supporters of Ojukwu and the Biafran cause, and the verdict has been the same. When Major-General Philip Effiong talked of disillusionment in his broadcast of surrender, he was expressing the general feeling of the people—and the disillusionment was mainly with Ojukwu himself.

In his aide-memoire to the President of the Ivory Coast Ojukwu explained the military situation in these words:

> "Biafra is no longer in a position to offer formal and organised military resistance to Nigeria. With the fall of Owerri and the lightning movements of the enemy the Biafran armed forces have been disorganised. *But this does not mean the end of the struggle.* Foreseeing the imminent disintegration of the armed forces, plans were made for elements of the regular army under specially trained leadership, to resort to guerilla struggle, with arms caches located in suitable places for the purpose. But, as the proper aim now must be to stop the complete destruction of Biafran leadership and talent, it may be wise for guerilla forces to lie low for a while."

It is difficult to believe this statement. The Biafran army never at any time had enough arms and ammunition to fight the war, let alone to spare for the "arms caches located in suitable places." In any case, things happened so fast in the last days that General Ojukwu could not even see his officers, let alone discuss such arrangements. But even if this were true, such a struggle could be inspired only be General Ojukwu's continued presence in Biafra to give leadership, or by his death as a martyr.

General Ojukwu, however, knew better than any one that with the final collapse of formal and organised military resistance, and his abrupt departure, the struggle had ended. The statement that "as the aim now must be to stop the complete destruction of Biafran leadership and talent, it may be wise for guerilla forces to lie low for a while" betrays this fact. It would not make military sense for the guerillas to lie low until the Federal troops had fully consolidated, if they were really in a position to fight.

All this may seem unkind, particularly coming from one who was supposed to work closely with General Ojukwu. But that is not the end of the story. Ojukwu's action was a real surprise to me, for it ran contrary to the heroism and gallantry shown by him in September 1968, when Aba and Owerri fell in quick succession, the

Biafran army had disintegrated, and there was nothing, not even a single armed soldier, standing between the Federal troops and Umuahia. Calm and collected, Ojukwu on that occasion called a meeting of his close associates in Umuahia and explained to them the hopelessness of the situation and then directed that immediate steps be taken to save what could be saved, particularly the talent of Biafra. As many university men, scientists, technicians, engineers, professionals and administrators as possible were to be evacuated to Gabon and other countries, except for those who voluntarily elected to remain behind.[1] As for him he was going to take to the bush and continue the struggle. He also suggested that someone who had the nearest resemblance to him should be selected to wear his clothing so that, in the event of his death, his double might keep up the appearance of his being alive.

His action drew much respect, admiration and sympathy. Everyone opted to remain with him. The soldiers were inspired to suicidal ventures. Nobody left the area. He showed a clear determination to martyr himself, and by so doing convinced everyone of his commitment and belief in what he was doing. Not even a single member of his family was sent out.

He also took into account the position of those four African countries whose leaders had risked their personal and political reputations to give recognition to Biafra, and had just taken a united stand in favour of Biafra at the Algiers meeting of the O.A.U. He therefore sent emissaries to them that very night to explain the hopeless military situation and what he had decided to do. The emissaries came back within two days bringing with them messages of encouragement to continue the fight "even if there was only one inch of Biafra left". The emissaries also brought back promises of immediate supplies of arms which would if necessary

1. General Ojukwu still showed his concern for the safety of Biafran talent and expressed this in his January 14th recorded speech in these words:

"The sole motive behind Nigeria's determination to draw an iron curtain over Biafra and exclude international observers, relief agencies, journalists whom they have not carefully picked themselves, is to make sure that the atrocities they will certainly carry out in Biafra are unseen and unreported in the world press. Once they have sealed off Biafra from the gaze of mankind, I hesitate to contemplate the fate of the Biafran leadership, the trained man-power, the scientists and professionals whom they will liquidate as planned before the world can interfere."

This alarm has turned out to be utterly unfounded. For under the terms of the general amnesty proclaimed by General Gowon, the talents of the former Eastern Region, caught in the secessionist enclave, have not only been spared but are actively being re-absorbed into the Nigerian community and encouraged to direct their talents to the common good of the country.

be dropped from the air. As far as I know, it was from this time, that Biafra started to receive regular arms aid from abroad which continued until the very end. No doubt those foreign leaders must have been as touched and impressed by Ojukwu's conduct as those at home had been. That was how the war which had virtually ended in September 1968, came to be continued for more than another year.

17 The Sudden Collapse of the Biafran Army

But what were the real causes of the sudden and unexpected collapse of Biafra? This is a question to which there has not till now been a complete answer, a question asked even by the visitors themselves. The timing, method and speed of the collapse took every one by complete surprise.

In his aide-memoire to President Houphouet-Boigny, to which references have already been made, Ojukwu explained the situation as follows:

> "(i) *Exhaustion of our troops through hunger.* With practically all the food-producing areas in Biafra controlled by the enemy it became impossible to give the troops even one square meal in two or three days at a stretch.
>
> (ii) *Lack of medical facilities.* With the blockade, drugs could not be brought in and, what is more, practically all important hospitals were within enemy-held territory.
>
> (iii) *Inadequate transport for troop movement.* Again with the blockade, spare parts for the maintenance of existing transport became difficult to come by, thereby making it impossible to make existing vehicles serviceable, not to mention the fact that vehicles destroyed could not be replaced with new ones.
>
> (iv) *Lack of clothing and shoes for our troops.*
>
> (v) *Lack of anything to match the enemy's fleets of armoured vehicles, aircraft and long-range artillery.*
>
> (vi) *The massive use of weapons, particularly armoured vehicles and the introduction of new and highly sophisticated weapons.* Determined to obtain a military victory at all costs, Britain and Russia not only massively increased the quantities and type of weapons previously supplied by them but introduced new and very highly sophisticated weapons in the use of which they spent months in training Nigerians. They also spent the periods in planning and training in new tactics.
>
> (vii) *Improved leadership in the Nigerian fighting forces.* In the final stages, Nigerian troops were led and officered for the most part by foreign personnel including those from Britain. The Russians also helped from the background in the accurate and effective use of certain sophisticated weapons. The enemy aircraft manned by skilled foreign pilots, became more heavily used in the front lines against our troops."

The above facts and assessments might be true coming from the man who was in overall control of the Biafran armed forces and so in a position to know exactly what was happening in the front. But most of those forces existed against the Biafran forces, as we knew or were repeatedly told, since the very beginning of the civil war. Exhaustion of troops through hunger, lack of medical supplies and inadequate transport for troop movements, certainly contributed to the sudden collapse. One might also add, without placing it in the same category as the three just mentioned, lack of clothing and shoes for the troops. But Biafran soldiers were known to be fighting very well without these things for months. The Federal troops definitely outmatched, by very large margins, the Biafran troops in numbers and weaponry; but this again had been the case all along.

There were therefore other causes which combined with all the above to bring about the sudden collapse and to these I must turn.

By his boastful and self-deceptive utterances General Ojukwu himself unconsciously contributed to the sudden collapse. The last and most effective of such utterances was his speech to the joint meeting of chiefs, elders and members of the consultative assembly at Akokwa a few weeks before the dramatic collapse. Ojukwu wanted, as he put it, a most rousing (i.e. pompous) speech, aimed at boosting the flagging morale both of the public and of the fighting forces. He also wanted to use the occasion for clarifying certain aspects of the "Ahiara declaration" which had caused serious concern, uneasiness and even disaffection among the people. (I have dealt specially with that "declaration" in a previous chapter.)

General Ojukwu took the draft speech and went over it for two complete days himself. He spoke of the spectacular achievements of the Biafran forces both on land and in the air. He boasted that our troops were marching almost uninterrupted towards Port Harcourt and should be within shelling range of the oil city any time from then. He spoke of how what had been described as the last of the last offensives of the Federal forces, mounted on all fronts, had been "completely shattered". The Federal troops had planned to be in Orlu long before the date of that speech, but here we were miles beyond Orlu towards the enemy, comfortably holding the meeting. The enemy was everywhere on the run, he boasted. He spoke of the exploits of the Biafran air force and informed the applauding and elated audience that soon the air force would be equipped with more powerful and long range aircraft capable of dealing devastating blows at Lagos and other Nigerian towns.

As anyone in a position to have an idea of the truth could imagine, that speech in fact boomeranged. The Federal troops were spurred to redeem their honour, while our front troops were embarrassed. True, the Federal troops had launched their very last offensive some weeks before. This fact was well known both through intercepts and actual experience on the fronts. For the first time in the history of the war, the offensives were launched on all fronts with equal intensity, with the Federal troops bringing their overwhelming numbers and weaponry to bear. Hitherto, it was the known and easily anticipated practice of the Federal strategy to launch massive offensives on one or two fronts, thus giving the Biafran high command opportunity to manoeuvre by moving its troops from one sector or front to another. This was not possible on this occasion, and the Federal troops were able to break through with amazing speed in the Ikot Ekpene-Aba sectors.

The occupation of these areas meant the capture of the last remaining sources of food supply both for the civil and military populations. This clearly was the last straw which broke the camel's back for everyone within the enclave. Morale suddenly dropped to zero everywhere. For once, people defied the risk of being branded as saboteurs and whispered or grumbled openly about the need to call off the resistance.

The problem of feeding the population had exercised the mind of the government for months before. The food-producing areas of the former Eastern Nigeria lay in the non-Ibo peripheries of the territory. It was these peripheries which were first occupied in turn by the engulfing Federal troops, until eventually the only areas left were parts of Aba, Annang, Arochukwu and Bende. It was in order to off-set the effects of the loss of the food-producing areas of Ogoja, Abakaliki, Nsukka, Enyong, Calabar, Onitsha, parts of Aba and Port Harcourt provinces and others, that the land army programme was established. But this never really got off to a good enough start to have any noticeable effect on the problem. The soil of the Ibo hinterland is naturally poor and incapable of producing anything but second-rate cassava. But even this required time to grow and mature for harvesting. All kinds of devices were made to increase the local food supply, but without success.

While parts of Aba, Annang, Arochuku and Bende remained in Biafran hands, some hope of food also remained, for in addition to the food actually produced in these areas, additional supplies could still be brought in across the lines from Federal-held territories. But prices had become intolerably high, with garri attracting the fantastic price of one Biafran pound or more to the cigarette cup. One can imagine from this what the more advanced classes of local foodstuff, such as yams could cost, if they were available at all. Considering the fact that wages of workers were cut rather than increased, and were still at or below the pre-war levels, and the fact that many people had lost their own businesses, this was killing. There were times before the war when one pound could buy between 240 to 720 cups of garri. Now these remaining areas, the last hope, were removed.

The question on the lips of readers now will be, what about the relief supplies? I have already touched briefly on this matter elsewhere. But let me say here that the relief supplies did much to save the lives of the civilian population, particularly children. The relief agencies, as far as I know, never knowingly allowed their supplies to go to the fighting forces. But this does not mean that they never got to the forces, through theft, loot, seizure of relief vehicles by soldiers on the way, or even from relatives of the fighting soldiers.

But what contributed to the sudden break-through of Federal troops in the Ikot Ekpene-Aba areas? One cannot, of course, minimise the skill and achievement of the Federal forces in this sector. But there were forces and circumstances aiding them which they knew nothing about; forces and circumstances not mentioned by General Ojukwu in his aide-memoire, extracts from which were produced at the beginning of this chapter.

The first of these forces was the non-cooperation of the Aba people. Hitherto, much—indeed most—of the reconnoitring work had been done by the local people for the Biafran fighting forces. It was the local people who organised food to feed the troops, and it was the local people who supplied men, when necessary, for recruitment and training. All these were not available at this critical time. The reason for this was clear.

A few weeks before, the Governor had received information that the local people were molesting and even killing and eating the soldiers. Ojukwu's reaction to the information was swift and vindictive. A meeting of representatives of all sections of what remained of Biafra was called one evening at a place called Oriagu. Aba leaders, attended without knowing what was going to happen. Ojukwu addressed the meeting, speaking without notes and with great emotion, using as his "text" a petition which had been written to him by Aba leaders, listing a number of complaints which included the non-promotion of some named Aba members of the public services, the removal of a leading Aba citizen from the rehabilitation commission, and the attitude of the soldiers who were accused of being in the regular habit of harvesting people's crops, either for their personal use or for sale.

After effectively and convincingly dismissing the complaints about unfair treatment of Aba indigenes in the public services, and condemning the attitude of the soldiers in harvesting people's crops, General Ojukwu confronted the Aba people with the information he had received about their treatment of Biafran soldiers. He accused them of cannibalism and burst into tears. To drive his point home, he produced from behind a screen four persons who had been caught and had confessed to the killing and eating of Biafran soldiers. He could not bear it any more and abruptly left the meeting.

The expected effect was complete. Speaker after speaker, it was reported (I had left the meeting when the Governor left) turned against the Aba people whom they branded collectively as saboteurs, traitors and cannibals. The following day General Ojukwu proclaimed whatever had remained of the Aba division to be a military area; he ordered that the people who were known to have killed and eaten Biafran soldiers should be rounded up and publicly shot or hanged; he imposed a dusk to dawn curfew in the area; closed all markets; appointed a military administrator and deputy to take charge of the area after dismissing the civilian administrator and his executive committee; ordered the arrest and removal of Dr. Jaja Nwachuku to Orlu; clamped a few other leaders in temporary detention; and set up a military tribunal for the area.

All this was humiliating, disgraceful and painful in the extreme to the Aba people. To make matters worse, the military administrator and his deputy, who were not natives of the area, exhibited undue exuberance and were anything but tactful in their dealings with the local people, no matter how highly placed. They threw their weight about, bullied and pushed everyone around. They regularly called in the local leaders to be harangued like naughty and incorrigible schoolboys, or juvenile delinquents whom they had come to reform.

The effect was totally disastrous to the Biafran cause in the area. The people withdrew all voluntary cooperation and only half-heartedly carried out instructions handed to them. They no longer undertook any reconnoitring work, nor told the Biafran commanders, as they were previously wont to do, of Federal troops' movements known to them. A number of them in fact were alleged to have actually cooperated with Federal troops by showing them the right paths to take to cut off Biafran forces.

There was also the influence of spiritualists. This had been a known feature in the Biafran army for some time, but now that influence appeared complete. The majority of Biafran commanders were clients of the spiritualists (as were in fact some top civilian leaders). Biafran officers would not carry out planned attacks without first of all consulting the spiritualists and obtaining their approval. Each military formation had a number of spiritualists and prophets serving with the soldiers. The brigade headquarters in Aba had a spiritualist chapel attached to it. A leading spiritualist in the area was reported to enjoy the privilege and honour of having a number of soldiers under a lieutenant to guard his residence! Officers were known to abandon their fronts to attend prayer houses miles away.

When matters got out of hand, General Ojukwu again took desperate measures. He banned the organisations, exposed and removed some army commanders known to be adherents. But as we have seen, the majority of the army officers and commanders were in fact believers. The steps taken could not but be discriminatory: to remove all known adherents would mean winding up the whole Biafran military command. Then, in the midst of all this, a leading and extremely popular and prosperous young Ibo leader of the sect, a Mr. Ezenweta, was tried and condemned by the special tribunal for vicarious murder, and immediately executed. His condemnation and death had an electric effect not just among his followers and admirers in the armed forces but also among the civilian population. It has been estimated that nearly fifty per cent of the population were adherents, secret or open, of some spiritualist organisation or another, even though such individuals might also belong to branches of the Christian church.

Thus, the soldiers who had so absolutely depended on the divinatory wisdom of the spiritualists became totally helpless, or possibly even resentful, and would not fight. Officers would not give orders and, if they gave them, they were not obeyed. General Ojukwu's personal appearances at the Aba front to salvage morale completely failed. The Federal troops were moving in and occupying everywhere without firing a shot. Some of them actually moved in singing, with their rifles slung on their soldiers.

There are certain deductions which can be made concerning the spiritualists' influence over the Biafran army, particularly in the Ikot Ekpene-Aba sector where the total collapse, involving a whole army division, occurred. The whole territory, embracing Calabar, Ibibio, Annang and Aba areas, was well known as the strongholds of spiritualist organisations even before the war. Their leaders and headquarters were in those areas. It was reported that the people of these areas, particularly the non-Ibos, were supporters of the Federal cause. Just as the Christian church leaders on both sides prayed to God to grant victory to their respective sides, the spiritualists who supported the Federal cause may well have decided to be more practical, exploiting their intimate knowledge of Biafran military plans and weaknesses to advantage—who knows? There were, of course, Ibo cranks who made a great deal of money out of it all, even though they may not have deliberately intended to sabotage military plans.

Nothing in what I have said should be interpreted as inferring that the Federal forces did not deserve their victory. I have only tried to show what might have made that victory so sudden and dramatic. The Federal troops were, of course, bound to win, even if not so suddenly and surprisingly. The plans for the success of the last final offensive were foolproof. They had received new weapons, some of them never before used; they were using new tactics; and their air force, more than ever before, was giving direct and more effective assistance to the ground forces in the actual fighting areas and no longer bombing civilian populations, markets and hospitals.

The collapse of the Biafran army, though abrupt was not unexpected by the Biafran leadership. General Ojukwu saw the signs more clearly than others, but continued to inspire false confidence. The army had shown signs of complete exhaustion both through hunger and grave physical strain. No member of the Biafran army had been allowed on leave, or even had days off since the start of the conflict. It was indeed one of the miracles of the tragedy that they lasted so long. When General Ojukwu knew that the game was nearly up, his tactics appeared to be that of holding on for as long as possible in the hope—as he very often openly and tactlessly told the world—that the Nigerian army would crack up first, either through exhaustion or through some political event on the Federal side. In this he was encouraged by reports given by foreign visitors who had been in contact with Nigeria, and also by Biafran intelligence agents. "Give us six months, and Nigeria is bound to crack up," he told foreign journalists in September or October 1969, in one of those very many public utterances which could only strengthen the Federal side in its resolve and could also reveal Biafra's own unsure position. There was also the hope that some peace settlement would be reached even though we on the Biafran side, because of the rigid and arrogant position held, never did enough to encourage such efforts.

General Ojukwu did not normally tell the whole truth about the military situation. Where he did he would gloss over known difficulties. Every military reverse or critical situation was always explained away with assurances that something was going to be done to achieve a miracle. Thus, on a certain date in November or December, when Ojukwu called a meeting of all senior army officers, and invited leading civilians to attend as well, many of us began to wonder. All the military commanders and officers, except those who could not leave the fronts because of operations, attended the meeting. The leading civilians invited also attended, as did the head of the Biafran police—something quite unusual.[1]

General Ojukwu opened the meeting by stating plainly that he had called in the military leaders so that they might say in the presence of Biafran elders whether they still had the will to continue the fight. One did not have to be a psychologist to see from the faces of those present that, even if the spirit was willing, the body was definitely and absolutely weak. Given the chance to speak their minds, some of them would have done so. But Ojukwu never allowed them that chance. He proceeded at once to state firmly that as far as he himself was concerned he saw no alternative but to fight on. It was what Biafra expected of everyone, and anything different would be a betrayal of the cause. He was sure, no one present in that room could even conceivably be a party to such an unpardonable betrayal. All that was required was some reorganisation of the army. He seasoned his long speech as usual with much blackmail and intimidation.

The G.O.C., who knew the feelings of his officers, tried in vain to evoke the expression of those feelings. After one or two non-military members of the audience had spoken, the meeting ended after midnight with beer and coffee. The following day, Ojukwu, as the Commander-in-Chief, issued his reorganisation proposals. The main effect was to split what used to be a unified army command into two army divisions under two independent commands. The task of the G.O.C. would now be that of co-ordinating the activities of the two different and independent commands, the heads of which, at the same time, could have direct access to, and receive direct instructions from, the Commander-in-Chief. The ways of the military can be quite incomprehensible to the civilian, and as a civilian administrator, I could not see how the arrangements just described could be efficacious. It did however betray the fact that

1. As far as Ojukwu was concerned it was sacrilegious for any civilian, no matter how highly placed, to say anything about the army or its operations.

all was not perfect, at that time, in the relations between the Commander-in-Chief and his high military command.

The suffering and death had been quite terrible. There had been fervent prayers everywhere for these to end. God answered the prayers and brought the war to an end in a way and at a time beyond all human calculations. That is the Christian answer to the question which this chapter has attempted to answer.

APPENDIX

THE CONCLUDING PARTS OF GOVERNOR OJUKWU'S AHIARA DECLARATION

APPENDIX

The Concluding Parts of Governor Ojukwu's Ahiara Declaration

The Principles of the Revolution

I stand before you tonight not to launch the Biafran Revolution, because it is already in existence; it came into being two years ago when we proclaimed to all the world that we had finally extricated ourselves from the sea of mud that was, and is, Nigeria. I stand before you to proclaim formally the commitment of the Biafran State to the Principles of the Revolution and to enunciate those Principles.

Some people are frightened when they hear the word Revolution. They say: Revolution? Heaven help us! It is too dangerous. It means mobs rushing around destroying property, killing people and upsetting everything.

But these people do not understand the real meaning of revolution. For us, a revolution is a change—a quick change, a change for the better. Every society is changing all the time. It is changing for the better or for the worse, it is either moving forward or moving backwards; it cannot stand absolutely still. A revolution is a forward movement. It is a rapid, forward movement which improves a people's standard of living and their material circumstances and purifies and raises their moral tone. It transforms for the better those institutions which are still relevant, and discards those which stand in the way of progress.

The Biafran Revolution believes in the sanctity of human life and the dignity of the human person. The Biafran sees the wilful and wanton destruction of human life not only as a grave crime but as an abominable sin. In our society every human life is holy, every individual person counts. No Biafran wants to be taken for granted or ignored, neither does he ignore nor take others for granted. This explains why such degrading practices as begging for alms were unknown in Biafran society. Therefore, all forms of disabilities and inequalities which reduce the dignity of the individual or destroy his sense of person have no place in the New Biafran Social Order. The Biafran Revolution upholds the dignity of men.

The Biafran Revolution stands firmly against genocide—against any attempt to destroy a people, its security, its right to life, property and progress. Any attempt to deprive a community of its identity is abhorrent to the Biafran people. Having ourselves suffered genocide, we are all the more determined to take a clear stand now and at all times against this crime.

The New Biafran Social Order places a high premium on Patriotism—Love and Devotion to the Fatherland. Every true Biafran must love Biafra, must have faith in Biafra and its people, and must strive for its greater unity. He must find his salvation here in Biafra. He must be prepared to work for Biafra. He must be prepared to defend the sovereignty of Biafra wherever and by whomsoever it is challenged. Biafran patriots do all this already, and Biafra expects all her sons and daughters of today and tomorrow, to emulate their noble example. Diplomats who treat insults to the Fatherland and the Leadership of our struggle with levity are not patriotic. That young man who sneaks about the village, avoiding service in his country's Armed Forces is unpatriotic; that young, able-bodied school teacher who prefers to distribute relief when he should be fighting his country's war, is not only unpatriotic but is doing a woman's work. Those who help these loafers to dodge their civic duties should henceforth re-examine themselves.

All Biafrans are brothers and sisters bound together by ties of geography, trade, inter-marriage and culture and by their common misfortune in Nigeria and their present experience of the armed struggle. Biafrans are even more united by the desire to create a new and better order of society which will satisfy their needs and aspirations. Therefore, there is no justification for anyone to introduce into the Biafran Fatherland divisions based on ethnic origin, sex or religion. To do so would be unpatriotic.

Every true Biafran must know and demand his civic rights. Furthermore, he must recognise the rights of other Biafrans and be prepared to defend them when necessary. So often people complain that they have been ill-treated by the police or some other public servant. But the truth very often is that we allow ourselves to be bullied because we are not man enough to demand and stand up for our rights, and that fellow citizens around do not assist us when we do demand our rights.

In the New Biafran Social Order sovereignty and power belong to the People. Those who exercise power do so on behalf of the People. Those who govern must not tyrannise over the People. They carry a sacred trust of the People and must use their authority strictly in accordance with the will of the People. The true test of success in public life is that the People—who are the real masters—are contented and happy. The rulers must satisfy the People at all times.

But it is no use saying that power belongs to the People unless we are prepared to make it work in practice. Even in the old political days, the oppressors of the People were among those who shouted loudest that power belonged to the People. The Biafran Revolution will constantly and honestly seek methods of making this concept a fact rather than a pious fiction.

Arising out of the Biafran's belief that power belongs to the People is the principle of public accountability. Those who exercise power are accountable to the People for the way they use that power. The People retain the right to renew or terminate their mandate. Every individual servant of the People, whether in the Legislature, the Civil Service, the Judiciary, the Police, the Armed Forces, in business or in any other walk of life, is accountable at all times for his work and the work of those under his charge. Where, therefore, a ministry department runs inefficiently or improperly, its head must accept personal responsibility for such a situation and, depending on the gravity of the failure, must resign or be removed. And where he is proved to have misused his position or trust to enrich himself, the principle of public accountability requires that he be punished severely and his ill-gotten gains taken from him.

The Task of a Leader

Those who aspire to lead must bear in mind the fact that they are servants and as such cannot ever be greater than the People, their masters. Every leader in the Biafran Revolution is the embodiment of the ideas of the Revolution. Part of his role as leader is to keep the revolutionary spirit alive, to be a friend of the People and protector of their Revolution. He should have right judgement both of people and of situations and the ability to attract to himself the right kind of lieutenants who can best further the interests of the People and of the Revolution. The leader must not only say but always demonstrate that the power he exercises is derived from the People. Therefore, like every other Biafran public servant, he is accountable to the People for the use he makes of their mandate. He must get out when the People tell him to get out. The more power the leader is given by the People, the less is his personal freedom and the greater his responsibility for the good of the People. He should never allow his high office to separate him from the People. He must be fanatical for their welfare.

A leader in the Biafran Revolution must at all times stand for justice in dealing with the People. He should be the symbol of justice which is the supreme guarantee of good government. He should be ready, if need be, to lay down his life in pursuit of this ideal. He must have physical and moral courage and must be able to inspire the people out of despondency.

He should never strive towards the perpetuation of his office or devise means to cling to office beyond the clear mandate of the People. He should resist the temptation to erect memorials to himself in his life-time, to have his head embossed on the coin, name streets and institutions after himself, or convert government into a family business. A leader who serves his people well will be enshrined in their hearts and minds. This is all the reward he can expect in his lifetime. He will be to the People the symbol of excellence, the quintessence of the Revolution. He will be BIAFRAMAN.

Social Justice

One of the corner-stones of the Biafran Revolution is Social Justice. We believe that there should be equal opportunity for all, that appreciation and just reward should be given for honest work and that society should show concern and special care for the weak and infirm. Our people reject all forms of social inequalities and disabilities and all class and sectional privileges. Biafrans believe that society should treat all its members with impartiality and fairness. Therefore, the Biafran State must not apportion special privileges or favours to some citizens and deny them to others. For example, how can we talk of Social Justice in a situation where a highly paid public servant gets his salt free and the poor housewife in the village pays five pounds for a cup? The State should not create a situation favourable to the exploitation of some citizens by others. The State is the Father of all, the source of security, the reliable agent which helps all to realise their legitimate hopes and aspirations. Without Social Justice, harmony and stability within society disappear and antagonisms between various sections of the community take their place. Our Revolution will uphold Social Justice at all times. The Biafran State will be the Fountain of Justice.

Property and the Community

In the New Biafra, all property belongs to the Community. Every individual must consider all he has, whether in talent or material wealth, as belonging to the community for which he holds it in trust. This principle does not mean the abolition of personal property but it implies that the State, acting on behalf of the community, can intervene in the disposition of property to the greater advantage of all. Over-acquisitiveness or the inordinate desire to amass wealth is a factor liable to threaten social stability, especially in an under-developed society in which there are not enough material goods to go round.

This creates lop-sided development, breeds antagonisms between the haves and the have-nots and undermines the peace and unity of the people.

While the Biafran Revolution will foster private economic enterprise and initiative, it should remain constantly alive to the dangers of some citizens accumulating large private fortunes. Property-grabbing, if unchecked by the State, will set the pattern of behaviour for the whole society which begins to attach undue value to money and property. Thus a wealthy man, even if he is known to be a crook, is accorded greater respect than an honest citizen who is not so well off. A society where this happens is doomed to rot and decay. Moreover, the danger is always there of a small group of powerful property owners using their influence to deflect the State from performing its duties to the citizens as a whole and thereby destroying the democratic basis of society. This happens in many countries and it is one of the duties of our Revolution to prevent its occurrence in Biafra.

Finally, the Biafran Revolution will create possibilities for citizens with talent in business, administration, management and technology to fulfil themselves and receive due appreciation and reward in the service of the State, as has indeed happened in our total mobilisation to prosecute the present war.

An Egalitarian Society

The Biafran Revolution is committed to creating a society not torn by class consciousness and class antagonisms. Biafran society is traditionally egalitarian. The possibility for social mobility is always present in our society. The New Biafran Social Order rejects all rigid classifications of society. Anyone with imagination, anyone with integrity, anyone who works hard, can rise to any height. Thus, the son of a truck-pusher can become the Head of State of Biafra. The Biafran Revolution will provide opportunities for Biafrans to aspire and to achieve their legitimate desires. Those who find themselves below at any particular moment must have the opportunity to rise to the top.

Our New Society is open and progressive. The people of Biafra have always striven to achieve a workable balance between the claims of tradition and the demand for change and betterment. We are adaptable because as a people we are convinced that in the world "no condition is permanent". And we believe that human effort and will are necessary to bring about changes and improvements in the condition of the individual and of society. The

Biafran would thus make the effort to improve his lot and the material well-being of his community. He has the will to transform his society into a modern progressive community. In this process of rapid transformation he will retain and cherish the best elements of his culture, drawing sustenance as well as moral and psychological stability from them. But being a Biafran he will never be afraid to adapt what needs to be adapted or change what has to be changed.

Putting the Revolution Into Practice

The Biafran Revolution will continue to discover and develop local talent and to use progressive foreign ideas and skills so long as they do not destroy the identity of our culture or detract from the sovereignty of our Fatherland. The Biafran Revolution will also ensure through education that the positive aspects of Biafran traditional culture, especially those which are likely to be swamped out of existence by introduced foreign influences, are conserved. The undiscriminating absorption of new ideas and attitudes will be discouraged. Biafrans can, in the final analysis, only validly express their nation's personality and enhance their corporate identity through Biafran culture, through Biafran art and literature, music, dancing and drama, and through the peculiar gestures and social habits which distinguish them from all other people.

Our new society is rooted in Christian ethnics.

Those then are the main principles of our Revolution. They are not abstract formulations but arise out of the traditional background and the present temper of our people. *They grow out of our native soil and are the product of our peculiar climate*. They belong to us. If anyone here doubts the validity of these principles let him go out into the streets and into the villages, let him ask the ordinary Biafran. Let him go to the Army, ask the rank and file and he will find, as I have found, that they have very clear ideas about the kind of society we should build here. They will not put them in the same words I have used tonight but the meaning will be the same. From today, let no Biafran pretend that he or she does not know the main-spring of our national action, let him or her not plead ignorance when found indulging in un-Biafran activities. The principles of our Revolution are hereby clearly set out for everyone to see. They are now the property of every Biafran and the instrument for interpreting our national life.

But principles are principles. They can only be transformed into reality through the institutions of society, otherwise they remain inert and useless. It is my firm conviction that in the Biafran Revolution principles and practice will go hand in hand. It is my duty and the duty of you to bring this about.

Looking at the institutions of our society, the very vehicles for carrying out our Revolutionary principles, what do you find? We find old, jaded and rusty machines creaking along most inefficiently and delaying the People's progress and the progress of the Revolution.

The problem of our institutions is partly that they were designed by other people, in other times and for other purposes. Their most fundamental weakness is that they came into being during the colonial period when the relationship between the colonial administrators and the people was that of master and servant. *Our public servants, as heirs of the colonial masters, are apt to treat the People with arrogant condescension.* In the New Biafran Social Order, we say that power belongs to the People, but this central principle tends to elude many of the public servants who continue to behave in a manner which shows that they consider themselves master—the People their servants. The message of the Revolution has tended to fly over their heads. Let them beware, the Revolution, gathering momentum like a flood, washes clear all impediments on its way.

Take any of the institutions and the history is the same. First, it was fashioned for the British Colonial Service, then it saw service in that ill-fated country called Nigeria. It would be a miracle, fellow countrymen, if it should be found to be adequate for the need of revolutionary Biafra. What is surprising is not that these institutions fail us today but that there should be Biafrans, and some of them apparently very intelligent people, who sit back and expect good results from them. The fact is that one does not require extraordinary common-sense or insight to see the need for overhauling these machines and discarding those that are obsolescent.

The Legislature

For example, the Legislature, which should be the primary instrument for effecting the will of the People, was too often in the past used to frustrate the People. As I have said over and over again, power derives from the People. Ideally, all the People should be involved in the actual process of law-making. As a matter of fact, in our traditional society all adults who had attained the age of reason were directly involved in discussion, debate and decision-making on all things affecting the whole people. That was the original government by consensus. That was possible when the community was small and compact. With the emergence of the nation-state which is larger and heterogenous, this ideal procedure became impracticable. Therefore, the process of delegation of power was evolved to meet a practical need. But this does not invalidate the original principle that power belongs to the People. A man who is delegated by the People to represent their interests, therefore, is acting on behalf of the People and ceases to act for them the moment they withdraw their mandate. Like the ideal leader, the People's representative should get out when the People tell him to get out. He must constantly reassure the People that he is acting in their best interest.

In the past, the People's representatives, while paying lip-service to the primacy of the People and the supremacy of their interest made sure that in actual practice their own personal will prevailed over the will of the People and their own personal interest over the interest of the nation. Thus we had politicians who spent their time amassing wealth, who did everything conceivable to remain in office, who would kill, loot, throw acid and do anything to remain in power. The will of the People meant nothing to them.

In the New Biafra, the Legislature must be constituted to reflect the spirit and the Principles of the Revolution.

Legislators must understand that responsibility goes with power. Those who wield power must appreciate the responsibilities attached to that power. The legislator is a servant of the People given special powers to enable him discharge special responsibilities. Power is not given to him to turn him into a big man; to enable him sit inside huge American cars and build himself palaces. The conscientious legislator who strives to carry out his responsibility will find no time to pursue his own lucrative interests. He will find no time for membership of boards of corporations and directorships of public and private companies; or for doing deals with foreign business interests.

Politics and the Revolution

In revolutionary Biafra, certain basic reforms in politics and political institutions are necessary in order to safeguard the liberty of the People and protect their interest. For example, it will be imperative to separate the functions of the Legislature from those of the Executive. A member of the Legislature cannot at the same time be a member of the Executive. In the past, it was possible for a legislator to be a minister of state which is an executive post, in which case he neglected either his duty to his constituency or his duty to the state. Very often he neglected both.

In revolutionary Biafra there will be an executive leader elected by the people with full powers to choose his lieutenants. If he chooses a legislator or a public servant, such a person must resign his original appointment.

Another important principle is that people should be free to vote and be voted for wherever they live in Biafra. An Ikot Ekpene man living in Etiti should be free to vote and be voted for at Etiti. He does not have to go to Ikot Ekpene to vote or be voted for as happened in the past.

The principle of delegation of power from the People is so important that every revolutionary government of Biafra must encourage democratically organised groups of youths, students, women, workers, farmers, professional bodies, managerial and business organisations, traders and others to participate actively in political debate and discussion. The Revolution belongs to them.

Then, let us look at our Civil Service. It is too rigid and inflexible, too slow and ponderous for the needs of today. Too often when quick action and initiative are called for, what the public gets is cold, formal and aloof treatment. What is required in the future is a modernised and energised Civil Service, a Service which will fit into our Revolution and become the instrument of change. Its members must embody the spirit of the New Order by identifying with the values of change and progress and promoting these values in the conduct of public affairs.

The Judiciary

Since our Revolution has its foundation in the Rule of Law, the Judiciary becomes a most important arm of the State. It is the instrument for the protection and defence of our people's liberties, for interpreting the will of our Revolution and for promoting the values of the New Order. It will be necessary, in the first place, to review our body of laws and bring it into line with the values of concepts of the New Order. It will be essential to stream-line this machinery so as to facilitate its processes and make legal redress available to all citizens. Every Biafran should find it possible and easy to have recourse to law courts when his rights or liberties are interfered with or threatened. In this he should be able to count on the support of his fellow citizens.

In the past, justice and its processes were often very remote from the life of the ordinary citizen. The ways of justice were beyond his understanding. And yet justice was meant to exist for his benefit. In revolutionary Biafra, the citizen should understand what law and justice are about. Our Revolution, therefore, aims at involving the citizen in the process of justice so that he will participate actively in the protection of his life and liberties and in the defence of the integrity, stability, and moral health of the nation.

The Police Force

Like the Judiciary, the Police Force is a very important institution, very important because it is given the special responsibility of maintaining the law and order and guarding the security of the People and the nation. Like other institutions of our society, the Police Force needs to be reformed so that it can better fulfil its function in the Revolution. Its members must absorb the ideals of the New Biafran Social Order. The Police have often been criticised by the public. They have been accused of corruption, bribery and inefficiency. We say that some of these evils and weaknesses can be traced to the fact that the Police Force, like many other institutions of our society, had a colonial beginning and was vitiated in Nigeria. Today, we are involved in a task of building a New Society with new values and new outlooks. Our Police Force must be part of this New Order. It must promote the ideals of the New Order—ideals of change and progress. The conduct of its members must, in the spirit of the Revolution, be scrupulously honest. The Biafran Police must be a People's Police, that is to say, a champion of the People's rights. The Policeman is not there simply to arrest criminals. He is also there to help people avoid going wrong. He must never exploit the People's ignorance of their civic rights. On the contrary, it is his duty, where such ignorance exists, to teach the citizen his rights. Above all, he must be a dedicated patriot fanatically devoted to prosecuting the safety and security of the State. Fortunately, we know there are members of our Police Force imbued with these ideals. It is on them that the Force will be rebuilt.

The Armed Services

The Biafran Armed Forces hold a key position in the Biafran Revolution. They have been rightly in the front-line defence of the Biafran nation and the People in the past two years. They have performed this task creditably, for which the Nation is indebted to them. But like the others, our military institutions carry the stamp of their Colonial and Nigerian origin. For our Revolution, the Biafran Armed Forces must be transformed into a true People's Army.

The New Biafran Armed Forces should have love, unity and cooperation between the officers and other ranks, between them and the People.

They must rid themselves of the starchiness and rigid class distinctions which are the hall-marks of an establishment army; they should always ensure that their members never maltreat fellow citizens; that they never loot or "liberate" the People's property; that they treat Biafran womanhood with respect and decorum, and that they pay a fair price for whatever they buy and return whatever they borrow from the People.

The Biafran Armed Forces must unite with the People to build the New Society and must share with the People the Biafran ideology which sustains the Revolution.

The Public Services

What emerges from our examination of the public services is that the public servant is yet to learn that he is a servant of the People, not their master; that he must love the People and seek their welfare. There is no room in the New Biafra for the public servant who is arrogant, insolent and overbearing. The public servant is created to provide an efficient service for the People. It is the responsibility of the public servant to provide this efficient service. There is no room in revolutionary Biafra for the inefficient or indolent public servant, for that man who sits at his desk filling out football coupons; for that woman who makes endless telephone calls, or for that worker who comes late and watches the clock for an hour before closing time. There is no room for the public servant who is corrupt or who uses public facilities to promote his private ends. I think of that man who uses official transport to evacuate his personal belongings and abandons the property of the State to the enemy. I think of that public servant in the Ministry of Lands who allocates State land to himself, his wife and his friends. I think of that Army officer who drives past in any empty car, leaving a wounded soldier to bleed to death. I see these things and I say to myself: these men have yet to grasp the lesson of our Revolution or else the Revolution will grasp them.

I ask myself: what can be done to bring the lesson home to them? Nothing at all, unless they are ready to do something for themselves. The revolution cannot wait for the indolent, inefficient and corrupt public servant. He has to catch up with the Revolution, or the Revolution will catch up with him. The public servant who cannot, or will not, do the work for which he is hired, will be fired. It is no good saying: I have been in this job for twenty years. The Revolution cannot go into your long record. We repeat that if you cannot do the job of the Revolution, someone else will be found to do it.

However, we recognise that some devoted public servants may be inefficient simply because they have not received the right and adequate training for what they are required to do. In this respect, our Revolution will do one or two things. Either move them to a job they can do, or provide the right training-on-the-job if this is likely to produce worthwhile results.

Training and Education

Our experience during this struggle has brought home to us the need for versatility. Many of our citizens have found themselves having to do emergency duties different from their normal peace-time jobs. In the years after the present armed conflict, we may find that in the defence of the Revolution the general state of mobilisation and alertness will remain. One of the ways of preparing ourselves for this emergency will be to ensure that every citizen will be trained in two jobs—his normal peace-time occupation and a different skill which will be called into play during a national emergency. Thus, for example, a clerk may be given training to enable him to operate as an ambulance-driver during an emergency, or a university lecturer as a post-master or a Signal Sergeant in one of the Armed Forces.

We realise here that the problem is more than that of providing narrow, technical training. It has to do with reorientation of attitudes. It has to do with the cultivation of the right kind of civic virtue and loyalty to Biafra. We all stand in need of this.

It is quite clear that to attain the goals of the Biafran Revolution will require extensive political and civic education of our People. To this effect, we will, in the near future, set up a National Orientation College (N.O.C.) which will undertake the needful function of formally inculcating the Biafran ideology and the Principles of the Revolution. We will also, pursue this vital task of education through seminars, mass rallies, formal and informal address by the leaders and standard-bearers of the Revolution. All Biafrans who are going to play a role in the promotion of the Revolution, especially those who are going to operate the institutions of the New Society, must first of all expose themselves to the ideology of the Revolution.

The full realisation of the Biafran ideology and the promise of the Biafran Revolution will have the important effect of drawing the People of Biafra into close unity with the Biafran State. The Biafran State and the Biafran People thus become one. The People jealously defend and protect the integrity of the State. The State guarantees the People certain basic rights and welfare. In this third year of our independence, we re-state those basic rights and welfare obligations which the revolutionary State of Biafran guarantees to the People.

The Right to Work

In the field of employment and labour, the Biafran Revolution guarantees every able Biafran the right to work. All those who are lazy or refuse to work forfeit their right to this guarantee. "He who does not work should not eat" is an important principle in Biafra.

Our Revolution provides equal opportunities for employment and labour for all Biafrans irrespective of sex. For equal output a woman must receive the same remuneration as a man.

Our revolutionary Biafran State will guarantee a rational system of remuneration of labour. Merit and output shall be the criteria for reward in labour. "To each according to his ability, to each ability according to its product" shall be our motto in Biafra.

Our Revolution guarantees security for workers who have been incapacitated by physical injury, old age or disease. It will be the duty of the Biafran State to raise the standard of living of the Biafran People, to provide them with improved living conditions and to afford them modern amenities that enhance their human dignity and self-esteem. We recognise at all times the great contributions made by the farmers, the craftsmen and other toilers of the Revolution to our national progress. It will be a cardinal point of our economic policy to keep their welfare constantly in view. The Biafran Revolution will promulgate a Workers' Charter which will codify and establish workers' rights.

Health and Welfare

The maintenance of the health and physical well-being of the Biafran citizen must be the concern and the responsibility of the State. The revolutionary Biafran State will at all times strive to provide medical service for all its citizens in accordance with the resources available to it; it will wage a continuous struggle against epidemic and endemic diseases; and will promote among the People knowledge of hygienic living. It will develop social and preventive medicine, set up sanatoriums for endurable and infectious diseases and mental cases, and a net-work of maternity homes for ante- and post-natal care of Biafran mothers. Furthermore, Biafra will set great store by the purity of the air which its People breathe. We have a right to live in a clean, pollution-free atmosphere.

Culture and Higher Education

Our Revolution recognises the vital importance of the mental and emotional needs of the Biafran People. To this end, the Biafran State will pay great attention to Religion, Education, Culture and the Arts. We shall aim at elevating our cultural institutions and promoting educational reforms which will foster a sense of national and racial pride among our People and discourage ideas which inspire a feeling of inferiority and dependence on foreigners and foreign interests. We must produce the kind of manpower that will nurture the Biafran Revolution. It will be the prime duty of the revolutionary Biafran State to eradicate illiteracy from our society, to guarantee free education to all Biafran children to a stage limited only by existing resources. Our nation will encourage the training of scientists, technicians and skilled workers needed for quick industrialisation and the modernisation of our agriculture. We will ensure the development of higher education and technological training for our people, encourage our intellectuals, writers, artists and scientists to research, create and invent in the service of the State and the People. We must prepare our People to contribute significantly to knowledge and world culture.

Finally, the present armed struggle, in which many of our countrymen and women have distinguished themselves and made numerous sacrifices in defence of the Fatherland and the Revolution, has imposed on the State of Biafra extra responsibility for the welfare of its People. Biafra will give special care and assistance to soldiers and civilians disabled in the course of the pogrom and the war; it will develop special schemes for resettlement and rehabilitation. The nation will assume responsibility for the dependants of the heroes of the Revolution who have lost their lives in defence of the Fatherland.

In talking about the rights of the Biafrans and the welfare obligations the State owes to them, I have had cause to refer to our limited resources. These limitations are particularly severe at the moment as a result of the war. But even without the war we would be short of adequate resources for putting into effect all the principles and policies for transforming our society. This is partly because of the wrong economic policies of the past, policies that we must immediately tackle if the Revolution is to fulfil its promise to the People, for the Revolution is also the servant of the People.

Self-reliance

One of the key problems of the economy of under-developed countries is the fact that they are controlled and exploited by foreign monopoly interests.

Under-developed countries cannot advance unless they break the strangle-hold of the foreign monopolies. The only hope of success lies in the state pursuing an active policy of self-reliance in putting its own economic house in order. But it cannot do this unless it takes control of the main springs of the economy—the means of production, distribution and exchange. This will ensure central mobilisation of the national economy through proper planning and control.

This is what Biafra must do; this is what African countries must do; this is what the under-developed world must do, if they are to save themselves.

As primary producers, we are economically at the mercy of the industrialised countries. We are obliged to sell our products cheap to them and to buy their manufactures dear from them. Like other under-developed countries, our economy is fragile, and because we do not earn enough for what we produce we remain poor and cannot improve the standard of living of our people. And because we are poor we cannot develop our economy. How then can we break this vicious circle? If we try to unite with other primary producers to obtain better terms of trade, we find that because of our poverty we cannot hold out long enough against the aggressive policies of these rich industrialised countries.

Here, as in all other spheres of our Revolution, the answer must come from within, from ourselves. We must pursue an enlightened dynamic policy which will concentrate on employing our primary products in various domestic manufactures. The present war has already opened our eyes to what we can do by relying on our own resources in material and men. It is unthinkable that after the war we shall return to the old system of selling our primary products to someone in Europe at his own price so that he can turn them into manufactured goods and sell back to us, again at his own price. Our primary products shall henceforth be used mainly to feed Biafra's growing industries.

Another economic goal of the Biafran Revolution is self-sufficiency in food production. Our experience during the present war has emphasised to us the importance of this. The work of the Biafran Land Army has also shown us the tremendous possibilities that exist for a major agrarian revolution. The Biafran Revolution will intervene actively to end the exploitation of the countryside by the town—a baneful process which is often easily lost sight of. The Biafran Revolution will encourage farmers, craftsmen and tradesmen to form cooperatives and communes, and will make them take pride in their work by according them the recognition and prestige they deserve. The programme for industrial progress in revolutionary Biafra will achieve balanced development between industry and agriculture, between regions or provinces within Biafra, between town and country and finally between Biafra and other African countries who desire to do business with us.

Again and again, in stating the Principles of our Revolution, we have spoken of the People. We have spoken of the primacy of the

People, of the belief that power belongs to the People; that the Revolution is the servant of the People. We make no apologies for speaking so constantly about the People, because we believe in the People; we have faith in the People. They are the bastion of the Nation, the makers of its culture and history.

The Qualities of the Individual

But in talking about the People we must never lose sight of the individuals who make up the People. The single individual is the final, irreducible unit of the People. In Biafra that single individual counts. The Biafran Revolution cannot lose sight of this fact.

The desirable changes which the Revolution aims to bring to the lives of the People will first manifest themselves in the lives of individual Biafrans. The success of the Biafran Revolution will depend on the quality of individuals within the state. Therefore, the calibre of the individual is of the utmost importance to the Revolution. To build the New Society we will require new men who are in tune with the spirit of the New Order. What then should be the qualities of this Biafran of the New Order?

He is patriotic, loyal to his State, his Government and its leadership; he must not do anything which undermines the security of his State or gives advantage to the enemies of his country. He must not indulge in such evil practices as tribalism and nepotism which weaken the loyalty of their victims to the state. He should be prepared, if need be, to give up his life in defence of the Nation.

He must be his brother's keeper; he must help all Biafrans in difficulty, whether or not they are related to him by blood; he must avoid, at all costs, doing anything which is capable of bringing distress and hardship to other Biafrans. A man who hoards money or goods is not his Brother's keeper because he brings distress and hardship to his fellow citizens.

He must be honourable; he must be a person who keeps his promise and the promise of his office, a person who can always be trusted.

He must be truthful: he must not cheat his neighbour, his fellow citizens and his country. He must not give or receive bribes or corruptly advance himself or his interests.

He must be responsible: he must not push across to others the task which properly belongs to him, or let others receive the blame or punishment for his own failings. A responsible man keeps secrets. A Biafran who is in a position to know what our troops are planning and talks about it is irresponsible. The information he gives out will spread and reach the ear of the enemy. A responsible man minds his own business; he does now show off.

He must be brave and courageous: he must never allow himself to be attacked by others without fighting back to defend himself and his rights. He must be ready to tackle tasks which other people might regard as impossible.

He must be law-abiding: he obeys the laws of the land and does nothing to undermine the due processes of law.

He must be freedom-loving: he must stand up resolutely against all forms of injustice, oppression and suppression. He must never be afraid to demand his rights. For example, a true Biafran at a post office or bank counter will insist on being served in his turn.

He must be progressive: he should not slavishly and blindly adhere to old ways of doing things; he must be prepared to make changes in his way of life in the light of our new revolutionary experience.

He is industrious, resourceful and inventive; he must not fold his arms and wait for the Government to do everything for him; he must also help himself.

My fellow countrymen and women, proud and courageous Biafrans, two years ago, faced with the threat of total extermination, we met in circumstances not unlike today's. At that august gathering, the entire leaders of our people being present, we as a people decided that we had to take our destiny into our own hand, to plan and decide our future and to stand by these decisions no matter the vicissitude of this war which by then was already imminent. At that time, our major preoccupation was how to remain alive, how to restrain an implacable enemy from destroying us in our own homes. In that moment of crisis we decided to resume our sovereignty.

In my statement to the leaders of our community before that decision was made, I spoke about the difficulties, explained that the road which we were about to tread was to be carved through a jungle of thorns and that our ability to emerge through this jungle was, to say the least, uncertain. Since that fateful decision, the very worst has happened. Our people have continually been subjected to genocide. The entire conspiracy of neo-colonialism has joined hands to stifle our nascent independence. Yet, undaunted by the odds, proud in the fact of our manhood, encouraged by the companionship of the Almighty, we have fought to this day with honour, with pride, with glory so that today, as I stand before you, I see a proud people acknowledged by the world. I see a heroic people, men with heart-beats as regular and blood as red as the best on earth.

On that fateful day two years ago, you mandated me to do everything within my power to avert the dangers that loomed ahead, the threat of extermination. Little did we, you and I, know how long the battle was to be, how complex its attendant problems. From then on, what have been achieved are there for the entire world to see and have only been possible because of the solidarity and support of our people. For this I thank you all. I must have made certain mistakes in the course of this journey but I am sure that whatever mistakes I have made are mistakes of the head and never of the heart. I have tackled the sudden problems as they unfold before my eyes and I have tackled them to the best of my ability with the greater interest of our people in mind.

Today, I am glad that our problems are less than they were a year ago; that arms alone can no longer destroy us; that our victory, the fulfilment of our dreams, is very much in sight. We have forced a stalemate on the enemy and this is likely to continue, with any advances likely to be on our side. If we fail, which God forbid, it can only be because of certain inner weakness in our being. It is in order to avoid these pitfalls that I have today proclaimed before you the principles of the Biafran Revolution.

We in Biafra are convinced that the Black man can never come into his own until he is able to build modern states based on indigenous African ideologies, to enjoy true independence, to be able to make his mark in the arts and sciences and to engage in meaningful dialogue with the white man on a basis of equality. When he achieves this, he will have brought a new dimension into international affairs.

Biafra will not betray the Black man. No matter the odds, we will fight with all our might until Black men everywhere can point with pride to this Republic, standing dignified and defiant, an example of African nationalism triumphant over its many and age-old enemies.

We believe that God, humanity and history are on our side, and that the Biafran Revolution is indestructible and eternal.

Oh God, not my will but Thine for ever.

Ahiara Village
Biafra

June 1st, 1969

Index